THE MACMILLAN SHAKESPEARE
ADVISORY EDITOR: PHILIP BROCKBANK
Professor of English and Director of the
Shakespeare Institute, University of Birmingham
GENERAL EDITOR: PETER HOLLINDALE
Senior Lecturer in English and Education,
University of York

HAMLET

THE MACMILLAN SHAKESPEARE

HAMLET

Edited by
Nigel Alexander
Senior Lecturer in English,
University of Nottingham

M

MACMILLAN EDUCATION

First published 1973
Reprinted 1975, 1976, 1978, 1979, 1982, 1983,
1984 (twice), 1985 (twice)

Published by
MACMILLAN EDUCATION LTD
Houndmills, Basingstoke, Hampshire RG21 2XS
and London
Companies and representatives
throughout the world

Printed in Great Britain by
Anchor Brendon Ltd
Tiptree, Essex

ISBN 0 333 01515 0

CONTENTS

INTRODUCTION

Note: The following abbreviations are used in the Introduction and notes:

Q1: First Quarto
Q2: Second Quarto
F: Folio

Plays are conditioned by the circumstances of their performance. In an author's note to the published text of *Jumpers*, Tom Stoppard writes:

> In preparing previous plays for publication I have tried with some difficulty to arrive at something called a 'definitive text', but I now believe that in the case of plays there is no such animal. Each production will throw up its own problems and very often the solution will lie in some minor changes to the text, either in the dialogue or in the author's directions, or both.[1]

Any reader or potential performer of *Hamlet* should be aware, or be warned, that the 'definitive text' of Shakespeare's play is equally elusive. The text, however, is not so enigmatic as the play itself. If scholars are not quite sure what Shakespeare wrote, it seems that critics are totally uncertain of what he meant. We still await the final solution to the problem of *Hamlet* which will make every obscurity clear and resolve all our doubts. A long wait is likely since the problems of the text are not susceptible of easy solution and tragedy treats of a world where all is far from clear and our difficulties never will be resolved since they are the price paid by humanity for being an animal that is as rash as it is rational, controlled neither by its instincts nor its intelligence, but by both in an uneasy, and tragic, alliance.

The student approaching *Hamlet* must make up his mind about three clear questions connected with the text in front

[1] Tom Stoppard, *Jumpers*, p.11 (Faber & Faber, 1972)

of him and three less certain, but even more important, questions about the nature of what he reads, or intends to perform. The first three questions are: 1 What is the nature of our present text and how far does it represent what Shakespeare wrote for his own company? 2 What is its relationship to the story and saga of Hamlet in history and legend? Has Shakespeare made a ludicrous mistake by inserting a portrait of a Renaissance prince into an entirely inappropriate context? 3 What is the relationship between Shakespeare's play and the old play on the Hamlet story which appears to have been performed between 1588 and 1594? The second set of questions are: 1 Is the play in any sense a unity? Does an Elizabethan company of players have any relevance to an ancient Danish court? 2 What is the nature of Hamlet's problem? Is this a portrait of a prince and philosopher, or merely a set of theatrical attitudes and tricks? 3 What kind of reaction is expected of the audience? Are they meant to see any significance in these actions or is it enough that they have sat in their seats during a performance whose main attractions might be described as perverted sex and violence?

All scholarship and criticism of the play has to address itself to these problems. The answers remain uncertain, but every actor or company which undertakes to perform the play is compelled to provide some sort of answer in the way they treat the text and the emphasis they give to the complex pattern of actions and images which form the play. The choice imposed upon the central character – the choice which criticism has rightly supposed is symbolised in the soliloquy, 'To be – or not to be' – involves both actors and spectators in a series of difficult discriminations between co-existent yet contradictory thoughts and emotions. Their doubts and hesitations are, it will be suggested, a measure of the playwright's success as he struggles to dramatise one of the most complex and compelling of all human choices in a play whose problems are not accidental but are the result of his own deliberate and dazzling artistic creation.

THE TEXT

The difficulties of the text are the result of theatrical conditions similar to those described by Tom Stoppard and the
even greater complexities associated with the process of
printing and publishing plays in sixteenth- and seventeenth-
century England. There was no copyright as we understand
it. Once a play had been printed it belonged, not to its
author, but to the member of the Stationers' Company who
had printed it after duly recording his title and intention to
do so in the register of the Company. The monopoly of the
Stationers' Company, which had been established to control printing and facilitate government censorship, extended
only as far as the actual printed text. Once a group of actors
bought a copy there was nothing, except government censorship, to prevent them performing the play. It is, therefore, understandable that the theatrical companies were
unwilling to allow their chief commercial asset, the text of
their plays, be published in a form where they might be
stolen by rivals or read by members of the public who might
otherwise have paid to see a performance.

The printing and publishing of his plays, therefore, was
not an activity likely to occupy a great deal of the time of a
busy actor and dramatist. Shakespeare seems to have taken
a great deal of trouble with the publication of his poems,
Venus and Adonis and *The Rape of Lucrece*. It is improbable
that he supervised the publication of any of the plays
printed during his lifetime. After his death, two of his
friends and fellow actors, John Heminge and Henry Con-
dell, collected his works and published them in the great
Folio volume of 1623 now called the First Folio. They
provided for the printer the best texts that they could find,
and the book is a monument to their care and industry – but
there are many factors involved which prevent it from being
a completely accurate or entirely reliable text. Some of these
factors may be illustrated by a brief comparison of the early
editions upon which any modern edition of *Hamlet* has to
be based.

Two editions of Hamlet were printed in Shakespeare's lifetime and they, together with the Folio text, are the versions which must be consulted by the modern editor or enquiring student. They are:

1 A Quarto volume published in 1603 with a title page announcing that the play had been performed frequently in London and at the two universities of Oxford and Cambridge. This is now called the First Quarto or Bad Quarto of *Hamlet*.

2 A Quarto volume published in 1604/5 (the date on the title page was changed during printing). The play is said to be 'newly imprinted and enlarged to almost as much again as it was, according to the true and perfect copy'. This is now called the Second or Good Quarto.

3 The text of the play in the First Folio of 1623. It is evident from the title page of the 1604/5 Quarto that its publishers regarded the 1603 version as inadequate. A reader would expect there to be differences. What he might not be prepared for is the obvious and even vital differences that exist between the Second Quarto and the Folio. Only the Folio attempts act-division.

The First Quarto records Hamlet's most famous line as 'To be or not to be – aye, there's the point' and is as accurate, or at least different, in its versions of other important speeches and soliloquies. The nunnery scene between Hamlet and Ophelia occurs in the second act before the Player's speech and Hamlet's resulting 'Hecuba' soliloquy. It includes a scene between Horatio and the Queen in which she promises to help her son. The Second Quarto is a more developed and coherent version of the play but it too contains a number of strange readings and inexplicable omissions. At II. 2. 437 the *friendly Fankers* become *French Falconers* in the Folio. Hamlet, at III. 3. 79, says *Why, this is base and silly, not revenge* – while in the Folio he says *Why, this is hire and salary, not revenge*. It includes a number of passages that are omitted in 1623 (notably the 'vicious mole of nature' speech at I. 4. 17–38 and Hamlet's conversation with the Norwegian captain and seventh soliloquy at IV. 4. 10–66) but it leaves out parts of Hamlet's conversation with Rosencrantz and Guildenstern, especially the discussion of the companies of child actors.

There are occasions where the texts differ and it is difficult to choose between them. Does Horatio at I. 1. 167 watch the morn walk 'o'er the dew of *yon high Eastward hill*' (Q2) or *yon high Eastern hill* (F)? Does Ophelia regard Hamlet's mind at III. 1. 161 as 'Like sweet bells jangled, *out of time and harsh*' (Q2) or *out of tune and harsh* (F)? Does Marcellus at I. 1. 73 talk of *cost of brazen cannon* (Q1 and 2) or *cast of brazen cannon* (F)? Did Hamlet at I. 4. 49, see his father's body *interred* (Q1 and 2) or *enurned* (F)? In his first soliloquy, I. 2. 129, does he hope that this *too much grieved and sallied flesh would melt* (Q1), *too too sallied flesh would melt* (Q2), or *too too solid flesh would melt* (F)?

It might be possible to make a decisive choice among these readings if we could be sure either that: (*a*) one of the texts was superior to the others – having been printed from a manuscript written by Shakespeare or transcribed from his papers – and that the others had merely copied this existing printed version, or (*b*) that they were all independent reports and versions of some one original manuscript – for in this case where two of them agreed on a reading (as *interred* for *enurned*) it would have more authority than the single dissenting text. Unfortunately the exact relationship between the texts is still far from clear. What is apparent is that there are no grounds for automatically preferring one text before the others.

At first it was thought that the First Quarto must represent an earlier version of the play – a particularly attractive idea since there evidently was a play called *Hamlet* in existence as early as 1589. If this is an earlier version, however, it is strange that it should so exactly resemble the later texts at some points and descend to near gibberish at others. It becomes easier to explain if it is assumed that the

1603 version is, in fact, later than the 1604. The economic conditions of theatrical publishing made the existence of a black market in play texts profitable to actors who did not themselves share in the profits of the company but were hired for a fixed wage. They could – and sometimes clearly did – put together a version of the play from memory and sell it to a printer. It is probable that this had happened in the case of two earlier plays which had been popular successes – *The Second and Third Parts of Henry VI* – and it seems likely that this is what happened to *Hamlet*. The position, however, is complicated by the fact that some of the material used by the actors to fill the inevitable gaps in their memories may have come from the earlier *Hamlet* play.

The sudden appearance of the Good Quarto in 1604/5 is explained by the desire of the company and Shakespeare to replace the bad or 'pirated' version with their own text – since they could no longer prevent its circulation in print. It has been argued that Shakespeare's own manuscript was sent to the printers – since the company would have their own fair copy made up as the prompt book from which an individual actor's part would be copied and learnt. The Folio is thought to have been printed from that prompt book. Even if this is so, something peculiar seems to have happened in the course of printing. In printing a book it was normal for two compositors setting up the type to work sheet about, thus compositor X sets sheets A, C, E, G . . . and compositor Y sets B, D, F, H . . . It is possible to identify an individual compositor (in the fluid state of Elizabethan spelling) by the forms he preferred and by recognising the actual type that he used. If these tests are applied to the Second Quarto it turns out that compositor X set sheets B, C, D, F, I . . . and compositor Y set sheets E, G, H, K, L . . . (sheet A was reserved for the title page). One explanation offered of this unusual practice is that the manuscript was very difficult and compositor X was either using a marked copy of the First Quarto (accurate for the opening of the play since the reporting actors had played

Marcellus and Barnardo) or was at least consulting it. Since they only had one copy he set virtually the entire first act of the play.

If this is so, and it seems that something like it must have occurred, there is no reading in the Second Quarto that can be considered entirely independent of the First – for there can be no guarantee that this kind of consultation did not take place. Nor is it clear whether the compositors who set up the Folio text did, or did not, consult a copy of the Second Quarto. What does seem certain is that the texts cannot be treated as independent reports. Thus *interred* cannot be preferred to *enurned* on the grounds that it is a record of what was in Shakespeare's manuscript and what someone heard on a stage. It may be a mistake in the First Quarto merely copied into the Second. This, it may be said, does not matter very much. But if there are over five hundred such possible variations the texts would begin to look a little different.

There is one further and most important consideration. Some of these differences may be the result of changes in the text made by Shakespeare himself. There exist two manuscripts of *A Game at Chess* in Thomas Middleton's own handwriting. They show exactly the kind of change that we consider variants in the case of Shakespeare's text. It is possible, therefore, that Shakespeare wrote both *Eastward* and *Eastern hill* both *out of time and harsh* and *out of tune and harsh*[1]. If he did write both, which are we to prefer? The more one considers the problems the clearer it becomes that while an editor has a duty to himself and his readers to produce a final text he cannot be confident that he has produced a 'definitive text'.

THE STORY

The absence of a definitive text does not mean that Shakespeare's *Hamlet* has no certain existence. It is common to say

[1] E. A. J. Honigmann, *The Stability of Shakespeare's Text* (Edward Arnold, 1965)

that the power of Shakespeare's plays come from their poetry – but, if this is so, then words are only one of the elements used to create that poetic effect. What Shakespeare has constructed is a developing pattern of action and imagery which forces certain significant relationships (between different characters and between what individual characters say and do) upon the attention of the audience. It is this information, their perception of these relationships, which makes, for an audience, their experience of *Hamlet*. There are many versions of the *Hamlet* story but none of them share Shakespeare's special set of relationships. The power of art is thus fundamentally a power of organisation – the ability to take common elements or traditional forms and show them in a new relationship. This relationship may be so unexpected and disturbing that it requires people to revise their accepted, comfortable, familiar ways of perceiving or thinking. The enormous debate that has raged round *Hamlet* is one indication that it is a work of this powerful and disturbing kind.

The story of Hamlet has a long history. It has evidently provided entertainment for a great variety of readers and listeners in many countries. Its origins apparently lie in Scandinavian folk tale and legend. The first surviving literary version is contained in the third and fourth books of the *Danish History* compiled at the end of the twelfth century by Saxo Grammaticus. It combines folk-tale with history, but it is one of the great monuments of mediaeval historical scholarship. Saxo's presentation is exciting and dramatic and it is instructive to observe how many elements of the Hamlet story are already present.

In the legend Feng murders his brother Horwendil, King of Jutland, and marries Gerutha, his queen. He admits and justifies the crime, saying that he was protecting Gerutha from her husband's violent hatred. Amleth, the son of Horwendil, feigns madness for his own protection. Feng naturally fears a son's vengeance and makes several attempts to discover whether Amleth is really as idiotic as he appears.

Amleth is left alone in a deserted spot with a young woman
– since the King assumes that, if he is in his right mind, he
will make love to her. Amleth is warned of the plot by his
foster brother who fastens a straw to the tail of a gad-fly.
Seeing it, the Prince recognises a trap, and carries the girl
beyond the observation of the King's spies.

Feng now appears to go away on a journey. At the suggestion of one of the courtiers Gerutha sends for Amleth and
questions him while the courtier conceals himself in the
straw which covers the chamber. Amleth kills the spy, cuts
his body in pieces and throws it down the sewer where it is
eaten by the castle pigs. Confessing that he is only waiting to
take revenge, Amleth overwhelms his mother with re-
proaches and brings her over to his side. Feng, returning,
can find no trace of his faithful courtier. Amleth says he
went into the sewer and was eaten. The courtiers laugh at
this example of Amleth's madness and folly but Feng grows
suspicious. He resolves to have Amleth murdered in
England.

Amleth, too, has his suspicions. Before leaving he makes
his mother promise to hang a great tapestry in the hall and
celebrate his funeral exactly one year from the day he
leaves. Two lords accompany him bearing the orders for
execution on two pieces of wood. Amleth erases the King's
message and substitutes his own, ordering the death of the
two lords. In England he performs a number of feats of
intelligence and deduction. He tells the King that his father
was a palace slave and that the Queen's mother was a bond-
maid. The King not only puts the lords to death, but also
marries his daughter to Amleth.

One year later Amleth returns, alone, to Jutland and
enters the hall where his funeral feast is in progress. His
arrival causes much amusement – which Amleth adds to by
acting as cup-bearer and making everyone drunk. He keeps
pricking his finger with his sword and the lords, afraid that
he may injure himself, fix it with rivets into its scabbard.
When they have all fallen into a drunken sleep Amleth cuts

down the tapestry and fastens it over them with wooden pegs that he had fashioned while sitting by the hearth. He then sets fire to the hall, having ensured that no one can escape. Proceeding to Feng's separate sleeping quarters he substitutes his own sword for the King's and then wakes him. Amleth tells him that his lords are dying in the flames and that he, Amleth, has now come to take revenge. Feng is cut down while trying in vain to draw the fixed sword from its scabbard.

A shortened version of the story appears in the *Chronica Regnorum Aquilanorum* by the German historian Albert Krantz. Published in German in 1545 and in its original Latin in 1548 it continued to be popular and it has a number of features which make it a possible source for Shakespeare. Another version of the story was included by François de Belleforest, poet and historian, in his *Histoires Tragiques*. This work, begun as a continuation of the *Novelle* of Matteo Bandello, eventually contained stories from many languages and sources. Belleforest was known in England but, although Sir Geoffrey Fenton published a translation of some stories in 1567, no version of the Hamlet story appeared until 1608.

REVENGE TRAGEDY

It is possible that Shakespeare knew the versions of Saxo or Krantz. It is perhaps even probable that he had read Belleforest, but it is not certain. What is evident is that his dramatisation has lost none of the grim associations of the folk-tale. It is, as Horatio tells Fortinbras and the Danish court, a record

> Of carnal, bloody, and unnatural acts,
> Of accidental judgements, casual slaughters,
> Of deaths put on by cunning, and forced cause,
> And, in this upshot, purposes mistook
> Fall'n on the inventors heads.

It is a story concerned with murder, sudden violence and the slower but more deadly reaction to that violence. *Hamlet* is still a play concerned with a son's revenge for the murder of his father.

Revenge, the desire to retaliate for an injury, is a powerful, natural, and dangerous human emotion. It is as prevalent in the modern world as it ever was among the figures of the heroic and legendary past. It is frequently revenge, the desire to retaliate somehow, on someone, for the injuries they have suffered, which makes military units suddenly and savagely massacre the unfortunate civilians who happen to be in their path. It is still to be found in the bedchamber as commonly as on the battlefield. It can be a source of political and domestic horror, or a final sanction restraining the worst excesses of oppressors. Revenge never sleeps – as Thomas Kyd dramatically demonstrated in *The Spanish Tragedy*.

It is an emotion that naturally appeals to dramatists since it provides a coherent and logical framework for the depiction of human passions. A series of events can clearly be seen to start with some original crime and end once that crime has been avenged. The Greek tragedians used it many times and it reached the Elizabethans as part of the classical heritage through the literature of Rome. Aided by their own historical vision, and challenged by the particular requirements of their own theatre, they made the form their own to such an extent that the term 'revenge tragedy' can usually be understood as referring to tragedies written between 1580 and 1642.

The Spanish Tragedy by Thomas Kyd, and Shakespeare's own *Titus Andronicus* are early and successful examples of the dramatic use of revenge. In both plays an injured man has difficulty, first in identifying the people who have harmed him, and then in attacking them, since they are both powerful and well guarded. Patience, cunning and continuing resolution are necessary in order to achieve revenge. Hieronimo, the hero of *The Spanish Tragedy*, avenges the murder of his son Horatio by killing those responsible during the performance of a revenge tragedy in which he has persuaded them to take part. Titus Andronicus imitates Thyestes in Greek myth and Seneca's play *Thyestes* by serving up to his enemy, Tamora, Queen of the Goths, the minced bodies of her children cooked in a pie. After she has eaten them, he kills her. Like Amleth, these characters have all achieved a notable, memorable and satisfying revenge. Ben Jonson attacked those whose theatrical taste had not developed beyond this in the Induction to *Bartholomew Fair* ll. 108–11.

> He that will swear *Jeronimo* or *Andronicus* are the best plays yet, shall pass unexcepted at, here, as a man whose judgement shows it is constant, and hath stood still, these five and twenty, or thirty, years.

Yet the fact that he still finds it necessary to attack such plays indicates the powerful effect they had on the theatre-going public.

THE OLD PLAY

There was a play concerned with Hamlet performed at roughly the same time. It is assumed, that it must have resembled these early revenge tragedies. There are three important contemporary references to it:

1 In 1589 Robert Greene published his prose romance *Menaphon*. Thomas Nashe contributed a preface in the form of a letter 'To the Gentlemen Students of Both Universities' in which he contrasted Greene's admirable scholarship with the vulgar and ignorant use made of classical sources by the popular dramatists:

> It is a common practice nowadays amongst a sort of shifting companions, that run through every art and thrive by none, to leave the trade of *Noverint*, whereto they were born, and busy themselves with the endeavours of art, that could scarce Latinize their neck verse if they should have need. Yet English *Seneca* read by candle-light yields many good sentences, as

'Blood is a beggar', and so forth; and if you entreat him fair in a frosty morning he will afford you whole Hamlets – I should say handfuls – of tragical speeches.

2 In 1594 Philip Henslowe, the theatre owner and financier, records in his diary a series of performances given at Newington Butts by the Lord Admiral's and the Lord Chamberlain's companies. On the ninth of June they took eight shillings at a performance of *Hamlet*.

3 In *Wit's Miserie* (1596) Thomas Lodge refers to 'the ghost which cried so miserably at the Theatre, like an oyster wife, "Hamlet, revenge"'.

These references have been interpreted in various ways. Nashe is so determined to be 'witty' that his total effect and intention is obscure. However, he does refer at a later stage to the 'Kid in Aesop'. This, combined with the fact that Kyd had once been a scrivener, has made many commentators conclude that the early play on Hamlet (sometimes called the *Ur-Hamlet*) was written by Thomas Kyd. This view was particularly popular at a time when it was assumed that Shakespeare could have had no regular education in Stratford and must have begun his apprenticeship as a dramatist by rewriting or revising other men's plays. Since it is now clear that the Stratford grammar school was capable of providing a very good education, since it is possible that he may have been, according to one report, 'a schoolmaster in the country', and since few scholars now believe that the plays called *The Contention* and *The True Tragedy* are independent plays by other dramatists which Shakespeare rewrote as the second and third parts of *Henry VI*, it is no longer necessary to assume some lost 'source' play for Shakespeare. The evidence will bear a very different kind of interpretation.

In 1592–4 the London theatres were closed because of the risk of infection due to an epidemic of bubonic plague. The two companies which performed at Newington Butts were quite possibly playing together because of poverty caused by the lack of audiences and the necessity of touring in the provinces. The Admiral's Men were the company usually associated with Henslowe. The Chamberlain's Men were a new company; some of the actors had belonged to Lord Strange's Men who had been for some time associated with the Admiral's company. Their patron had died shortly after succeeding to the Earldom of Derby and when they re-formed as The Chamberlain's Men they added two other actors to their number, Richard Burbage and William Shakespeare. After their first recorded performance at Newington Butts the new company is known to have played at The Theatre from 1594 to 1596. It is this playhouse which Lodge refers to in *Wit's Miserie*. There is no record of Thomas Kyd ever working with this company. It seems probable that the old play of *Hamlet* was a piece in the repertory of The Chamberlain's Men and therefore it is perfectly possible that its author was William Shakespeare.

There is no doubt that Kyd is the object of Nashe's attack in his preface to Greene's *Menaphon*. This defence of Greene, however, was occasioned by the failure of his tragedy *Alphonsus, King of Aragon* to compete with Marlowe's *Tamburlaine*. Greene himself has inserted a sneer at Marlowe into his prose romance. We know that Marlowe and Kyd were for a time associated in working for the same company of actors under the patronage of a noble lord. If this nobleman was Lord Pembroke, as is suggested by the title page of *Edward II* and some remarks in a letter written by Kyd about his association with Marlowe, then we must add Shakespeare to the group. It appears that Nashe and Greene were attacking a more popular and more successful group of dramatists. It is important, therefore, to realise that we do not know who wrote the earlier *Hamlet* play. The evidence, however, does not warrant the assumption that it was written by Thomas Kyd. It could easily be the work of Shakespeare himself and the slow and continuous re-working of a play which was originally like *Titus Andronicus* could account both for the length of our present version of *Hamlet* and for the closely-worked intensity of the language and imagery.

There is another consideration which adds slight support to the idea that Shakespeare was the author of the early *Hamlet*. In 1599 or 1600 a company of child actors began playing at the Blackfriars Playhouse which had been reconstructed by James Burbage in 1596 but which he had been prevented from using as a theatre after a petition by the inhabitants of the Blackfriars. These are almost certainly the children referred to in Hamlet as 'little eyases' (II. 2. 346) and their impact upon the professional stage appears to have been considerable. They were noted for producing satiric plays and one of the objects of their satire was the old style of tragedy performed by the adult companies. *The Spanish Tragedy* was itself performed by the children, presumably in burlesque style, and their principal dramatist, John Marston produced a number of brilliant parodies of revenge drama in *Antonio's Revenge* and *The Malcontent*. Part of the reply of the adult companies is Shakespeare's *Hamlet* – a new version of an old story (perhaps previously dramatised by Shakespeare and therefore a target for the children) which adds an entirely new dimension to tragedy in the English theatre and is itself the object of imitation for the next forty years. The discussion between Hamlet and Rosencrantz and Guildenstern (which may, of course, be later than 1601 or even 1604 since it is omitted from the Quartos) indicates Shakespeare's interest and involvement in this important literary debate and controversy.

THE UNITY OF THE PLAY

One of the ways in which Shakespeare has transformed the old story is to make the actors themselves, the very adult company of which he was a part, visit Elsinore on the travels forced upon them by the success of the children in 'the city'. These actors are much more than a topical glance at a current literary quarrel. They, and the play which they perform within *Hamlet*, are one of the most vital parts of Shakespeare's design. They allow him to dramatise events and attitudes which could have been included in almost no other way. Hamlet says that the purpose of playing is to hold a mirror up to nature. For the Elizabethans, mirrors did not merely reflect – they reflected the truth. The looking-glass did not flatter, it showed a man what he was. The actors act as such a mirror for the King, for Hamlet and for the audience in the theatre. They remind the spectators, who are watching an audience on stage watching some actors performing a play, that they are engaged in an activity which may show them a true reflection of themselves – and that, like the King, they may be unprepared for the horrifying truth that is there revealed.

The excuse for this performance is that Hamlet wants to test the truth of the terrible story of murder, incest and adultery that he has heard from the Ghost. If Claudius is shown a re-enactment of the crime, a man pouring poison into the ear of a sleeping king, he may give himself away. The device is an old one, but most effective. It is still used by the writers of detective and mystery stories. *The Murder of Gonzago* does convince Hamlet, and the audience, of the King's guilt. It performs, however, a number of other vital functions. It shows the audience a dramatic representation of the original murder. It dramatises the nature of the task that Hamlet is called upon to perform – a revenge killing which bears a sinister resemblance to the act of murder – and it raises in acute form the questions of love and remembrance which are the subject of Hamlet's soliloquies and are at the heart of the turbulent relationships which form the tragic texture of the play.

A distinction must be made between the story of the play and its plot. The plot of *Hamlet* begins when the Ghost appears on the battlements to Horatio, Barnardo and Marcellus. The story began when Claudius poisoned his brother to obtain the crown and the love of Gertrude. It is this beginning which is now dramatised for the audience in the middle of the plot by the performance of the inner play. Up to this point they have merely heard about the murder. Now they have effectively seen it with their own eyes. It is, more than a simple re-enactment of the crime. The actual act of poisoning is performed twice, once in dumb show and once with words as well as gestures. Shakespeare uses a dumb show for the same reason that he uses an inner play – he requires that the image be realised in action upon his stage. Murder is performed twice because the inner play concerns two murders. The dumb show concerns the murder that is past – the murder of a king by an unknown hand. The rest of the play shows an image of the murder that is yet to come – the murder of a king by his nephew. It is not an accident that Hamlet ironically identifies the murderer for Claudius, 'This is one Lucianus, nephew to the King'.

It is significant that the figure of the poisoner remains the same throughout. If Hamlet were to complete the act of revenge and kill his uncle he would find himself playing the part of Lucianus – he would have become a man exactly like Claudius, a secret murderer by poison. Both images co-exist at the same time, dramatising, as nothing else could, the terrible dilemma of *Hamlet*. Murder should be revenged, but is revenge not also murder? How is it possible to act against Claudius without also acting in the same fashion as Claudius? The play indeed holds a mirror up to nature – but it shows a true and terrible reflection of Hamlet as well as of Claudius. Hamlet, apparently, is determined to play the part of Lucianus.

The inner play, which dramatises this apparently insoluble problem, also provides its resolution. Many commentators have asked why Claudius does not react at once when he sees the dumb show – some even go so far as to assert that he cannot have seen it. It is, however, essential to Shakespeare's design that the King should see the dumb show and hear the play. Hamlet has devised the play, with a dozen or fourteen lines of his own composition inserted, in

order to catch the conscience of the King (II. 2. 605–16).
In the mirror of the play, Claudius will suddenly be brought
face to face with himself. He is not the King of Denmark.
He is the man who murdered the King by pouring poison
into his ear. The conscience of Claudius, however, is
hardened and clouded over by the forgetfulness of the dead
which he is so anxious to urge upon the court. He remains
unmoved by the dumb show. He is made uneasy by the
debate about remembrance and remarriage between the
Player King and Player Queen and questions Hamlet
about the suitability of the argument or plot. He is moved to
action, and self-revelation, only when his alter ego in the
play, the poisoner Lucianus, begins a speech which is a
ceremony of witchcraft and stoops to pour his deadly drug
into the sleeping ear of the King. Claudius had won
Gertrude with the witchcraft of his wits and by poisoning
his brother's ear. He himself is now poisoned through his
ear – but on this occasion the poison is the witchcraft of
words spoken by an actor on a stage. It turns out, by one of
the great ironies of the play, that the performance of *The
Murder of Gonzago* is Hamlet's successful act of vengeance
against the King.

Shakespeare pivots the entire action of *Hamlet* round the
players. Before their performance the audience are faced
with a series of unresolved questions – after it death follows
death until 'the rest is silence'. On either side of the inner
play Shakespeare has placed a conversation about music
between Hamlet and Horatio, and Hamlet and Rosencrantz and Guildenstern. For the Renaissance, music
symbolised the proper harmony of the entire universe.
Horatio is the man who has his elements so well-balanced
that he is not a pipe to be played on by Fortune. Rosencrantz and Guildenstern, on the other hand, are men who
know no touch of music despite the fact that they seek to
play on Hamlet as on a pipe. The true friend and the false
ones are contrasted on either side of an action that must
make the audience question the nature of Hamlet's own

harmony and balance of soul. This question is intensified in the two great soliloquies which also fall on either side of the inner play.

When the players first arrive Hamlet calls at once for a speech. It is the tale told by Aeneas to Dido of the fall of Troy and, after it, Hamlet bitterly compares his own conduct to that of the actor who was prepared to weep at the sorrows of Hecuba. Compared to the passion displayed by the actor, his own lack of action seems pitifully inadequate. It is then that he resolves to 'catch the conscience of the King'. After the inner play, on his way to England in the company of Rosencrantz and Guildenstern, Hamlet encounters the army of Fortinbras on its way to the campaign in Poland. Hamlet now contrasts his apparent lack of action with the valour displayed by the soldiers who do not require 'great argument' to stir them to action but are risking their lives for a straw – but a straw which involves their honour. Again, Hamlet blames himself for thinking instead of acting – in the Hecuba soliloquy he believed that 'conscience does make cowards of us all'. He now says that 'thinking too precisely on th'event' is the cowardice which leaves him living to say 'This thing's to do'.

The irony of Shakespeare's design is that between these two soliloquies Hamlet has acted. He has presented *The Murder of Gonzago* and the consequences of that performance will transform his own part from that of an actor who adopts an 'antic disposition' but is unsure of his role, to a soldier engaged in a deadly secret battle with merciless adversaries. Before the play scene Claudius might be a murderer, but Hamlet could only strike at him in the way so boldly dramatised in the prayer scene – by an act of sudden murderous violence directed against an unsuspecting and unprepared man. The play catches the conscience of the King and, at the same time, warns him of his danger. His conscience does not make him repent. Instead, he resolves to protect himself and secure what he had gained from his crime – his crown, and queen. Claudius now plans to murder Hamlet, the son, as he had previously murdered Hamlet, the father. He sends Hamlet to execution in England and, when that fails, arranges the 'play' between Laertes and Hamlet in which one will have the advantage of a sharp and poisoned rapier. It is thus Claudius who begins to act out, for the second time, the part of the murderous Lucianus. In this attempt he fails. He is no longer faced by a sleeping brother but by a nephew roused to action with the perfect instrument of vengeance in his hand. Claudius finds that his judgement has failed and his luck run out. The search for security through murder ends in his own destruction.

The play also holds a mirror image of death up to Hamlet. It is one of the most remarkable features of Shakespeare's play that, although the nature of the act of vengeance is one of the central questions, Hamlet himself is never made to doubt or question his duty to revenge his father's murder. Instead, as so many commentators have done since, he blames himself for his delay. It is important to notice that to believe Hamlet's condemnation of his own actions is to assume that he ought, instantly, to have taken violent measures against the King. It is to accept the code of revenge as it is understood and later practised by Claudius and Laertes.

THE ROLE OF HAMLET

Hamlet appears to accept the code, but in the soliloquies and actions of the play, Shakespeare dramatises the considerations of conscience and the power of thought which prevent Hamlet, literally against his will, from achieving his desired blood revenge. It has often been observed that Hamlet is a man with a divided soul. It has not so frequently been noticed that Hamlet's troubled mind is the deliberate creation of Shakespeare and that he has presented it to his audience with a great deal of conscious artistic skill. In the course of the play Hamlet has seven long soliloquies. The first of these (I. 2. 129–59) occurs before he has seen the Ghost, the second (I. 5. 92–112) immediately after it has told its story of incest and adultery. Both speeches are concerned with memory (in the second, Hamlet actually dramatises the act of recording the Ghost's command in his brain) and the remembrance of his dead father. The next two soliloquies are concerned with thought or 'conscience'. The third (II. 2. 557–616) is spoken after the Player's recitation and is concerned with the power of thought which makes the actor pause for pity. It ends with the decision to catch the King's conscience. The fourth is 'To be, or not to be . . .' III. 1. 56–90 where thought faces the fact of death and conscience is said to make us cowards by restraining us from suicide. The fifth and sixth soliloquies are concerned with blood and will; one (III. 2. 395–406) is spoken on his way to his mother's private apartments, the other (III. 3. 73–96), the 'damnation soliloquy', behind the back of the apparently praying King. St Augustine had described the three powers of the soul as Memory, Understanding and Will. These six soliloquies dramatise exactly these powers in Hamlet's soul and show how his memory and understanding are irrevocably opposed to his will. One third of Hamlet desires to play the part of Lucianus and kill the King but he is prevented by the stronger, though unconscious, forces of his memory and conscience.

The seventh soliloquy (IV. 4. 32–66) is concerned with all three powers of the soul but the battle in Hamlet's mind is never decided at a conscious level. He never steps forward to tell us exactly what he is thinking and why he is acting in this fashion. If he did we should not believe him. A man who describes himself as a villain is probably telling the truth. A man who calls himself virtuous is certainly a liar, since he is already suffering from the unconscious sin of pride. In drama, therefore, as in life, it is easier for a villain to describe himself than an honest man. Shakespeare's resource is to make Hamlet call himself a coward and villain so often that the audience are bound to compare what he says with what he does. If his words stress his conscious doubts and desires, his actions show how much he is shaped by forces whose power he hardly acknowledges.

It is the battle within Hamlet's own mind which causes him to set the play as a trap for the King. His intention is to follow it with a brief but bloody revenge. In fact, since the play is also an instrument of memory and conscience, it has placed that revenge for ever out of Hamlet's reach. Claudius is no longer a-victim but a determined and deadly opponent who does succeed in killing Hamlet – though at the cost of his own life, and that of his queen. This dramatisation of the conscious and unconscious forces at work in Hamlet's mind has caused infinite problems for those who prefer simple explanations.

The split between Hamlet's understanding and his will is most clearly demonstrated in his relationship with Ophelia. It is clear that he has been appalled and depressed beyond measure by his mother's hasty marriage. He is aware that his reaction seems excessive to others (for the King and Queen tell him so) but he also believes that 'it is not, nor it cannot come to good'. He is right, because the marriage of Claudius and Gertrude is merely the visible sign of the monstrous rape that Claudius has perpetrated upon the 'body politic' of the state of Denmark – killing its king as well as marrying the Queen unlawfully. Once Hamlet has heard the revelation of the Ghost he takes farewell of Ophelia in the strange fashion that she describes to Polonius. He acts out the traditional role of a melancholy lover – but only the audience knows that he does so because love must now be superseded by the deadlier passion of revenge.

By the time that Hamlet meets Ophelia in the staged scene so carefully contrived by Claudius and Polonius, he has come to know more of the infinite corruption which infects the court. His melancholy has always been more than merely assumed and Shakespeare now shows in exact fashion how far it has affected his judgement. As he talks to Ophelia, Hamlet uses the symbolism of the three Graces – Chastity, Beauty and Passion who are usually shown in art as linked together in an eternal dance. In that dance, each combined with the others and supporting her partners, they represent the proper balance and combination of elements in the power of love. Alone and unsupported, Chastity may be cold and unloving, Beauty merely vain and self-regarding, and Passion the simple power of lust. Only when they join together are they truly at one. It is this combination which Hamlet says can never take place, since the combination of honesty (chastity) and beauty can only produce 'a bawd'–the grace of passion as mere animal desire. He sees his mother in this fashion and the attack upon Ophelia's 'paintings' as well as her speech and walk is a brutal attempt to identify her as the figure of lust.

In this Hamlet is clearly mistaken. Ophelia is indeed, at that moment, acting as a 'face' or decoy for the King and her father – but she is not herself part of the corruption which infects Denmark. She herself naturally treats such an attack as 'madness' and talks of a time when Hamlet appeared to be that rare Renaissance combination of the courtier, scholar and soldier. This ideal is strongly linked to the Augustinian concept of the three powers of the soul. A man ought to be able to pursue an active, contemplative and passionate life at one and the same time. The contemplative is associated with memory, the passionate with understanding and the active with will. There is a picture by Raphael in the National Gallery, London, in which Scipio is seen lying in full armour under a tree, dreaming of his fame. His dream is of two female figures – one of whom offers him a book and a sword, the symbols of the contemplative and active lives, while the other carries a flower, the symbol of passion. It is clear that Ophelia is at least partly correct. Hamlet's balance has been affected. In his passionate life he sees all women as whores and is about to give himself up to the uncontrolled passion of murderous revenge. He does not do so – but his passion has already contributed to Ophelia's destruction.

Ophelia, and her brother Laertes act out in the second

half of the play the terrible dilemma posed in Hamlet's 'To be, or not to be' soliloquy. Laertes chooses 'to be' and adopts for himself the complete role of revenger. Ophelia, clearly torn (in the incredibly painful songs of her scene of madness) between her love for her father and for Hamlet, chooses 'not to be' and goes to a death which the church, at least, regards as suicide. What is particularly tragic about her death is that Hamlet's language to her in the nunnery scene and at the play, although it is both sexually obscene and apparently insulting, is also the language of passionate love. What clouds it is Hamlet's own view of love, at that time, as a degrading force. Only in the graveyard, once he has faced the skulls which speak in their dumb show of the certainty of death, is he capable of asserting the love for Ophelia that might have saved them both, if the words to express it had existed. Yet Ophelia's death is a clear and necessary part of Shakespeare's design since the whole play is about the kind of human love that lives in memory and understanding, and will, in the last resort, attempt to outface death itself. It is a contest in which death inevitably triumphs – yet the power of human love remains, however improbably, unconquered.

THE SIGNIFICANCE OF THE ACTION

If it is once admitted that Shakespeare has used the players and *The Murder of Gonzago* to provide a great central reflecting mirror for the action of his play, and has, in Hamlet and Ophelia, dramatised minds brought to the brink of destruction by the terrifying power of competing and incompatible emotions, then the other elements in the design become clear. The Ghost is a powerful and formidable figure whose armour reminds the spectators of the duties of the active life – and in calling upon Hamlet to revenge his murder he summons memory, understanding and will to his aid. He commands Hamlet, however, to remember as well as to revenge – to spare his mother and not to taint his mind. These are commands difficult to reconcile and almost impossible to execute simultaneously No one can tell whether the Ghost comes from heaven or from hell. The call to avenge a father's murder is one to which few fail to respond (hence the strong feeling that Hamlet should have acted immediately) but few can also escape the conclusion that revenge, if practised in the manner of Lucianus, or Laertes, is damnable and inhuman. The responsibility of action remains Hamlet's alone since only Hamlet can transform the terrifying pull of these contrasting demands into deeds.

In the end, the play shows us three sons all faced with the task of avenging their fathers and defining, at the same time, their own place in the world. Fortinbras takes the traditional course of attempting to reassert his rights by force of arms. When he is compelled to recognise the justice of the compact between his father and King Hamlet he feels able to restore his honour by a campaign in Poland. It is on his return from that campaign that he appears, as a man in full armour, to speak the last lines of the play and remind the audience of the important role that is inevitably played in human affairs by force of arms and the virtues of the active life.

Laertes, on the other hand, is more a representative of the passionate life. His memory of his father causes him to cast aside all restraints of law or conscience. His attitude to Hamlet is that he is prepared to 'cut his throat i'th'church'. It is impossible not to sympathise with this attitude but Shakespeare also takes care to let his audience see that it is self-destructive as well as horrible. In breaking every law and custom of honour and courtesy in order to kill Hamlet, Laertes also devises the method of his own death.

Hamlet takes rather a different course. In the first place, he pauses for thought – the only time that he does not do so he kills Polonius and thus himself becomes a victim of vengeance as well as an avenger. Three times in the play he acts and each time his action is an appeal to the conscience of another character. He troubles the King's conscience in the inner play and the reaction of Claudius is to repeat his crime. He successfully rouses his mother's conscience in the closet scene and, finally, he appeals to the conscience of Laertes immediately before the duel with the poisoned sword. In the end even that appeal to an implacable avenger finds its mark – though not until both Hamlet and Laertes are dying. The forgiveness and mutual charity which they then exchange is the only way in which the long cycle of revenge can be broken and men can live in harmony and love within the sacred eternal dance of the Graces.

The alternative is clearly demonstrated during the duel scene. In one of the play's most terrible moments Gertrude leaves the side of the husband whom she loves (it is her tragedy that she did call it love) and comes down to wipe the sweat from Hamlet's forehead. The poisoned drink is standing beside her. She raises it to her lips: 'The Queen carouses to thy fortunes, Hamlet.' Claudius attempts to stop her: 'Good Gertrude, do not drink!' – 'I will my lord, I pray you pardon me.' There should be a long silence in the theatre as the King stands and watches her drinking the poison without uttering the words which could, even at that moment, have saved her. The love for which he committed murder, and is prepared to kill again and again, is the consuming passion of self-love.

Hamlet is far from a perfect character. His depression and melancholy, however understandable, cause him to misunderstand Ophelia and the Queen. He kills Polonius by mistake, but he also sends Rosencrantz and Guildenstern to their deaths with clear calculation. Yet throughout the pattern of deaths by poison, the constant playing of deceitful parts, and the duel of wits and words which becomes the final deadly encounter with the poisoned rapier, it is Hamlet who, by his constant questions, continually draws the attention of the audience to the possibility of the existence of honour, conscience and human love, even in the graveyard which is Elsinore. The skull of Yorick, the King's jester, reminds Hamlet, and the audience, that all mankind ends by playing the part of death continually grinning at its own 'grave' joke. It is Hamlet's insistence that even that part should be faced with courage, good humour and understanding which distinguishes him from the other characters and makes the play of *Hamlet* his tragedy.

Tragedy is a crisis in which intelligence and integrity doom their possessor to destruction more surely than any combination of vices. Compared to the settled persistence of mendacity and viciousness, or the uncomprehending vacillation of surviving mediocrity, this doubtful death seems less catastrophic than heroic. Tragedy ends with a funeral, which also celebrates a victory.

HAMLET

THE CHARACTERS

CLAUDIUS, King of Denmark
HAMLET, son to the late, and nephew to the present king
FORTINBRAS, Prince of Norway
HORATIO, friend to Hamlet
POLONIUS, Lord Chamberlain
LAERTES, his son
VOLTIMAND ⎫
CORNELIUS ⎪
ROSENCRANTZ ⎬ courtiers
GUILDENSTERN ⎪
OSRIC ⎭
MARCELLUS ⎫ officers
BARNARDO ⎭
FRANCISCO, a soldier
REYNALDO, servant to Polonius
GERTRUDE, Queen of Denmark and mother to Hamlet
OPHELIA, daughter to Polonius

A Gentleman
A Priest
A Captain
English Ambassadors
Players, two Clowns (Gravediggers)

Lords, Ladies, Officers, Soldiers, Sailors, Messengers
and Attendants

The ghost of Hamlet's father

ACT ONE, scene 1

For the act-division see p. 4. Shakespeare probably only divided the play into scenes.

The place where this first scene takes place is later (I. 2. 211) identified as a 'platform'. This is a gun-platform, specially prepared as a site for cannon. In Elizabethan times the great Danish batteries of guns commanding the entrance to the Baltic sea were particularly famous.

[1] Who's there? *Barnardo is the relieving sentinel and the fact that he challenges first is an instant indication that he is afraid of seeing more than his fellow soldier on guard.*

[2] Stand . . . unfold *Halt and identify yourself, reveal who you are*

[6] carefully . . . hour *you have taken care to arrive at the exact moment you are due to relieve me*

[9] sick at heart *extremely upset, mentally and physically. Another indication that their duty is somehow dangerous and sinister.*

[13] rivals *those who have an equal share in this period of guard duty*

[15] liegemen . . . Dane *soldiers or subjects who have sworn an oath of allegiance or loyalty to the King of Denmark*

[19] piece *Horatio indicates that, owing to the cold and the fact that it is the middle of the night, he is only 'half there'.*

ACT ONE

Scene 1. *Enter* BARNARDO *and* FRANCISCO, *two sentinels*

BARNARDO Who's there?
FRANCISCO Nay, answer me. Stand and unfold
    yourself.
BARNARDO Long live the King.
FRANCISCO Barnardo?
BARNARDO He.
FRANCISCO You come most carefully upon your hour.
BARNARDO 'Tis now struck twelve. Get thee to bed,
    Francisco.
FRANCISCO For this relief much thanks. 'Tis bitter
    cold,
    And I am sick at heart.
BARNARDO Have you had quiet guard?
FRANCISCO   Not a mouse stirring.   10
BARNARDO Well, good night.
    If you do meet Horatio and Marcellus,
    The rivals of my watch, bid them make haste.

        Enter HORATIO *and* MARCELLUS

FRANCISCO I think I hear them. Stand, ho! Who is
    there?
HORATIO Friends to this ground.
MARCELLUS   And liegemen to the Dane.
FRANCISCO Give you good night.
MARCELLUS   O, farewell honest soldier,
    Who hath relieved you?
FRANCISCO   Barnardo hath my place.
    Give you good night.
                      [*Exit*

MARCELLUS   Holla, Barnardo!
BARNARDO   Say,
    What, is Horatio there?
HORATIO   A piece of him.

[25] Touching *Concerning*

[29] approve *corroborate, confirm*

[31] assail *Barnardo describes Horatio's ears and understanding as a fortified position which has to be taken by their story. The continuous use of military metaphors is a striking feature of the play.*

[35] Last night of all *Last night out of all other nights; i.e. only last night*

[36] star *Barnardo uses the progress of the stars across the sky to fix the exact time. In Julius Caesar (II. 1. 2.) Brutus refers to the same method of telling the time at night.*

[37] illume *lighten*

[41] figure *form, shape. Neither the guards nor Horatio say that the Ghost is the dead King. They say it looks like him, implying that it is a spirit who has assumed his shape.*

[42] scholar *As an educated man Horatio might be expected to know the proper religious terms to use in addressing a ghost. Since the Ghost might be a devil and a threat to their immortal souls this was an important consideration.*

[44] harrows *lacerates the emotions with fear and wonder as the harrow (a heavy agricultural tool) breaks up the ground*

BARNARDO Welcome, Horatio. Welcome, good
    Marcellus.   20

MARCELLUS What, has this thing appeared again
    tonight?

BARNARDO I have seen nothing.

MARCELLUS Horatio says 'tis but our fantasy,
    And will not let belief take hold of him
    Touching this dreaded sight, twice seen of us.
    Therefore I have intreated him along
    With us to watch the minutes of this night,
    That, if again this apparition come,
    He may approve our eyes and speak to it.

HORATIO Tush, tush, 'twill not appear.

BARNARDO   Sit down awhile,   30
    And let us once again assail your ears,
    That are so fortified against our story,
    What we have two nights seen.

HORATIO   Well, sit we down,
    And let us hear Barnardo speak of this.

BARNARDO Last night of all,
    When yon same star that's westward from
        the pole,
    Had made his course t'illume that part of
        heaven
    Where now it burns, Marcellus and myself,
    The bell then beating one –

Enter GHOST

MARCELLUS Peace, break thee off – look where it
    comes again.   40

BARNARDO In the same figure, like the King that's
    dead.

MARCELLUS Thou art a scholar; speak to it, Horatio.

BARNARDO Looks it not like the King? Mark it
    Horatio.

HORATIO Most like, it harrows me with fear and
    wonder.

[46] usurp'st   *use wrongfully. The spirit is a usurper because it appears in the night, which ought to be a time of rest and quiet, and assumes the form of the dead King.*

[49] charge   *command*

[57] sensible . . . avouch   *the sense impression received by my eyes which provides a true assurance or guarantee of the Ghost's appearance. Horatio would not have believed it unless he had seen it for himself.*

[61] ambitious Norway   *the ambitious King of Norway*

[62] parle   *parley – conversation held between enemies under a flag of truce*

[63] sleaded poleaxe   *a fighting axe with a long staff or handle bound round with iron to prevent it from splitting. It was frequently carried by officers as a symbol of authority. This line is sometimes read as 'sledded Polacks' implying that the King had engaged Polish troops on sledges. In this care 'parle' would have to mean 'battle' which is unlikely.*

[65] jump   *just, exactly*

[67–8] particular . . . opinion   *I do not know with which particular thought I ought to start (my explanation of these events) but in the largest and most general terms my opinion is . . .*

[69] bodes   *forecasts (with the suggestion of future ill fortune)*

strange eruption   *unusual calamity (like an earthquake or disease)*

BARNARDO It would be spoke to.

MARCELLUS   Speak to it, Horatio.

HORATIO What art thou that usurp'st this time of
          night
          Together with that fair and warlike form
          In which the majesty of buried Denmark
          Did sometimes march? By heaven I charge
          thee, speak!

MARCELLUS It is offended.

BARNARDO   See, it stalks away.   50

HORATIO Stay, speak, speak, I charge thee, speak.

                              [*Exit* GHOST

MARCELLUS 'Tis gone, and will not answer.

BARNARDO How now, Horatio? You tremble and
          look pale.
          Is not this something more than fantasy?
          What think you on't?

HORATIO Before my God, I might not this believe
          Without the sensible and true avouch
          Of mine own eyes.

MARCELLUS   Is it not like the King?

HORATIO As thou art to thyself.
          Such was the very armour he had on   60
          When he the ambitious Norway combated.
          So frowned he once when, in an angry parle,
          He smote the sleaded poleaxe on the ice.
          'Tis strange.

MARCELLUS Thus twice before, and jump at this dead
          hour,
          With martial stalk hath he gone by our watch.

HORATIO In what particular thought to work I know
          not;
          But, in the gross and scope of mine opinion,
          This bodes some strange eruption to our state.

MARCELLUS Good now, sit down, and tell me – he
          that knows –   70
          Why this same strict and most observant watch

35

[72] toils . . . land *why the subjects of the land are made to work so hard every night keeping this rigorously maintained and particularly alert guard*

[74] foreign mart *resort to foreign markets to buy weapons*

[75] impress *conscription, directed labour*

sore *laborious to the extent of being painful*

[76] divide *The work makes no division between the working days of the week and Sunday, the Christian day of rest.*

[77] toward *imminent, impending*

[80] whisper *rumour*

[83] prickt on *driven on as a horse is spurred on*

emulate *rivalrous. His pride made him desire to equal or surpass King Hamlet.*

[85] this side *everyone in this hemisphere, i.e. all those who might be expected to have heard of him*

[87] ratified *made valid*

[89] seized *possessed. 'To seize' in this sense is to put a person in possession of a feudal holding. It could also mean land acquired by conquest.*

[90] moiety competent *equal part of land*

[91] gagèd *wagered*

returned *reverted, been transferred*

[93] comart *joint bargain, agreement*

[94] carriage . . . design *the meaning carried by the words in the specific article of the agreement*

[96] unimprovèd *not reproved, uncontrolled, not cultivated*

mettle *spirit, temperament, courage. Fortinbras is described as being hot and full of this as yet uncontrolled fierce spirit. 'Mettle' and 'metal' were originally the same word and it may also imply a sense of Fortinbras being of as yet untried or untempered metal – hot before it is tempered in cold water.*

[98] Sharked up *Looked for hastily, without selection*

list *military muster roll*

resolutes *dissolute (but perhaps determined) characters*

[99] food . . . diet *either a) men who fight for no pay but regular meals or, b) men who are accustomed to the food and diet of an enter- prise requiring stomach or courage – since the stomach was thought to determine a man's courage. Men who are accustomed to undertake dangerous exploits.*

So nightly toils the subject of the land;
And why such daily cast of brazen cannon,
And foreign mart for implements of war?
Why such impress of shipwrights, whose
    sore task
Does not divide the Sunday from the week?
What might be toward, that this sweaty haste
Doth make the night joint-labourer with the
    day:
Who is't that can inform me?

HORATIO   That can I –

At least, the whisper goes so. Our last King,   80
Whose image even but now appeared to us,
Was, as you know, by Fortinbras of Norway –
Thereto prickt on by a most emulate pride –
Dared to the combat; in which our valiant
    Hamlet
(For so this side of our known world
    esteemed him)
Did slay this Fortinbras – who, by a sealed
    compact,
Well ratified by law and heraldry,
Did forfeit (with his life) all those his lands
Which he stood seized of, to the conqueror.
Against the which a moiety competent   90
Was gagèd by our King, which had returned
To the inheritance of Fortinbras
Had he been vanquisher – as, by the same
    comart
And carriage of the article design,
His fell to Hamlet. Now sir, young
    Fortinbras,
Of unimprovèd mettle hot and full,
Hath in the skirts of Norway, here and there,
Sharked up a list of lawless resolutes
For food and diet to some enterprise
That hath a stomach in't: which is no other,   100

[103] terms compulsory *terms which Denmark is compelled to accept by force of arms*

[107] post haste *urgent business conducted at speed by means of post horses*

romage *commotion, turmoil*

[109] sort *agree (with this explanation)*

[111] question *cause of dispute*

[112] mote *speck of dust – a probable reference to Matthew 7. 3*

mind's eye *the memory*

[113] palmy *triumphant, glorious – since the palm was the emblem of triumph and victory*

[117] stars . . . fire *comets. It seems probable that either a) something is here missing from the text or, b) the lines have been displaced and 117–20 ought to follow after 125.*

[118] Disasters *an astrological term meaning the unfavourable aspect of a star or planet*

moist star *the moon – which controls the tides of the sea*

[119] Neptune's empire *the sea. Neptune was the Roman god of the sea.*

[120] sick . . . doomsday *of a sickly colour, pale. Eclipses of the sun or moon were considered especially bad omens. Doomsday is the Christian day of judgement when Christ is said to come again to judge the living and the dead. Matthew 24. 29 associated this with darkness in the sun and moon. Horatio says that the eclipse of the moon was almost as serious as that final darkness.*

[121] precurse *forerunner*

[122] harbingers *officers who went ahead of the King to announce his arrival and prepare his lodging*

[123] prologue *an introduction, or one who speaks it before a stage play*

omen coming on *approaching prophetic sign – the Ghost itself. Horatio says that the unnatural events which foretold the death of Julius Caesar in Rome have already appeared as 'prologue' to the Ghost.*

[125] climatures *regions*

[127] cross it *a) cross its path, b) make the sign of the cross at it. To cross the path of a spirit was to risk putting oneself in its power; making the sign of the cross at it ought to make it speak if it is a heavenly spirit or prevent it doing harm if it is a devil.*

blast *strike with a curse, blight*

As it doth well appear unto our state,
But to recover of us, by strong hand
And terms compulsatory, those foresaid lands
So by his father lost. And this (I take it)
Is the main motive of our preparations,
The source of this our watch, and the chief
    head
Of this post haste and romage in the land.

BARNARDO I think it be no other but e'en so.
Well may it sort, that this portentous figure
Comes armèd through our watch – so like the
    King   110
That was, and is, the question of these wars.

HORATIO A mote it is to trouble the mind's eye.
In the most high and palmy state of Rome
– A little ere the mightiest Julius fell –
The graves stood tenantless, and the sheeted
    dead
Did squeak and gibber in the Roman streets,
As stars with trains of fire, and dews of blood,
Disasters in the sun – and the moist star,
Upon whose influence Neptune's empire
    stands,
Was sick almost to doomsday with eclipse.   120
And even the like precurse of feared events,
As harbingers preceding still the fates
And prologue to the omen coming on,
Have heaven and earth together demonstrated
Unto our climatures and countrymen.

Enter GHOST

But soft, behold. Lo, where it comes again.
I'll cross it though it blast me. Stay illusion,

HORATIO *spreads his arms*

If thou hast any sound or use of voice,
Speak to me.

[130] good thing *a good act, perhaps omitted in life, which troubles the spirit and makes it walk until the act is performed*

[133] privy *have secret knowledge of*

[134] happily *by chance*

[137] Extorted *Taken by force — which therefore ought to be returned*

womb *The earth is regularly treated as a female figure or goddess. Another example of an act performed in life which might trouble the conscience of the spirit and make it walk as a ghost.*

[140] partisan *a weapon used by foot soldiers consisting of a long-handled spear with a projecting hook or blade set at right angles to the spear point*

[144] show *display*

[146] malicious mockery *an evil pantomime — their blows are a mockery because they are mock or imitation blows, being quite ineffective. They are also malicious because they are delivered with evil intent. They are thus also a mockery or insult to the majestic figure of the Ghost.*

[150] trumpet *trumpeter — who accompanies a military commander and announces his presence by blowing a call. The cock is the morn's trumpeter.*

[152] god of day *Apollo, the sun god. It is significant that Horatio, the scholar, talks in terms of classical mythology. The soldier Marcellus offers a Christian interpretation.*

[154] extravagant and erring *a spirit wandering (erring) beyond the bounds of its proper place*

[156] made probation *gave proof*

[158] 'gainst *by the time that*

season *the twelve days of Christmas*

If there be any good thing to be done   130
That may to thee do ease, and grace to me,
Speak to me.
If thou art privy to thy country's fate,
Which happily foreknowing may avoid,
O speak.
Or if thou hast uphoarded in thy life
Extorted treasure in the womb of earth,
For which they say you spirits oft walk in
          death,

          The cock crows

Speak of it. Stay, and speak – stop it
          Marcellus!
MARCELLUS Shall I strike at it with my partisan?   140
HORATIO Do, if it will not stand.
BARNARDO   'Tis here.
HORATIO   'Tis here!
MARCELLUS 'Tis gone.

                                        [*Exit* GHOST
We do it wrong, being so majestical,
To offer it the show of violence,
For it is as the air, invulnerable,
And our vain blows malicious mockery.
BARNARDO It was about to speak, when the cock crew.
HORATIO And then it started like a guilty thing
Upon a fearful summons. I have heard
The cock, that is the trumpet to the morn,   150
Doth with his lofty and shrill sounding throat
Awake the god of day, and at his warning,
Whether in sea or fire, in earth or air,
Th' extravagant and erring spirit hies
To his confine – and of the truth herein
This present object made probation.
MARCELLUS It faded on the crowing of the cock.
Some say that ever 'gainst that season comes
Wherein our Saviour's birth is celebrated

[161] abroad   *beyond the bounds of its proper place*

[162] strike   *exert an evil influence even to the extent of killing or destroying*

163] takes   *enchants*

[175] convenient   *conveniently, suitably for our purpose*

ACT ONE, scene 2

[1] Hamlet   *King Hamlet, brother of Claudius and father of Prince Hamlet*

[2] green   *fresh*

befitted   *it was fitting or proper for us*

[4] brow   *forehead. The kingdom is thought of as having a face which is contracted or drawn together in grief.*

[5] discretion   *reason. The King has used his reason to combat his natural feelings of grief to produce the wisest sorrow which remembers the living as well as the dead.*

[8] sometime   *former*

[9] jointress   *A jointure was property held in common between husband and wife. A jointress is therefore a widow who is entitled in her own right to her share of the common property.*

This bird of dawning singeth all night long,   160
And then, they say, no spirit dare stir abroad,
The nights are wholesome, then no planets
   strike,
No fairy takes, nor witch hath power to charm,
So hallowed and so gracious is that time.
HORATIO So have I heard – and do in part believe it.
But look, the morn in russet mantle clad
Walks o'er the dew of yon high eastward hill.
Break we our watch up and, by my advice,
Let us impart what we have seen tonight
Unto young Hamlet, for, upon my life,   170
This spirit, dumb to us, will speak to him.
Do you consent we shall aquaint him with it,
As needful in our loves, fitting our duty?
MARCELLUS Let's do't, I pray; and I this morning
   know
Where we shall find him most convenient.
                                [*Exeunt*

Scene 2. *Flourish. Enter* CLAUDIUS *King of Denmark,*
GERTRUDE *the Queen,* HAMLET, POLONIUS, LAERTES *and
his sister* OPHELIA, LORDS *attendant*

KING Though yet of Hamlet our dear brother's death
The memory be green, and that it us befitted
To bear our hearts in grief, and our whole
   kingdom
To be contracted in one brow of woe,
Yet so far hath discretion fought with nature
That we with wisest sorrow think on him
Together with remembrance of ourselves.
Therefore our sometime sister – now our
   queen –
Th' imperial jointress to this warlike state,
Have we, as 'twere with a defeated joy,   10

[11] auspicious   *favourable, fortunate*
dropping   *tearful*

[13] delight   *pleasure*
dole   *sorrow, pain*

[14] Taken to wife   *Married. Such a marriage would be illegal in Shakespeare's England since the Church considered such a relationship incestuous. A man could only legally marry his dead brother's widow after 1921. Claudius carefully leads up to this statement in an attempt to make it appear normal and natural conduct.*

[15] better wisdoms   *considered opinion. Claudius has asked his council for their approval, and obtained it.*

[20] disjoint   *disjointed, disorganized*
out of frame   *out of order. The metaphor is of an ordered or square structure which has been pushed out of shape. The irony for the audience is that the Ghost's appearance has already suggested that Denmark is out of frame.*

[21] Coleaguèd   *United*

[23] Importing   *Signifying*

[29] impotent   *powerless*

[31] further gait   *further course of action*

[31-3] levies . . . subject   *Since the troops are raised, mustered, and their entire number made up from the King of Norway's subjects, he can prevent their use by Fortinbras.*

[38] delated   *set down — the terms set down in the legal commission which they carry*

[43] suit   *request, petition*

With an auspicious and a dropping eye,
With mirth in funeral, and with dirge in
    marriage,
In equal scale weighing delight and dole,
Taken to wife. Nor have we herein barred
Your better wisdoms, which have freely gone
With this affair along. For all, our thanks.
Now follows that you know: young Fortinbras,
Holding a weak supposal of our worth,
Or thinking by our late dear brother's death
Our state to be disjoint and out of frame,   20
Coleaguèd with this dream of his advantage,
He hath not failed to pester us with message
Importing the surrender of those lands
Lost by his father, with all bonds of law,
To our most valiant brother. So much for him.
Now for ourself, and for this time of meeting,
Thus much the business is – we have here writ
To Norway, uncle of young Fortinbras,
(Who impotent and bedrid scarcely hears
Of this his nephew's purpose) to suppress   30
His further gait herein, in that the levies,
The lists, and full proportions, are all made
Out of his subject; and we here dispatch
You, good Cornelius, and you, Voltemand,
For bearers of this greeting to old Norway,
Giving to you no further personal power
To business with the King more than the scope
Of these delated articles allow.
Farewell, and let your haste commend your
    duty.
CORNELIUS   ⎱ In that, and all things, will we show
VOLTEMAND ⎰   our duty.   40
KING We doubt it nothing, heartily farewell.
          [*Exeunt* VOLTEMAND *and* CORNELIUS
And now, Laertes, what's the news with you?
You told us of some suit, what is't Laertes?

45

[44] speak of reason   *make a reasonable request*

[45] lose your voice   *fail to gain the King's approval. There is a play upon the meaning of 'voice' = Laertes' organ of speech, and 'voice' = approval expressed by speech cf.* A Midsummer Night's Dream *I. 1. 54.*

[46] offer   *Whatever Laertes asks will be given by the King as if it were a free gift and not the result of a petition.*

[47] native   *closely related*

[48] instrumental   *essential to the service of*

[50] dread   *held in awe or reverence*

[56] pardon   *permission to depart*

[60] will   *desire*

sealed   *gave the seal or approval of my hard-won consent*

[62] fair hour   *the time which is now at its most favourable for you. The King speaks as if time were a precious gift which he could give to Laertes to spend at his pleasure, with the help of his own best qualities (graces).*

[64] cousin   *a formal term of respect used by a sovereign when he addresses other kings or his own nobles*

son   *.implies that Claudius has taken the place of Hamlet's father and will treat him as a father should treat his son*

[65] kin . . . kind   *a little more than a distant relative but yet less than a close member of the family. There is a pun intended on 'kind' = of the same birth, descent, and 'kind' = friendly, loving.*

[66] clouds   *of grief, melancholy*

[67] sun   *Men suffering from melancholy were supposed to shun sunlight and seek the dark. Hamlet therefore accepts the King's remark as alluding to his condition but rejects, by an aggressive pun on 'sun' and 'son', the claim to close relationship.*

[68] nighted   *colour made black as night – refers both to the clouds of melancholy and the conspicuous black of Hamlet's clothes*

[69] friend . . . Denmark   *allow yourself to look like a friend (and not a scowling enemy) on Denmark – both the King and people*

You cannot speak of reason to the Dane
And lose your voice. What would'st thou
    beg Laertes,
That shall not be my offer, not thy asking?
The head is not more native to the heart,
The hand more instrumental to the mouth,
Than is the throne of Denmark to thy father.
What would'st thou have, Laertes?

LAERTES   My dread lord,   50
Your leave and favour to return to France;
From whence though willingly I came to
    Denmark
To show my duty in your coronation,
Yet now, I must confess, that duty done,
My thoughts and wishes bend again toward
    France,
And bow them to your gracious leave and
    pardon.

KING Have you your father's leave? What says
    Polonius?

POLONIUS He hath, my lord, wrung from me my slow
    leave
By laboursome petition; and at last
Upon his will I sealed my hard consent.   60
I do beseech you, give him leave to go.

KING Take thy fair hour, Laertes, time be thine,
And thy best graces spend it at thy will.
But now, my cousin Hamlet, and my son –

HAMLET [*Aside*] A little more than kin, and less than
    kind.

KING How is it that the clouds still hang on you?

HAMLET Not so, my lord; I am too much i' th' sun.

QUEEN Good Hamlet, cast thy nighted colour off,
And let thine eye look like a friend on
    Denmark.
Do not forever with thy vailèd lids   70
Seek for thy noble father in the dust.

[72] common   *common to all men, universal*

[73] nature   *natural life*

[75] particular   *as if it were something that applied only to yourself*

[76] Seems   *Hamlet interprets Gertrude's 'seems' = appears, to mean false-seeming or hypocrisy and defends himself against that implied charge.*

[78] customary   *the black clothes worn by custom at funerals*

[79] suspiration   *sighing. Hamlet implies that the sighs of mourners may be windy, forced and feigned.*

[80] fruitful   *producing many tears*

[82] shapes   *make-up and costume appropriate to a theatrical part*

[84] play   *act, perform. 'Play' and 'player' are the regular Shakespearian terms for 'act' and 'actor'.*

[86] trappings   *external display or decorations*

[91] term   *period of time*

[92] obsequious   *sorrow suitable for obsequies or funeral rites*

[93] condolement   *sorrowing, lamentation*

[95] incorrect   *not corrected – by submitting to the will of God*

[97] unschooled   *uninstructed in philosophy and theology*

[99] vulgar   *common, usual. Claudius argues that death is as common and natural as any of the commonest sense impressions experienced by man.*

[102] nature   *The common theme of the natural condition of humanity is death and therefore the fault against nature is the one which seems most absurd to the reason.*

Thou know'st 'tis common – all that lives
   must die,
Passing through nature to eternity.
HAMLET Ay, madam, it is common.
QUEEN   If it be,
   Why seems it so particular with thee?
HAMLET Seems, madam? Nay, it is. I know not seems.
   'Tis not alone my inky cloak, good mother,
   Nor customary suits of solemn black,
   Nor windy suspiration of forced breath,
   No, nor the fruitful river in the eye,   80
   Nor the dejected haviour of the visage,
   Together with all forms, moods, shapes of
      grief,
   That can denote me truly. These indeed
      'seem',
   For they are actions that a man might play.
   But I have that within which passes show –
   These but the trappings and the suits of woe.
KING 'Tis sweet and commendable in your nature,
      Hamlet,
   To give these mourning duties to your father.
   But you must know your father lost a father,
   That father lost, lost his – and the survivor
      bound   90
   In filial obligation for some term
   To do obsequious sorrow. But to persever
   In obstinate condolement is a course
   Of impious stubbornness, 'tis unmanly grief.
   It shows a will most incorrect to heaven,
   A heart unfortified, a mind impatient,
   An understanding simple and unschooled.
   For what we know must be, (and is as common
   As any the most vulgar thing to sense)
   Why should we, in our peevish opposition,   100
   Take it to heart? Fie, 'tis a fault to heaven,
   A fault against the dead, a fault to nature

[105] **first corse** *first corpse. According to Genesis 4 the first corpse was that of Abel, murdered by his brother Cain. It is a deliberately unfortunate illustration of Claudius's claim that all death is natural.*

[107] **unprevailing** *ineffective – because it can never overcome death*

[109] **most immediate** *person next in line of succession. Norway and Denmark are elective monarchies where the son does not necessarily succeed his father. Claudius here gives Hamlet his voice or vote on the elective council of nobles as Hamlet later gives his dying voice (V. 2. 360) for Fortinbras.*

[112] **impart** *bestow, give*

[113] **school in Wittenberg** *Shakespeare makes Hamlet a student at the University of Wittenberg, in Germany, founded in 1502. Martin Luther became professor of philosophy in 1508 and the university acquired a considerable reputation on account of its connection with the Protestant reformation.*

[114] **retrograde** *contrary*

[115] **bend** *to turn away from a straight line – hence, to direct incline, change, persuade*

[118] **lose** *waste*

[125] **jocund health** *joyful toast using the formula 'here's a health unto his Majesty' while drinking*

[127] **rouse** *carousel, bout of drinking*

bruit again *echo. To bruit is to make a noise or report. The King intends the heavens to echo the cannon which mark his drinks as a symbol of his royal power and prudence.*

[129] **solid** *hard, dense. Flesh is one of the solid elements in the body in Elizabethan physiology. Hamlet is particularly conscious of its hardness or heaviness because its weight or mass contributes to his melancholy – hence his desire to be eased of its burden. Many editors here prefer the reading of Q1 and Q2 'sallied' or 'troubled' (though 'sallied' may be a form of 'solid'), and some interpret it as meaning 'sullied' or 'stained'. The use of 'melt', 'thaw', 'resolve' make 'solid' is in my opinion the more probable reading.*

[130] **resolve** *to pass by dissolution, change, into another, simpler form*

[132] **canon** *law*

self slaughter *suicide. The Church regarded suicide as damnable because it indicated despair of the Providence of God.*

(To reason most absurd) whose common theme
Is death of fathers, and who still hath cried
From the first corse till he that died today,
'This must be so'. We pray you throw to earth
This unprevailing woe, and think of us
As of a father. For, let the world take note,
You are the most immediate to our throne,
And with no less nobility of love   110
Than that which dearest father bears his son
Do I impart toward you. For your intent
In going back to school in Wittenberg,
It is most retrograde to our desire;
And we beseech you, bend you, to remain
Here in the cheer and comfort of our eye,
Our chiefest courtier, cousin, and our son.

QUEEN Let not thy mother lose her prayers Hamlet.
    I pray thee stay with us, go not to
      Wittenberg.

HAMLET I shall in all my best obey you, madam.   120

KING Why, 'tis a loving and a fair reply,
    Be as ourself in Denmark. Madam, come.
    This gentle and unforced accord of Hamlet
    Sits smiling to my heart; in grace whereof
    No jocund health that Denmark drinks today,
    But the great cannon to the clouds shall tell,
    And the King's rouse the heaven shall bruit
      again,
    Respeaking earthly thunder. Come away.

Flourish. Exeunt all but HAMLET

HAMLET O that this too too solid flesh would melt,
    Thaw, and resolve itself into a dew.   130
    Or that the Everlasting had not fix'd
    His canon 'gainst self slaughter. O God, God,
    How weary, stale, flat, and unprofitable
    Seem to me all the uses of this world!
    Fie on't, ah, fie – 'tis an unweeded garden

[136] rank   *luxuriant, with an offensive smell, corrupt, festering*
gross   *coarse, rough, repulsive*

[137] merely   *absolutely, completely*

[140] Hyperion   *in Greek mythology one of the race of giants, son of Uranus the sky god and Gaia the earth mother, and father of Helios the sun god. The name is frequently used, as Shakespeare appears to use it, as a title for the sun.*

satyr   *In Greek mythology a small woodland god, half-human and half-goat or horse. They were the companions of Pan and Dionysus and devoted to wine and lechery.*

[141] beteem   *permit, allow*

[144] increase of appetite   *as if her appetite (for love) had grown greater the more she fed on what should satisfy it*

[146] Frailty   *if Frailty were thought of as having human shape then her name would be woman or womankind – one of Hamlet's witty and sarcastic phrases which have become proverbial*

[147] little   *short*

[149] Niobe   *in Greek mythology the wife of Amphion, King of Thebes, who wept so much for the death of her children that she was transformed into a mountain rock which continued to shed tears. She had boasted that her twelve children were superior to Apollo and Artemis the divine children of Leto.*

[150] discourse of reason   *process or faculty of reasoning*

[153] Hercules   *in Greek mythology the chief mortal hero of Greece, son of Zeus the leader of the Olympian gods and Alcmena Queen of Tiryns. He performed the twelve labours but is more famous in the Renaissance for the Choice of Hercules in which he chose the way of virtue in preference to an easy and happy life.*

[155] flushing   *a sudden flowing of blood to the face or of tears from the eyes causing redness*

galled   *made sore by rubbing*

[156] post   *move speedily as if using posthorses*

[157] incestuous   *compare line 14 and note*

[159] break . . . tongue   *It is impossible for Hamlet to express this cause of his melancholy openly in the court. He must remain silent even if it breaks his heart. Unexpressed grief was supposed to be dangerous.*

[160] well   *Hamlet clearly does not look at the person who addresses him and replies with conventional politeness at first.*

That grows to seed. Things rank and gross in
   nature
Possess it merely. That it should come to this.
But two months dead – nay not so much, not
   two –
So excellent a king that was to this
Hyperion to a satyr. So loving to my mother,   140
That he might not beteem the winds of heaven
Visit her face too roughly. Heaven and earth,
Must I remember? Why she would hang on
   him
As if increase of appetite had grown
By what it fed on; and yet, within a month,
– Let me not think on't. Frailty, thy name
   is woman –
A little month, or ere those shoes were old
With which she followed my poor father's body
Like Niobe, all tears; why she, even she
(O God, a beast that wants discourse of reason   150
Would have mourned longer) married with my
   uncle,
My father's brother, but no more like my father
Than I to Hercules. Within a month,
Ere yet the salt of most unrighteous tears
Had left the flushing in her gallèd eyes,
She married. O most wicked speed to post
With such dexterity to incestuous sheets!
It is not, nor it cannot come to good.
But break, my heart, for I must hold my
   tongue.

Enter HORATIO, MARCELLUS *and* BARNARDO

HORATIO Hail to your lordship.
HAMLET   I am glad to see you well.   160
      Horatio – or I do forget myself!
HORATIO The same, my lord, and your poor servant
      ever.

53

[163] change *exchange. Horatio calls Hamlet 'lord' and himself 'servant', Hamlet replies that they are friends and can exchange roles since friends are each the servant of the other.*

[164] what make you... ? *what are you doing here? what business takes you away from Wittenberg?*

[170] violence *you shall not compel me to believe my own ears and trust your own report against yourself*

[174] drink deep *another reference to the intemperate habits of Claudius. Hamlet will, in fact, prevent Horatio from drinking deep from the poisoned cup in the last act, V. 2. 347.*

[178] hard upon *closely*

[179] baked meats *It was customary to provide a feast at funerals. Hamlet suggests that as a result of court haste and economy the cuts and joints of meat baked for his father's funeral were served again cold at his mother's second marriage. There is a play upon 'cold' and 'thrift' which suggests that the whole episode was somehow mean and uncharitable.*

[181] dearest *closest, most deadly. 'Dear' was used of whatever came near in either love or hate.*

[183] see *Horatio, who has come to tell Hamlet of the Ghost, is startled by this reference. The dramatist uses the half joke to impress the importance of Hamlet's memory on the audience.*

[184] mind's eye *memory*

[186] all in all *Two meanings are possible: a) Hamlet's father, despite some natural failings, was a better man than any other he is likely to see b) he was a man in which the qualities of the four humours were so mixed that he was superior to any other man.*

[190] Season *Qualify, moderate*
      admiration *astonishment*

HAMLET Sir, my good friend. I'll change that name
       with you.
      And what make you from Wittenberg,
       Horatio?
      Marcellus.
MARCELLUS My good lord.
HAMLET I am very glad to see you.
      [*To* BARNARDO] Good even, sir.
      But what, in faith, make you from
       Wittenberg?
HORATIO A truant disposition, good my lord.
HAMLET I would not hear your enemy say so;
      Nor shall you do my ear that violence,   170
      To make it truster of your own report
      Against yourself. I know you are no truant.
      But what is your affair in Elsinore?
      We'll teach you to drink deep ere you depart.
HORATIO My lord, I came to see your father's funeral.
HAMLET I prithee do not mock me, fellow student;
      I think it was to see my mother's wedding.
HORATIO Indeed, my lord, it followed hard upon.
HAMLET Thrift, thrift, Horatio. The funeral baked
       meats
      Did coldly furnish forth the marriage tables. 180
      Would I had met my dearest foe in heaven
      Or ever I had seen that day, Horatio.
      My father – methinks I see my father.
HORATIO Where, my lord?
HAMLET   In my mind's eye, Horatio.
HORATIO I saw him once; he was a goodly king.
HAMLET He was a man, take him for all in all,
      I shall not look upon his like again.
HORATIO My lord, I think I saw him yesternight.
HAMLET Saw who?
HORATIO My lord, the King your father.
HAMLET   The King my father!
HORATIO Season your admiration for a while   190

[191] attent   *attentive*

[196] dead waist   *motionless or slow centre. 'The waist of the night' is its middle portion, described as dead because it appears to move so slowly or is the centre where time stands still. There is also a play upon the fact that at this time the dead walk.*

[198] at point   *at all points, completely*
      cap-a-pe   *from head to foot*

[202] truncheon's length   *the length of a short thick staff carried by a commander as a symbol of his authority*

      distilled   *nearly transformed or converted into jelly because they were shaking so much with fear*

[205] dreadful secrecy   *extreme secrecy*

[207] delivered   *reported*

[211] platform   *a level place constructed for mounting a battery of cannon*

[214] address   *began to make movements indicating it was about to speak*

With an attent ear, till I may deliver,
Upon the witness of these gentlemen,
This marvel to you.

HAMLET   For God's love let me hear.

HORATIO Two nights together had these gentlemen,
      Marcellus and Barnardo, on their watch,
      In the dead waist and middle of the night,
      Been thus encountered. A figure like your
        father
      Armèd at point exactly, cap-a-pe,
      Appears before them, and with solemn march
      Goes slow and stately by them. Thrice he walk'd 200
      By their oppress'd and fear surprisèd eyes
      Within his truncheon's length – whilst they,
        distilled
      Almost to jelly with the act of fear,
      Stand dumb and speak not to him. This to me
      In dreadful secrecy impart they did,
      And I with them the third night kept the
        watch,
      Where – as they had delivered – both in time,
      Form of the thing, each word made true and
        good,
      The apparition comes. I knew your father,
      These hands are not more like.

HAMLET   But where was this?   210

MARCELLUS My lord, upon the platform where we
      watch.

HAMLET Did you not speak to it?

HORATIO   My lord, I did;
      But answer made it none. Yet once methought
      It lifted up its head and did address
      Itself to motion, like as it would speak:
      But even then the morning cock crew loud,
      And at the sound it shrunk in haste away
      And vanish'd from our sight.

HAMLET   'Tis very strange.

[220] **writ down**   *as if it were written down in our orders or oath of allegiance*

[228] **beaver**   *the front part of the helmet which was hinged so that it could be swung up exposing the face*

[233] **constantly**   *steadily, firmly*

[238] **grizzled**   *grey*

[240] **sable silvered**   *black touched with grey or silver at the edge*
[241] **I warrant**   *I am sure, convinced*

[243] **gape** *Hell is often depicted in art and literature as a mouth with teeth which opens and swallows the damned.*

HORATIO As I do live, my honoured lord, 'tis true;
   And we did think it writ down in our duty 220
   To let you know of it.
HAMLET Indeed, indeed, sirs, but this troubles me.
   Hold you the watch tonight?
MARCELLUS ⎫
BARNARDO ⎭ We do, my lord.
HAMLET Armed, say you?
MARCELLUS ⎫
BARNARDO ⎭   Armed, my lord.
HAMLET From top to toe?
MARCELLUS ⎫
BARNARDO ⎭ My lord, from head to foot.
HAMLET Then saw you not his face?
HORATIO O yes, my lord; he wore his beaver up.
HAMLET What, look'd he frowningly?
HORATIO A countenance more in sorrow than in anger. 230
HAMLET Pale or red?
HORATIO Nay, very pale.
HAMLET   And fix'd his eyes upon you?
HORATIO Most constantly.
HAMLET   I would I had been there.
HORATIO It would have much amazed you.
HAMLET Very like, very like. Stayed it long?
HORATIO While one with moderate haste might tell
   a hundred.
MARCELLUS ⎫
BARNARDO ⎭ Longer, longer.
HORATIO Not when I saw't.
HAMLET His beard was grizzled – no?
HORATIO It was, as I have seen it in his life,
   A sable silvered.
HAMLET   I will watch tonight.   240
   Perchance 'twill walk again.
HORATIO   I warrant it will.
HAMLET If it assume my noble father's person,
   I'll speak to it, though hell itself should gape

[246] tenable *kept back, held in control*

[254] doubt *suspect*

ACT ONE, scene 3

[1] necessaries *essential baggage*

[2] give benefit *are favourable*

[3] convoy . . . assistant *a ship is available to carry your letter*

[5–6] trifling . . . blood *Laertes contrasts 'trifling' and 'toy' with 'fashion' and 'favour'. Hamlet is showing affection (favour) to Ophelia in a way which cannot be serious (trifling). It is a passing mood (fashion) and idle fancy (toy) caused by sexual desire (blood).*

[7] violet *one of the traditional flowers for lovers. Hamlet's love appears like a violet in spring and will vanish as quickly.*

primy *in its prime, springtime*

[9] suppliance *that which supplies, or provides for, the desires of one minute*

[11] crescent *as it increases, grows, develops*

[12] thews *sinews, strength*

bulk *size*

temple *the body*

waxes *grows bigger*

And bid me hold my peace. I pray you all,
If you have hitherto concealed this sight
Let it be tenable in your silence still;
And whatsomever else shall hap tonight,
Give it an understanding, but no tongue;
I will requite your loves. So, fare you well –
Upon the platform, 'twixt eleven and twelve,   250
I'll visit you.

ALL   Our duty to your honour.

HAMLET Your loves, as mine to you; farewell.

                                   [*Exeunt all but* HAMLET
My father's spirit in arms! All is not well.
I doubt some foul play. Would the night were
    come.
Till then, sit still, my soul. Foul deeds will
    rise,
Though all the earth o'erwhelm them, to
    men's eyes.

                                              [*Exit*

Scene 3. *Enter* LAERTES, *and* OPHELIA *his sister*

LAERTES My necessaries are embarked. Farewell.
And, sister, as the winds give benefit
And convoy is assistant, do not sleep,
But let me hear from you.

OPHELIA   Do you doubt that?

LAERTES For Hamlet, and the trifling of his favour,
Hold it a fashion and a toy in blood,
A violet in the youth of primy nature,
Forward, not permanent; sweet, not lasting,
The perfume and suppliance of a minute,
No more.

OPHELIA   No more but so?

LAERTES   Think it no more;   10
For nature crescent does not grow alone
In thews and bulk, but as this temple waxes

[14] **grows wide** *has a larger range, takes a broader view. Laertes implies that Hamlet's love for Ophelia belongs to his youth. As he grows older his mind too will change and he will be forced to take note of considerations other than his own desires.*

[15] **soil** *stain, blot, moral fault*

cautel *act of craft, deceit*

[17] **greatness weighed** *high position considered*

will . . . own *he cannot follow his own desires or intentions*

[19] **unvalued** *of no worth or account, unimportant*

[20] **Carve . . . himself** *Take what he wants – as a prince would never be expected to carve his own meat at table so he cannot select female flesh according to his desire*

choice *choice of a wife as future Queen*

[21] **sanctity** *holiness, sacred quality.*

[25] **fits . . . wisdom** *it is proper for you, as an intelligent girl, to believe him only so far as . . .*

[30] **credent** *ready to believe*

list *listen to*

[31] **chaste treasure** *precious reputation for chastity. It also has the possible meaning of permitting sexual intercourse.*

[32] **unmastered importunity** *persistent requests for love or attention which are uncontrolled and troublesome*

[36] **chariest** *most careful, cautious, wary, fastidious*

prodigal *lavish*

[37] **unmask** *uncover. At court balls it was sometimes the fashion for the dancers to be masked (as in* Much Ado About Nothing). *A girl who wished to preserve her reputation for chastity should remove her mask only in the presence of the moon, not with her partners. There is also a sense that Ophelia should only ever undress and expose her naked beauty by moonlight – sacred to Diana goddess of chastity.*

[38] **Virtue** *even the personified figure of Virtue herself cannot escape the blows of Calumny. Calumny, or evil report, is the great enemy of reputation, or good report.*

[39] **canker** *an insect larva which destroys plants*

galls *harms, causes to swell*

infants of the spring *roses*

[40] **button** *buds. Laertes probably does not intend the possible meaning of pregnancy and infant mortality carried by the lines but they are important for Shakespeare's imagery.*

[42] **Contagious blastments** *Infections which deform or destroy*

The inward service of the mind and soul
Grows wide withal. Perhaps he loves you now,
And now no soil nor cautel doth besmirch
The virtue of his will; but you must fear,
His greatness weighed, his will is not his own,
For he himself is subject to his birth.
He may not, as unvalued persons do,
Carve for himself, for on his choice depends   20
The sanctity and health of this whole state;
And therefore must his choice be
   circumscribed
Unto the voice and yielding of that body
Whereof he is the head. Then, if he says he
   loves you,
It fits your wisdom so far to believe it
As he in his particular act and place
May give his saying deed; which is no further
Than the main voice of Denmark goes withal.
Then weigh what loss your honour may
   sustain,
If with too credent ear you list his songs,   30
Or lose your heart, or your chaste treasure
   open
To his unmastered importunity.
Fear it, Ophelia. Fear it, my dear sister;
And keep you in the rear of your affection,
Out of the shot and danger of desire.
The chariest maid is prodigal enough
If she unmask her beauty to the moon.
Virtue itself scapes not calumnious strokes.
The canker galls the infants of the spring
Too oft before their buttons be disclosed,   40
And in the morn and liquid dew of youth
Contagious blastments are most imminent.
Be wary then; best safety lies in fear:
Youth to itself rebels, though none else near.

OPHELIA I shall th'effect of this good lesson keep

[47] ungracious pastors *clergymen who themselves lack the grace of God and who therefore do not act as the good shepherds of the Bible leading their flock to Heaven*

[49] puffed *proud – perhaps the deadliest of the seven deadly sins*

[50] primrose path *the way which appears decked with primrose flowers symbolising pleasure but is, in fact, the way to hell. Ophelia gives the Christian version of the choice of life, or ways, performed by the shepherd Hercules in the allegorical landscapes of Renaissance art.*

[51] recks . . . rede *pays no attention to his own instruction – another pastoral pun since 'reed' could also be the shepherd's pipe with which he summons his flock*

[53] double blessing *It was customary for children to ask their parents' blessing, especially on leaving home. Laertes thinks it doubly gracious to be blessed twice.*

[56] sits in the shoulder *is favourable – blowing from behind and billowing out the sail*

[58] precepts *principles*

[59] character *write – as if the memory were a wax tablet or note book*

[60] unproportioned *disproportioned, not arranged or considered in proper order*

[62] their adoption tried *when you have tested their relationship with you as friends*

[63] Grapple *Fix firmly together, grip hard*

[64] dull *make blunt, tarnish. Laertes should not blunt his power to confer friendship by the easy acceptance of every new acquaintance who professes to be a gentleman of courage but whose qualities – like those of a newly hatched bird which has never left the nest – have never been tried.*

[67] Bear't *Conduct it*

[69] Take . . . judgement *Consider everyone's critical views but hold back your own opinion without disclosing it*

[71] expressed in fancy *evidently expensive on account of the extraordinary cut or excessive amount of ornament*
       gaudy *showy but tasteless*

As watchman to my heart. But, good my
   brother,
Do not, as some ungracious pastors do,
Show me the steep and thorny way to heaven,
Whiles like a puffed and reckless libertine
Himself the primrose path of dalliance treads   50
And recks not his own rede.

LAERTES   O fear me not,

Enter POLONIUS

I stay too long – But here my father comes,
A double blessing is a double grace;
Occasion smiles upon a second leave.

POLONIUS Yet here, Laertes? Aboard, aboard, for
   shame!
The wind sits in the shoulder of your sail,
And you are stayed for. There – my blessing
   with thee,
And these few precepts in thy memory
Look thou character. Give thy thoughts no
   tongue,
Nor any unproportioned thought his act.   60
Be thou familiar, but by no means vulgar.
Those friends thou hast, and their adoption
   tried,
Grapple them to thy soul with hoops of steel;
But do not dull thy palm with entertainment
Of each new hatched, unfledged courage.
   Beware
Of entrance to a quarrel; but, being in,
Bear't that th'opposed may beware of thee.
Give every man thy ear, but few thy voice,
Take each man's censure, but reserve thy
   judgement.
Costly thy habit as thy purse can buy,   70
But not expressed in fancy; rich, not gaudy,
For the apparel oft proclaims the man;

[74] generous   *noble, rich in quality*
        choice   *The Quartos and Folio read 'chiefe' and 'cheff'. The sense is obscure and the text appears to be corrupt. The emendation (Collier's) is not certain.*

[80] false   *it is impossible to be false to anyone else since being true to oneself implies being 'most generous and free from all contriving' (IV. 7. 137)*

[83] invites   *requests or requires your presence (on board ship)*

[89] touching   *concerning*

[93] audience   *act of hearing, attention. Ophelia has not only seen Hamlet but listened to what he had to say.*

[94] put on me   *put to me, told to me*

[96–7] understand . . . honour   *you do not understand as clearly as you ought the kind of behaviour that is suitable to your position as my daughter and necessary to safeguard your reputation*

[99] tenders   *offers of love – either in the form of love tokens or words*

[101] green   *unripe, immature*

[102] Unsifted   *Unstrained – hence, inexperienced*

And they in France of the best rank and
   station
Are of a most select and generous choice in
   that.
Neither a borrower nor a lender be,
For loan oft loses both itself and friend,
And borrowing dulls the edge of husbandry.
This above all – to thine own self be true,
And it must follow, as the night the day,
Thou can'st not then be false to any man.   80
Farewell, my blessing season this in thee.

LAERTES Most humbly do I take my leave, my lord.

POLONIUS The time invites you. Go, your servants
   tend.

LAERTES Farewell, Ophelia, and remember well
What I have said to you.

OPHELIA   'Tis in my memory locked,
And you yourself shall keep the key of it.

LAERTES Farewell.

                                [*Exit*

POLONIUS What is't, Ophelia, he hath said to you?

OPHELIA So please you, something touching the Lord
   Hamlet.

POLONIUS Marry, well bethought.   90
'Tis told me he hath very oft of late
Given private time to you, and you yourself
Have of your audience been most free and
   bounteous.
If it be so – as so 'tis put on me,
And that in way of caution – I must tell you
You do not understand yourself so clearly
As it behoves my daughter and your honour.
What is between you? Give me up the truth.

OPHELIA He hath, my lord, of late made many tenders
Of his affection to me.   100

POLONIUS Affection? Puh! You speak like a green girl
Unsifted in such perilous circumstance.

[106] tenders *Polonius now picks up Ophelia's 'tenders' or offers of love and plays with the meaning. Here 'tenders' means offers of money.*

true pay *proper amount of money*

[107] not sterling *not of the proper quality of silver*

Tender yourself more dearly *Offer yourself at a higher rate – i.e. look after yourself more carefully*

[108] crack the wind *render breathless or broken-winded*

[109] Running *Pursuing*

tender me a fool *make me look a fool – though since 'fool' also can mean 'child' there is a second possible meaning of 'present me with a child'. The possibility of an unwanted pregnancy is hinted at by both Laertes and Polonius.*

[111] fashion *manner*

[112] fashion *passing mood or fancy – another example of the way Polonius puts the worst interpretation on Ophelia's words*

[113] given countenance *supported his words*

[115] springes *snares, traps*

[117] blazes *sudden flashes of fire. The metaphor is that Ophelia must not mistake these sudden blazes of passion for the burning flame of true love. The blaze like a shooting star gives neither light nor heat and is out almost as soon as it starts. Love warms, illuminates and continues to burn like the sun.*

[119] promise *apparent promise of light and heat*

[122] entreatments *military negotiations for a surrender*

[123] parle *conversation between enemies under a flag of truce. Polonius now talks of Ophelia as a town under siege which may be taken simply by the fair words of the enemy.*

[127] brokers *go-betweens. They may be of three kinds and Polonius unites all three functions in this complex series of images: a) dealers in finance who are not of the true colour or appearance (dye) which their authorising documents (investments) indicate but simply solicitors for improper requests who talk as if their proposals were holy and religious in order to deceive their clients, b) go-betweens in matters of love who are not the kind of men claimed by the garments they have borrowed (from the church) but simply makers of lewd and immoral suggestions who talk the language of marriage vows in order to deceive their victims, b) dealers in old clothes – though this meaning is less fully worked out. Hamlet is thus a shady financier, a pander who promises marriage, and an old clothes man.*

Do you believe his 'tenders', as you call them?

OPHELIA I do not know, my lord, what I should think.

POLONIUS Marry, I will teach you: think yourself a
baby
That you have ta'en these tenders for true pay
Which are not sterling. Tender yourself more
dearly
Or (not to crack the wind of the poor phrase
Running it thus) you'll tender me a fool.

OPHELIA My lord, he hath importuned me with love   110
In honourable fashion.

POLONIUS Ay – fashion you may call it; go to, go to.

OPHELIA And hath given countenance to his speech,
my lord,
With almost all the holy vows of heaven.

POLONIUS Ay, springes to catch woodcocks. I do
know,
When the blood burns, how prodigal the soul
Lends the tongue vows. These blazes,
daughter,
Giving more light than heat – extinct in both,
Even in their promise, as it is a-making –
You must not take for fire. From this time   120
Be something scanter of your maiden presence;
Set your entreatments at a higher rate
Than a command to parle. For Lord Hamlet,
Believe so much in him that he is young,
And with a larger tether may he walk
Than may be given you. In few, Ophelia,
Do not believe his vows; for they are brokers,
Not of that dye which their investments show,
But mere implorators of unholy suits,
Breathing like sanctified and pious bonds,   130
The better to beguile. This is for all,
I would not, in plain terms, from this time
forth
Have you so slander any moment leisure

[135] charge *command*

ACT ONE, scene 4

[1] shrewdly *sharply, piercingly*

[2] eager *keen, cutting*

[3] lacks of *lacks a few minutes until twelve – i.e. just before twelve*

two pieces *two cannon*

[8] wake *stays awake*

rouse *ceremonious forms of drinking healths and pledging*
[9] wassail } *each other. 'Wassail' is a form of the Old Norse 'ves heill', 'be in good health'.*

swagg'ring up-spring reels *the last and wildest dance at ancient Germanic festivals*

[10] Rhenish *wine from the vineyards of the Rhine*

[12] triumph *celebration*

pledge *toast*

[15] manner born *born and brought up to accept the custom as natural*

[16] More honoured *A custom that is more honourable to break than keep*

[17-18] heavy . . . nations *this drunken debauchery which leaves everyone with heavy heads causes us to have a bad reputation among nations both to the east and west – i.e. everywhere*

[18] traduced *slandered, ill spoken of*

taxed *blamed*

[19] clepe *call*

[19-20] swinish phrase . . . addition *blacken our titles or reputation by always adding to them the remark that we are swine or pigs*

[20] takes *detracts*

[21] at height *to the highest pitch, highest possible point*

As to give words or talk with the Lord Hamlet.
Look to't, I charge you. Come your ways.
OPHELIA I shall obey, my lord.

[*Exeunt*

Scene 4. *Enter* HAMLET, HORATIO *and* MARCELLUS

HAMLET The air bites shrewdly; it is very cold.
HORATIO It is a nipping and an eager air.
HAMLET What hour now?
HORATIO   I think it lacks of twelve.
MARCELLUS No, it is struck.
HORATIO Indeed? I heard it not. It then draws near
    the season
    Wherein the spirit held his wont to walk.

    A flourish of trumpets, and two pieces go off
    What does this mean, my lord?
HAMLET The King doth wake tonight and takes his
    rouse,
    Keeps wassail, and the swagg'ring up-spring
    reels,
    And, as he drains his draughts of Rhenish
    down,   10
    The kettle-drum and trumpet thus bray out
    The triumph of his pledge.
HORATIO   Is it a custom?
HAMLET Ay, marry, is't;
    But to my mind, though I am native here
    And to the manner born, it is a custom
    More honoured in the breach than the
    observance.
    This heavy-headed revel east and west
    Makes us traduced and taxed of other nations.
    They clepe us drunkards, and with swinish
    phrase
    Soil our addition; and, indeed, it takes   20
    From our achievements, though performed
    at height,

[22] pith   *the inner substance in the stems of plants, central core*
attribute   *reputation – destroys the inner core of our reputation which would allow it to grow and flourish*

[24] vicious mole of nature   *a hereditary defect, or one acquired at birth, which causes vicious or psychopathic conduct*

[25] their birth   *a) their parentage, b) hour of their birth which, in astrological terms, would determine their temperament*

[27] o'ergrowth . . . complexion   *the excess of one of the four humours. These were the four substances, choler, melancholy, phlegm and blood whose combination in the human body formed a man's temperament. The idea goes back to a Greek medical text ascribed to Hippocrates and formed the basis of physiology and psychology for over 2,000 years. They ought to be balanced or in proportion – the excess of any one could result in mental or physical illness.*

[28] pales and forts   *safeguards and defences. The reason is seen as defended by a stockade or palisade and guard towers or forts.*

[30] plausive   *acceptable, agreeable*

[32] nature's livery   *the clothes of nature – i.e. the features and temperament you are born with*
fortune's star   *the star of fortune – which is the luck or chance that governs a man's material possessions or position in the world. Astrologers believed that a man's fortune could be predicted from the influence of the stars. The defect is thus a matter of heredity or chance.*

[34] undergo   *experience*

[35] censure   *opinion*
take corruption   *acquire corruption – i.e. even his virtues will be considered evil or corrupt*

[36] dram   *drop, small quantity*
eale   *evil*

[37] o'erdouse   *intoxicate, poison*

[38] scandal   *disgrace, damage to reputation*

[39] ministers of grace   *servants of God's grace*

[43] questionable   *a) doubtful, alarming, b) a shape that ought to be questioned*

[47] canonized   *buried in sanctified ground in accordance with church or canon law*
hearsed   *placed on a bier or in a coffin*

[48] cerements   *grave clothes, shrouds or winding sheets wrapped closely round a dead body*

[49] enurned   *buried*

The pith and marrow of our attribute.
So, oft it chances in particular men
That, for some vicious mole of nature in them,
As in their birth, wherein they are not guilty
Since nature cannot choose his origin;
By the o'ergrowth of some complexion,
Oft breaking down the pales and forts of
    reason,
Or by some habit that too much o'er-leavens
The form of plausive manners – that these
    men,   30
Carrying, I say, the stamp of one defect,
Being nature's livery or fortune's star,
His virtues else (be they as pure as grace,
As infinite as man may undergo)
Shall, in the general censure, take corruption
From that particular fault. The dram of eale
Doth all the noble substance o'erdouse
To his own scandal

Enter GHOST

HORATIO   Look, my lord, it comes.
HAMLET Angels and ministers of grace defend us!
Be thou a spirit of health or goblin damned,   40
Bring with thee airs from heaven or blasts
    from hell
Be thy intents wicked or charitable,
Thou com'st in such a questionable shape
That I will speak to thee. I'll call thee Hamlet,
King, father, royal Dane. O, answer me.
Let me not burst in ignorance, but tell
Why thy canonized bones, hearsed in death,
Have burst their cerements? Why the
    sepulchre
Wherein we saw thee quietly enurned
Hath oped his ponderous and marble jaws   50
To cast thee up again? What may this mean

[52] complete steel *full armour*

[53] glimpses *moonlight – momentary shining giving an uncertain or imperfect view*

[54] fools of nature *a) weak in judgement because of nature – i.e. because still natural or mortal, b) dupes of the natural order*

[55] disposition *temperament, constitution*

[59] impartment *communication*

[61] removèd ground *more remote, secluded, place*

[67] immortal *Hamlet does not care if the Ghost kills him since he does not value his life at the price of a pin. The Ghost cannot kill his soul since it is immortal. Horatio is concerned that the Ghost might damn his soul by causing him to despair and commit suicide.*

[69] flood *sea*

[71] beetles *projects, overhangs*

[72] horrible form *The spirit has only assumed the shape of Hamlet's father, it could easily assume some other shape.*

[73] deprive *take away, remove*
    sovereignty of reason *supreme power of reasoning or thought*

[75] toys of desperation *fantasies of despair and self-destruction*

That thou, dead corse, again in complete steel
Revisits thus the glimpses of the moon,
Making night hideous, and we fools of nature
So horridly to shake our disposition
With thoughts beyond the reaches of our souls?
Say, why is this? Wherefore? What should we
  do?

        GHOST *beckons* HAMLET

HORATIO It beckons you to go away with it,
    As if it some impartment did desire
    To you alone.
MARCELLUS Look with what courteous action   60
    It waves you to a more removèd ground –
    But do not go with it.
HORATIO   No, by no means.
HAMLET It will not speak. Then I will follow it.
HORATIO Do not, my lord.
HAMLET   Why, what should be the fear?
    I do not set my life at a pin's fee,
    And for my soul, what can it do to that,
    Being a thing immortal as itself?
    It waves me forth again. I'll follow it.
HORATIO What if it tempt you toward the flood, my
      lord,
    Or to the dreadful summit of the cliff   70
    That beetles o'er his base into the sea,
    And there assume some other horrible form,
    Which might deprive your sovereignty of
      reason
    And draw you into madness? Think of it.
    The very place puts toys of desperation,
    Without more motive, into every brain
    That looks so many fathoms to the sea
    And hears it roar beneath.
HAMLET   It waves me still.
    Go on. I'll follow thee.

[81] fate   *destiny*

[83] Nemean lion's nerve   *sinew of the Nemean lion. The first labour of Hercules was to combat the Nemean lion. It withstood blows from his club and he had to wrestle with it and strangle it.*
[85] make a ghost   *kill*
  lets   *hinders*

[87] waxes   *grows, becomes*

[89] Have after   *Let us follow after him*
  issue   *result*

[91] direct   *govern its future course*

ACT ONE, scene 5

[2] hour   *appointed time*
[3] flames   *These appear to indicate that the Ghost comes from hell or purgatory.*

[6] bound   *ready, prepared. The Ghost implies that he will be 'bound', compelled to revenge once he has heard.*

MARCELLUS You shall not go, my lord.

HAMLET   Hold off your hands.   80

HORATIO Be ruled, you shall not go.

HAMLET   My fate cries out
          And makes each petty artery in this body
          As hardy as the Nemean lion's nerve.
          Still am I called. Unhand me, gentlemen.
          By heaven, I'll make a ghost of him that lets
               me!
          I say, away. Go on – I'll follow thee.
                              [*Exeunt* GHOST *and* HAMLET

HORATIO He waxes desperate with imagination.

MARCELLUS Let's follow. 'Tis not fit thus to obey him.

HORATIO Have after. To what issue will this come?

MARCELLUS Something is rotten in the state of
               Denmark.   90

HORATIO Heaven will direct it.

MARCELLUS   Nay, let's follow him.
                                                  [*Exeunt*

Scene 5. *Enter* GHOST *and* HAMLET

HAMLET Whither wilt thou lead me? Speak. I'll go no
               further.

GHOST Mark me.

HAMLET   I will.

GHOST   My hour is almost come,
          When I to sulph'rous and tormenting flames
          Must render up myself.

HAMLET   Alas, poor ghost.

GHOST Pity me not, but lend thy serious hearing
          To what I shall unfold.

HAMLET   Speak. I am bound to hear.

GHOST So art thou to revenge, when thou shalt hear.

HAMLET What?

GHOST I am thy father's spirit,
          Doomed for a certain term to walk the night,   10

[12] **foul crimes**   *human life is naturally sinful and unless the soul receives confession, absolution and the last rites of the Church it is in danger of hell. The Ghost makes the particular point that his sudden murder deprived King Hamlet of these last rites and he has therefore to be purified by fire.*

[16] **harrow up**   *break up – see I. 1. 44 and note*

[17] **start**   *leap, jump*

spheres   *In Ptolemaic astronomy the sun, moon, planets or wandering stars and the fixed stars were all thought of as revolving round the earth in their separate spheres. A star which jumped from its sphere was a shooting star and an indication of some exceptional event in the universe.*

[20] **fretful porpentine**   *disturbed porcupine – thought to extend its quills when angry. Dover Wilson points out that a porcupine with quills erect is the crest of the Sidney family – displayed on Leicester Hospital at Warwick, founded in 1571.*

[21] **eternal blazon**   *description of the secrets of eternity. A 'blazon' is a description in words of armorial bearings.*

[27] **as in the best**   *even in the most favourable circumstances murder must be considered a foul crime. This one was particularly 'unnatural' or contrary to the natural order since it was the murder of a) a brother, b) a sleeping man who had no chance to prepare his soul for death.*

[30] **meditation**   *contemplation, thoughts of God. Thoughts of God or of love could both be considered winged and therefore swift but it is an interesting choice of words since religion and love are traditionally the two great obstacles to the taking of blood revenge.*

[32] **duller**   *more stupid, less spirited, more forgetful*

[33] **Lethe**   *in Greek mythology a river of the underworld. Once the souls of the dead drank its waters they forgot their earthly existence. A weed on bankside 'wharf' of Lethe would have the same properties of forgetfulness.*

[34] **stir**   *act*

[35] **orchard**   *enclosed garden for herbs and fruit trees*

[36] **whole ear of Denmark**   *all the people of Denmark. The state is again considered as a body politic with organs like a human body.*

[37] **forgèd process**   *deliberately falsified official account*

[38] **Rankly abused**   *Corruptly deceived*

[39] **serpent**   *malicious deceitful person having the guile of the serpent which deceived Eve*

And for the day confined to fast in fires,
Till the foul crimes done in my days of nature
Are burnt and purged away. But that I am
   forbid
To tell the secrets of my prison house,
I could a tale unfold whose lightest word
Would harrow up thy soul, freeze thy young
   blood,
Make thy two eyes, like stars, start from their
   spheres,
Thy knotted and combinèd locks to part,
And each particular hair to stand on end
Like quills upon the fretful porpentine.   20
But this eternal blazon must not be
To ears of flesh and blood. List, list, O, list.
If thou did'st ever thy dear father love –

HAMLET O God!

GHOST Revenge his foul and most unnatural murder.

HAMLET Murder?

GHOST Murder most foul – as in the best it is –
But this most foul, strange, and unnatural.

HAMLET Haste me to know't, that I, with wings as
   swift
As meditation or the thoughts of love,   30
May sweep to my revenge.

GHOST   I find thee apt;
And duller should'st thou be than the fat weed
That roots itself in ease on Lethe wharf,
Would'st thou not stir in this. Now, Hamlet,
   hear:
'Tis given out that, sleeping in my orchard,
A serpent stung me; so the whole ear of –
   Denmark
Is by a forgèd process of my death
Rankly abused. But know, thou noble youth,
The serpent that did sting thy father's life
Now wears his crown.

[40] prophetic   *because Hamlet had already felt that 'it is not nor it cannot come to good' (I. 2. 158)*

[42] incestuous ⎱   *In marrying Gertrude, his brother's wife,*
    adulterate ⎰   *Claudius could be considered as committing both incest and adultery. The speech seems to suggest that adultery was contemplated before the murder of King Hamlet. The audience are never definitely informed whether it was committed or not.*

[43] gifts   *a) personal qualities, b) presents*

[46] will   *a) desire, b) sexual organs*

[48] dignity   *worth, merit*

[51] natural gifts   *natural talents, abilities, quality*

[53] moved   *changed, shifted, excited, persuaded*

[58] soft   *quiet! silence!*

[62] hebona   *The text may be corrupt or Shakespeare himself confused about the nature of the poison. It may be: a) henbane, or b) the yew tree (German 'eiben') thought to be poisonous.*

[64] leperous   *causing leprosy*

[66] quicksilver   *mercury – so called because of its fast movement*

[67] gates and alleys   *The human body is now seen as a body politic, a city with gates and alleys.*

[68] vigour   *force*
    posset   *make sour*

[69] eager   *sour, acid*

[71] tetter   *pustular eruption of the skin*
    barked about   *encrusted round like the bark of a tree*

[72] lazar-like   *like leprosy*

[75] dispatched   *killed, removed, deprived*

HAMLET   O my prophetic soul –   40
      My uncle?

GHOST   Ay, that incestuous, that adulterate beast,
      With witchcraft of his wits, with traitorous
        gifts
      (O wicked wit, and gifts that have the power
      So to seduce) won to his shameful lust
      The will of my most seeming virtuous queen.
      O Hamlet, what a falling off was there,
      From me, whose love was of that dignity
      That it went hand in hand even with the vow
      I made to her in marriage; and to decline   50
      Upon a wretch whose natural gifts were poor
      To those of mine.
      But virtue, as it never will be moved,
      Though lewdness court it in a shape of heaven,
      So lust, though to a radiant angel linked,
      Will sate itself in a celestial bed
      And prey on garbage.
      But soft – methinks I scent the morning air –
      Brief let me be. Sleeping within my orchard,
      My custom always of the afternoon,   60
      Upon my secure hour thy uncle stole,
      With juice of cursed hebona in a vial,
      And in the porches of my ears did pour
      The leperous distilment – whose effect
      Holds such an enmity with blood of man
      That swift as quicksilver it courses through
      The natural gates and alleys of the body;
      And with a sudden vigour it doth posset
      And curd (like eager droppings into milk)
      The thin and wholesome blood. So did it mine,   70
      And a most instant tetter barked about,
      Most lazar-like, with vile and loathsome crust,
      All my smooth body.
      Thus was I, sleeping, by a brother's hand
      Of life, of crown, of queen, at once dispatched.

[76] blossoms *cut off like a flower with my sins still in full bloom*

[77] Unhouseled *Without having taken the last sacrament of the Church*

   disappointed *unprepared (for death)*

   unaneled *unannointed with sacred oil as a sign of blessing – hence, in danger of damnation*

[78] reck'ning *reckoning of sins for confession and absolution*

   account *judgement – place where an account of his deeds has to be given and he is called to pay the penalty. The metaphor is of both a legal and a cash transaction.*

[79] on my head *without forgiveness*

[81] nature *natural feelings*

   bear *endure*

[83] luxury *lust*

[85] Taint . . . mind *Do not stain or corrupt your own mind with sinful desires*

[87] thorns *of conscience*

[93] couple *join, add, include*

[94] instant *instantly*

[95] stiffly *strongly. Hamlet is afraid the shock of seeing the Ghost may age him prematurely.*

[96–7] memory . . . globe *so long as memory can find a place to stay in this disordered, divided or perplexed world. The globe is a) the earth, b) the world of his own mind in his head.*

[98] table of my memory *Memory is now seen as a slate or wax tablet on which impressions may be written – as Polonius advised Laertes to 'character' write his precepts in his memory.*

[99] wipe away *the slate of memory is now to be wiped clean*

   trivial fond records *unimportant foolish items remembered*

[100] saws *wise sayings or proverbs copied from books*

   forms *examples*

   pressures *impressions*

[102] live *exist*

[103] book and volume of my brain *memory*

[104] baser matter *less vital, less important information*

[107] My tables *Most editors and directors make Hamlet reach for a property notebook and write at this point. This is possible but the lines make better sense if he is still talking of the table of his memory which he is now impressing with the newly confirmed image of his uncle as villain and future victim.*

Cut off even in the blossoms of my sin,
Unhouseled, disappointed, unaneled,
No reck'ning made, but sent to my account
With all my imperfections on my head.
O horrible, O horrible, most horrible.   80
If thou hast nature in thee, bear it not.
Let not the royal bed of Denmark be
A couch for luxury and damnèd incest.
But, howsomever thou pursuest this act,
Taint not thy mind, nor let thy soul contrive
Against thy mother aught. Leave her to heaven,
And to those thorns that in her bosom lodge
To prick and sting her. Fare thee well at
    once,
The glowworm shows the matin to be near
And 'gins to pale his uneffectual fire.   90
Adieu, adieu, adieu. Remember me.

                          [Exit

HAMLET O all you host of heaven. O earth. What
    else –
And shall I couple hell? O, fie. Hold, hold, my
    heart
And you, my sinews, grow not instant old,
But bear me stiffly up. Remember thee?
Ay, thou poor ghost, whiles memory holds a
    seat
In this distracted globe. Remember thee,
Yea, from the table of my memory
I'll wipe away all trivial fond records,
All saws of books, all forms, all pressures past, 100
That youth and observation copied there,
And thy commandment all alone shall live
Within the book and volume of my brain,
Unmixed with baser matter. Yes, by heaven!
O most pernicious woman.
O villain, villain, smiling, damned villain!
My tables – meet it is I set it down

[110] word *memory word. Quintilian advised his students to remember passages by picking out one or more significant words from each paragraph. The Ghost's last words serve as Hamlet's memory aid to call his story instantly to mind. It could also imply 'watchword'.*

[113] secure him *keep him safe*
[114] Illo ho ho *cry used by a falconer calling his falcon or hawk*

[123–4] villain . . . knave *a display of wit to turn aside a question he cannot answer*

[128] circumstance *ceremony, formality*

That one may smile, and smile, and be a
    villain;
At least I am sure it may be so in Denmark.
So, uncle, there you are. Now, to my word: 110
It is 'Adieu, adieu. Remember me'.
I have sworn't.

HORATIO [*Within*] My lord, my lord!
MARCELLUS [*Within*]   Lord Hamlet!

Enter HORATIO *and* MARCELLUS

HORATIO Heavens secure him!
HAMLET So be it.
MARCELLUS Illo, ho, ho, my lord!
HAMLET Hillo, ho, ho, boy! Come, bird, come.
MARCELLUS How is't, my noble lord?
HORATIO   What news, my lord?
HAMLET O, wonderful.
HORATIO Good my lord, tell it.
HAMLET   No, you will reveal it.
HORATIO Not I, my lord, by heaven.
MARCELLUS   Nor I, my lord.   120
HAMLET How say you then – would heart of man once
    think it?
    But you'll be secret?
BOTH   Ay, by heaven, my lord.
HAMLET There's never a villain dwelling in all
    Denmark
    But he's an arrant knave.
HORATIO There needs no ghost, my lord, come from
    the grave
    To tell us this.
HAMLET Why, right. You are in the right.
    And so, without more circumstance at all,
    I hold it fit that we shake hands and part;
    You as your business and desire shall point you
    (For every man hath business and desire,   130
    Such as it is) and for mine own poor part –

[135] offence   *Horatio means there is no cause for them to feel aggrieved or offended with Hamlet; Hamlet uses it in its stronger sense of crime.*

[136] Saint Patrick   *was a) the keeper of purgatory, b) had banished snakes from Ireland. The Ghost has come from purgatory to rid Denmark of the serpent Claudius.*

[138] honest   *truthful – i.e. not a demon*

[147] sword   *The hilt of the sword forms a cross and can therefore bind the consciences of men who are soldiers and Christians. Hamlet does not rely merely on their word but insists on a formal oath. An oath to bind the conscience might be invalid if sworn with the devil a party to it – hence the strange shifting of ground to avoid the Ghost. Hamlet does not believe that it is the devil, but he takes no chances.*

[150] truepenny   *honest fellow*

[151] cellerage   *space under the stage, hell*

   Look you – I will go pray.

HORATIO These are but wild and whirling words, my
   lord.

HAMLET I am sorry they offend you – heartily;
   Yes, faith, heartily.

HORATIO   There's no offence, my lord.

HAMLET Yes, by Saint Patrick, but there is, Horatio –
   And much offence too. Touching this vision
   here –
   It is an honest ghost, that let me tell you.
   For your desire to know what is between us,
   O'ermaster it as you may. And now, good
   friends,   140
   As you are friends, scholars, and soldiers,
   Give me one poor request.

HORATIO What is't, my lord? We will.

HAMLET Never make known what you have seen
   tonight.

BOTH My lord, we will not.

HAMLET   Nay, but swear't.

HORATIO   In faith
   My lord, not I.

MARCELLUS   Nor I, my lord, in faith.

HAMLET Upon my sword.

MARCELLUS We have sworn, my lord, already.

HAMLET Indeed, upon my sword, indeed.

    GHOST *cries under the stage*

GHOST Swear.

HAMLET Ha, ha, boy, say'st thou so? Art thou there
   truepenny   150
   Come on. You hear this fellow in the
   cellerage:
   Consent to swear.

HORATIO   Propose the oath, my lord.

HAMLET Never to speak of this that you have seen,
   Swear by my sword.

[156] Hic et ubique   *Here and everywhere – attributes of God, or the devil*

[163] pioneer   *military engineer, digger of mines*

[165] as a stranger . . . welcome   *welcome it as you would a stranger*

[167] philosophy   *natural philosophy, science*

[172] antic disposition   *grotesque incongruous behaviour*

[174] encumb'red   *folded*
[175] doubtful phrase   *ambiguous remark*

[182] Rest, rest . . . spirit   *not a way of addressing the devil*

[184] poor a man   *a man so humble, poor in power to recompense your love*

GHOST Swear.

HAMLET Hic et ubique? Then we'll shift our ground.
　　　　Come hither, gentlemen,
　　　　And lay your hands again upon my sword.
　　　　Never to speak of this that you have heard,
　　　　Swear by my sword.　　　　　　　　　　160

GHOST Swear by his sword.

HAMLET Well said, old mole. Can'st work i'th'earth so
　　　　fast?
　　　　A worthy pioneer. Once more remove, good
　　　　friends.

HORATIO O day and night, but this is wondrous
　　　　strange.

HAMLET And therefore as a stranger give it welcome.
　　　　There are more things in heaven and earth,
　　　　　Horatio,
　　　　Than are dreamt of in your philosophy.
　　　　But come,
　　　　Here, as before, never, so help you mercy,
　　　　How strange or odd some'er I bear myself　　170
　　　　(As I perchance hereafter shall think meet
　　　　To put an antic disposition on)
　　　　That you, at such times, seeing me, never shall,
　　　　With arms encumb'red thus, or this headshake,
　　　　Or by pronouncing of some doubtful phrase,
　　　　As, 'Well, well, we know' or 'We could, an
　　　　　if we would'
　　　　Or 'If we list to speak' or 'There be, an if
　　　　　they might'
　　　　Or such ambiguous giving out, to note
　　　　That you know aught of me – this do swear
　　　　So grace and mercy at your most need help
　　　　you.　　　　　　　　　　　　　　　　180

GHOST Swear.

HAMLET Rest, rest, perturbèd spirit. So, gentlemen,
　　　　With all my love I do commend me to you;
　　　　And what so poor a man as Hamlet is

[188] out of joint   *compare 'disjoint' and 'out of frame' (I. 2. 20).*
The state of the world and the kingdom is now proved to be disordered.
cursed spite   *curse the malice of fortune*

May do t'express his love and friending to you,
God willing, shall not lack. Let us go in
   together;
And still your fingers on your lips, I pray.
The time is out of joint. O cursed spite,
That ever I was born, to set it right.
Nay, come, let's go together.   190
                  [*Exeunt*

ACT TWO, scene 1

[1] notes   *letters*

[3] marvellous wisely   *behave in an extremely wise fashion*

[4] inquire   *inquiry*

[7] Danskers   *Danes. The word actually means citizens of Danzig. It is not clear if this is an error or if Shakespeare thought that Danzig was part of Denmark.*

[8] what means   *how much money they have*
     keep   *live, lodge*

[10] encompassment   *questions which circle round and hem in the main object*
     drift   *intention, aim*

[11–12] come . . . touch it   *you will approach closer to what you want to than you could by asking direct questions*

[20] forgeries   *inventions*
     rank   *gross, foul, flagrant*

[23] companions noted   *frequently observed to accompany*

ACT TWO

Scene 1. *Enter old* POLONIUS *with his man, or two*

POLONIUS Give him this money and these notes,
        Reynaldo.
REYNALDO I will, my lord.
POLONIUS You shall do marvellous wisely, good
        Reynaldo,
      Before you visit him, to make inquire
      Of his behaviour.
REYNALDO   My lord, I did intend it.
POLONIUS Marry, well said. Very well said. Look you,
        sir,
      Enquire me first what Danskers are in Paris;
      And how, and who, what means, and where
        they keep,
      What company, at what expense; and finding
      By this encompassment and drift of question   10
      That they do know my son, come you more
        nearer
      Than your particulars demands will touch it.
      Take you, as 'twere, some distant knowledge
        of him;
      As thus: 'I know his father and his friends,
      And in part him'. Do you mark this,
        Reynaldo?
REYNALDO Ay, very well, my lord.
POLONIUS 'And in part him – but' you may say 'not
        well;
      But if't be he I mean, he's very wild;
      Addicted so and so'; and there put on him
      What forgeries you please; marry, none so rank   20
      As may dishonour him, take heed of that,
      But, sir, such wanton, wild, and usual slips
      As are companions noted and most known
      To youth and liberty.

[26] Drabbing *Whoring*

[28] season *qualify, temper*
      charge *accusation, imputation*

[30] open to incontinency *entirely without sexual restraint*
[31] quaintly *skilfully*
[32] taints *faults natural to freedom*

[34] unreclaimed blood *untamed passion*
[35] general assault *which attack, or affect, everyone*

[37] drift *intention, aim*
[38] fetch of warrant *a justified stratagem*
[39] sullies *stains, faults*
[40] soiled . . . working *worn or blemished by its natural operation*

[42] sound *chart, discover, find out the depth of*
[43] prenominate *named before*
[44] breathe of *speak of*
[45] closes with you *comes close to grips with you, meets you*
      in this consequence *with this result*
[47] addition *title*

REYNALDO   As gaming, my lord.

POLONIUS Ay, or drinking, fencing, swearing, quarrelling,

Drabbing – you may go so far.

REYNALDO My lord, that would dishonour him.

POLONIUS Faith, no; as you may season it in the charge.

You must not put another scandal on him,

That he is open to incontinency;   30

That's not my meaning. But breathe his faults so quaintly

That they may seem the taints of liberty;

The flash and outbreak of a fiery mind,

A savageness in unreclaimed blood,

Of general assault.

REYNALDO   But, my good lord –

POLONIUS Wherefore should you do this?

REYNALDO   Ay, my lord,

I would know that.

POLONIUS   Marry, sir, here's my drift,

And I believe it is a fetch of warrant.

You laying these slight sullies on my son,

As 'twere a thing a little soiled wi'th'working,   40

Mark you,

Your party in converse, him you would sound,

Having ever seen in the prenominate crimes

The youth you breathe of guilty, be assured

He closes with you in this consequence –

'Good sir' or so, or 'friend' or 'gentleman'

According to the phrase or the addition

Of man and country.

REYNALDO   Very good, my lord.

POLONIUS And then, sir, does he this – he does – What was I about to say? By the mass, I was about to say   50 something. Where did I leave?

[57] o'ertook in's rouse   *overcome by intoxication while drinking*

[60] Videlicet   *That is to say*
[61] take   *catch*
     carp   *a freshwater fish thought to be particularly subtle – but it also means to find fault with, slander*
[62] of wisdom . . . reach   *out of our wisdom and far-sightedness*
[63] windlasses   *a circuit made to intercept game in hunting – hence to proceed indirectly, craftily*
     assays   *attempts, trials*
     of bias   *curved, weighted, indirect. A bowl has a weight upon one side called the bias so that it has to be bowled in a curved path to reach the mark.*
[64] By indirections . . . out   *Find out people's intentions by indirect methods*
[65] lecture   *lesson, instruction*
[69] inclination   *nature, character*
     in yourself   *in your own person, by your own observation*

[76] closet   *a private apartment for religious or domestic use, a lady's dressing room. A 'closet' is not a bedroom.*
[77] unbraced   *unfastened*
[78] fouled   *tangled*
[79] down-gyvèd   *fallen down round his ankles like 'gyves' or fetters*

REYNALDO At 'closes in the consequence', at 'friend
   or so' and 'gentleman'.

POLONIUS At 'closes in the consequence' – ay, marry,
       He closes thus: 'I know the gentleman,
       I saw him yesterday – or t'other day –
       Or then, or then; with such or such, and, as
         you say,
       There was he gaming, there o'ertook in's rouse,
       There falling out at tennis', or perchance,
       'I saw him enter such a house of sale'
       Videlicet, a brothel, or so forth. See you now   60
       Your bait of falsehood take this carp of truth.
       And thus do we of wisdom and of reach,
       With windlasses and with assays of bias,
       By indirections find directions out.
       So, by my former lecture and advice,
       Shall you my son. You have me, have you not?

REYNALDO My lord, I have.

POLONIUS   God buy you. Fare you well.

REYNALDO Good my lord.

POLONIUS Observe his inclination in yourself.

REYNALDO I shall, my lord.   70

POLONIUS And let him ply his music.

REYNALDO   Well, my lord.

POLONIUS Farewell!

                     [*Exit* REYNALDO

Enter OPHELIA

       How now, Ophelia. What's the matter?

OPHELIA O my lord, my lord. I have been so
       affrighted.

POLONIUS With what, i'th'name of God?

OPHELIA My lord, as I was sewing in my closet,
       Lord Hamlet, with his doublet all unbraced,
       No hat upon his head, his stockings fouled,
       Ungartered, and down-gyvèd to his ankle,
       Pale as his shirt, his knees knocking each other, 80

[81] purport   *effect, meaning*

[84] Mad   *This is not a foolish conclusion on the part of Polonius since Ophelia has just been describing the traditional symptoms of love melancholy.*

[88] hand thus   *Hamlet is shading his eyes in order to scrutinise her face closely. The gesture is commonly seen in portraits of the period.*

[94] bulk   *physical presence, body*

[99] bendèd   *turned*

[101] ecstasy   *madness*
[102] property   *quality*
  fordoes   *destroys*
[103] will   *the part of the mind or soul concerned with action. According to St Augustine the soul had three powers – memory, understanding and will, all of which had to be used to reach the Eternal City of God. The will is particularly subject, therefore, to the passions.*
  desperate undertakings   *actions of despair – such as suicide*

[110] heed   *attention*
[111] quoted   *marked, noticed, observed*
[112] wreck   *destroy by seducing*
  beshrew   *curse, shame upon*
  jealousy   *suspicion*

And with a look so piteous in purport
As if he had been loosèd out of hell
To speak of horrors – he comes before me.
POLONIUS Mad for thy love?
OPHELIA   My lord, I do not know,
But truly I do fear it.
POLONIUS   What said he?
OPHELIA He took me by the wrist, and held me hard.
Then goes he to the length of all his arm,
And with his other hand thus o'er his brow
He falls to such perusal of my face
As he would draw it. Long stayed he so.   90
At last, a little shaking of mine arm,
And thrice his head thus waving up and down,
He raised a sigh so piteous and profound
As it did seem to shatter all his bulk
And end his being. That done, he lets me go,
And with his head over his shoulder turned
He seemed to find his way without his eyes
For out adoors he went without their helps
And to the last bendèd their light on me.
POLONIUS Come, go with me. I will go seek the King. 100
This is the very ecstasy of love,
Whose violent property fordoes itself,
And leads the will to desperate undertakings
As oft as any passion under heaven
That does afflict our natures. I am sorry –
What, have you given him any hard words of
   late?
OPHELIA No, my good lord; but, as you did command,
I did repel his letters, and denied
His access to me.
POLONIUS   That hath made him mad.
I am sorry that with better heed and judgement 110
I had not quoted him. I feared he did but trifle
And meant to wreck thee; but beshrew my
   jealousy.

[113] proper   *natural*

[114] cast beyond   *contrive too far, overreach*
       opinions   *judgements*
       It is as common for old men to exercise too much judgement and be too cautious as it is for young ones to be reckless and not exercise enough judgement.

[117] close   *hidden, secret*
       move   *cause, create*

[118] grief   *pain*
       This must be made known to the King since (if kept secret) this love might cause more pain for all of us because we hid it than it will create hatred now if we speak about it. The affections of the heir to the throne are, as Laertes suggested, a matter of state.

ACT TWO, scene 2

[2] Moreover that   *Besides the fact that*

[3] provoke   *incite, stimulate*

[5] transformation   *complete change in character*

[6] exterior   *body and dress*
    inward   *mind and soul*

[9] understanding of himself   *comprehension of his own nature and the way in which it is proper for him to behave (cf. I. 3. 96)*

[10] deem   *judge*

[11] being . . . him   *having been brought up with him as children*

[12] sith   *since, afterwards*
     neighboured . . . haviour   *so close to his young manhood and Form of behaviour*

[13] vouchsafe   *grant*
     rest   *stay*

[16] occasion   *accident, chance, opportunity*

[18] opened   *made clear, made known, revealed*

[21] adheres   *is close to*

[22] gentry   *courtesy*

By heaven, it is as proper to our age
To cast beyond ourselves in our opinions
As it is common for the younger sort
To lack discretion. Come, go we to the King.
This must be known, which, being kept
    close, might move
More grief to hide than hate to utter love.
Come.

                                [Exeunt

Scene 2. *Enter* KING, QUEEN, ROSENCRANTZ *and* GUILDEN-
STERN *with others*

KING Welcome, dear Rosencrantz and Guildenstern.
      Moreover that we much did long to see you,
      The need we have to use you did provoke
      Our hasty sending. Something have you heard
      Of Hamlet's transformation. So I call it,
      Sith nor th'exterior nor the inward man
      Resembles that it was. What it should be,
      More than his father's death, that thus hath
        put him
      So much from th'understanding of himself
      I cannot deem of. I entreat you both   10
      That, being of so young days brought up
        with him,
      And sith so neighboured to his youth and
        haviour,
      That you vouchsafe your rest here in our court
      Some little time. So by your companies
      To draw him on to pleasures, and to gather,
      So much as from occasion you may glean,
      Whether aught to us unknown afflicts him thus
      That, opened, lies within our remedy.
QUEEN Good gentlemen, he hath much talked of you;
      And sure I am two men there is not living   20
      To whom he more adheres. If it will please you
      To show us so much gentry and good will

[24] supply *assistance*
     profit *benefit, advancement, improvement*

[26] fits *as is suitable for i.e. a gift large enough for it to be representative of the thanks of a king*

[28–9] Put . . . entreaty *Expressed your wishes, which we are bound to respect, more in the form of a command than a request*

[30] bent *inclination*

[38] practices *what we perform – but it also carries the sense of crafty devices*

[44] hold *keep for the service of*

[47] Hunts not the trail *Does not follow the scent so keenly*
     policy *the business of politics – but 'policy' often has a pejorative sense for the Renaissance. Cesare Borgia was the prime example of a politician with Machiavelli the chief theoretician of 'policy'. Polonius will later fall victim to his own hunt when Hamlet cries 'a rat' in III. 4. 24*

As to expend your time with us awhile
For the supply and profit of our hope,
Your visitation shall receive such thanks
As fits a king's remembrance.

ROSENCRANTZ   Both your Majesties
Might, by the sovereign power you have of us,
Put your dread pleasures more into command
Than to entreaty.

GUILDENSTERN   But we both obey,
And here give up ourselves, in the full bent,   30
To lay our service freely at your feet,
To be commanded.

KING Thanks Rosencrantz, and gentle Guildenstern.

QUEEN Thanks Guildenstern, and gentle Rosencrantz.
And I beseech you instantly to visit
My too much changèd son. Go, some of you,
And bring these gentlemen where Hamlet is.

GUILDENSTERN Heavens make our presence and our
          practices
Pleasant and helpful to him.

QUEEN   Aye amen.
          [*Exeunt* ROSENCRANTZ *and* GUILDENSTERN

Enter POLONIUS

POLONIUS Th'ambassadors from Norway, my good
          lord,   40
Are joyfully returned.

KING Thou still hast been the father of good news.

POLONIUS Have I, my lord? I assure you, my good
          liege,
I hold my duty – as I hold my soul –
Both to my God and to my gracious King;
And I do think (or else this brain of mine
Hunts not the trail of policy so sure
As it hath used to do) that I have found
The very cause of Hamlet's lunacy.

KING O speak of that! That do I long to hear.   50

[52] fruit   *the last course*

[53] grace   *do them honour*

[55] distemper   *derangement or disturbance of the balance of the four humours in a man's temperament*

[56] doubt   *suspect, fear*

main   *the main, chief, cause*

[58] sift him   *examine him closely*

[61] first   *first request – the first article of the commission given to them by Claudius*

[63] preparation   *expedition prepared to fight against*

the Polack   *the King of Poland*

[67] borne in hand   *used, exerted, managed. Fortinbras misused his uncle's authority on account of his sickness, age and feebleness.*

arrests   *orders stopping his course of action*

[69] in fine   *in conclusion*

[71] assay   *attempt: 'give th'assay' make an armed attempt against*

[74] commission   *royal permission and order*

[76] herein further shown   *Voltemand must clearly give Claudius a property document or roll of parchment.*

[77] quiet pass   *peaceful passage. It seems probable that Shakespeare imagined a) that Poland had a continuous land frontier with Denmark [Polish controlled territories such as Pomerania did in fact have such a frontier], b) that Norwegian territory lay just across the Baltic Sound from Elsinore [the Elizabethan traveller Fynes Moryson made this mistake]. Fortinbras would thus have to cross the Sound and pass close to Elsinore on his way to Poland.*

[79] regards   *considerations, conditions*

allowance   *approval, permission*

POLONIUS Give first admittance to th'ambassadors.
　　　　My news shall be the fruit to that great feast.
KING Thyself do grace to them, and bring them in.
　　　　　　　　　　　　　　　　[*Exit* POLONIUS
　　　　He tells me, my dear Gertrude, he hath found
　　　　The head and source of all your son's
　　　　　distemper.
QUEEN I doubt it is no other but the main,
　　　　His father's death and our o'erhasty marriage.

　　　　Enter POLONIUS, VOLTEMAND *and* CORNELIUS

　　　　Well, we shall sift him. Welcome, my good
　　　　　friends.
　　　　Say, Voltemand, what from our brother
　　　　　Norway?
VOLTEMAND Most fair return of greetings and desires.　60
　　　　Upon our first, he sent out to suppress
　　　　His nephew's levies – which to him appeared
　　　　To be a preparation 'gainst the Polack,
　　　　But, better looked into, he truly found
　　　　It was against your highness. Whereat grieved
　　　　That so his sickness, age, and impotence
　　　　Was falsely borne in hand, sends out arrests
　　　　On Fortinbras; which he, in brief, obeys,
　　　　Receives rebuke from Norway, and, in fine,
　　　　Makes vow before his uncle never more　　70
　　　　To give th'assay of arms against your Majesty.
　　　　Whereon old Norway, overcome with joy,
　　　　Gives him threescore thousand crowns in
　　　　　annual fee,
　　　　And his commission to employ those soldiers
　　　　So levied as before against the Polack;
　　　　With an entreaty, herein further shown,
　　　　That it might please you to give quiet pass
　　　　Through your dominions for this enterprise,
　　　　On such regards of safety and allowance
　　　　As therein are set down.

[81] more considered time *when we have had time to give the matter more consideration*

[86] expostulate *debate, argue*

[87] majesty . . . duty is *the nature of kingly behaviour and duty. Polonius wishes to draw attention to his own good service in discovering Hamlet's love for Ophelia. Since he cannot praise himself directly he covers the matter with figures of rhetoric that he may be discovered an honest man.*

[90] soul *essential part*

[91] outward flourishes *appearance and dress*

[93] Mad call I it . . . *a hasty blurring of his meaning since it may not be tactful to call the heir to the throne mad. It also reminds the audience, through the joke, that Hamlet's madness is something other than insanity.*

[95] matter *subject matter*

[98] figure *figure of rhetoric. Polonius's style is a parody of the chiasmic order (a, b, b, a) favoured by those imitating the rhetorical style of Greek or Roman orators.*

[101] effect *result, consequence*

[102] defect *imperfection*

[103] effect *outward sign, appearance. Hamlet's outward actions or appearance become defective or mad as a result of some cause.*

[105] Perpend *Weigh exactly, ponder, consider*

[106] have . . . mine *control while she is still unmarried*

[108] gather *put together, collect what knowledge you can from this surmise conjecture, imagine (the rest)*

[109] beautified *made beautiful – since it comes immediately after 'soul's idol' it seems that a pun on 'beatified' is intended. Hamlet calls her one of the saints of love who has created her own beauty. The letter ironically praises her for exactly those qualities Hamlet says he hates most in the nunnery scene.*

KING   It likes us well;   80
        And at our more considered time we'll read,
        Answer, and think upon this business.
        Meantime we thank you for your well-took
            labour.
        Go to your rest. At night we'll feast together.
        Most welcome home.
                            [*Exeunt* AMBASSADORS
POLONIUS   This business is well ended.
        My liege, and madam, to expostulate
        What majesty should be, what duty is,
        Why day is day, night night, and time is time,
        Were nothing, but to waste night, day, and time.
        Therefore, since brevity is the soul of wit,   90
        And tediousness the limbs and outward
            flourishes,
        I will be brief. Your noble son is mad.
        Mad call I it (for to define true madness,
        What is't but to be nothing else but mad?)
        But let that go.
QUEEN   More matter with less art.
POLONIUS Madam, I swear I use no art at all.
        That he's mad, 'tis true. 'Tis true 'tis pity,
        And pity 'tis 'tis true. A foolish figure –
        But farewell it, for I will use no art.
        Mad let us grant him then, and now remains   100
        That we find out the cause of this effect;
        Or rather say the cause of this defect,
        For this effect defective comes by cause.
        Thus it remains, and the remainder thus.
        Perpend.
        I have a daughter – have while she is mine –
        Who in her duty and obedience, mark,
        Hath given me this. Now gather and surmise.
                    [*Reads the letter*]
        To the celestial, and my soul's idol, the most
        beautified Ophelia

[115] Doubt   *a) Be in doubt, b) suspect. Hamlet is evidently a poet of the new school that came to be called metaphysical. Many devices that became common in seventeenth-century verse and admired in Donne are here parodied – a typically Shakespearian stylistic device to parody intellectual poetry in one of the most intellectual plays of the age.*

[119] numbers   *verses*

[120] reckon   *count up. He is unable to count his groans because there are too many of them and he lacks the art to put them into verses, numbers.*

[123] machine   *construct – the human body as constructed by God*

[130] fain   *gladly, willingly*

[135] played the desk or table book   *played a part as silent (and yet as involved in the affair) as the desk on which the letter was written or the book of tables or notebook in which the poem was inscribed*

[136] given my heart a winking   *caused my heart to wink at, connived at*

[137] idle sight   *carelessly – as if it didn't matter*

[138] round   *directly, in straightforward fashion*

– That's an ill phrase, a vile phrase. 'Beauti-   110
fied' is a vile phrase – but you shall hear, thus:
In her excellent white bosom, these, &c

QUEEN Came this from Hamlet to her?

POLONIUS Good madam, stay awhile, I will be
    faithful.

          Doubt thou the stars are fire,
          Doubt that the sun doth move,
          Doubt truth to be a liar,
          But never doubt I love.

    O dear Ophelia, I am ill at these numbers
    I have not art to reckon my groans; but that   120
    I love thee – best, O most best, believe it.
                    Adieu.
    Thine evermore, most dear lady, whilst this
    machine is to him.

                           Hamlet.

This, in obedience, hath my daughter shown
me.
And more above, hath his solicitings
As they fell out by time, by means, and place,
All given to mine ear.

KING   But how hath she
Received his love?

POLONIUS   What do you think of me?

KING As of a man faithful and honourable.

POLONIUS I would fain prove so. But what might you
    think,   130
When I had seen this hot love on the wing,
(As I perceived it, I must tell you that,
Before my daughter told me) what might you,
Or my dear majesty your queen here, think,
If I had played the desk or table book,
Or given my heart a winking, mute and dumb,
Or looked upon this love with idle sight –
What might you think? No, I went round to
    work,

[140] **out of thy star** *out of the sphere in which your star is fixed i.e. beyond your place and fortune*

[141] **prescripts** *orders, instructions*

[142] **resort** *continual attempts to see her*

[144] **the fruits of my advice** *carried out my commands. Good advice bears fruit when it is carried out in action.*

[147] **watch** *inability to sleep, wakefulness*

[148] **lightness** *light headedness, confusion of mind. Polonius's account of Hamlet's progressive decline into love melancholy was offered as serious comment in treatises on melancholy: see Andreas Laurentius,* A Discourse on the Preservation of Sight *1599, p. 118.*

[155] **Take this from this** *The line must be accompanied by a gesture and probably means take my head from my body. Polonius is prepared to wager his head on the truth of his opinion.*

[156] **circumstances** *surrounding details, particulars, current conditions*

[158] **centre** *the centre of the earth – which is also the central point of the universe in Ptolemaic astronomy*

      try *test, examine*

[159] **together** *at one time*

[160] **lobby** *the ante-room of the palace where people waited for audience with the King in the hall or throne-room*

[161] **loose** *free, release from constraints. It also has the sense of 'to shoot an arrow': Polonius fires the arrow of Ophelia at Hamlet to determine if he has been hit by love's arrow. As an adjective, 'loose' also carries the meanings of unclad, very lightly dressed and sexually unrestrained. These are not intended by Polonius but they could be regarded as part of the symbolism of sexuality with which Shakespeare surrounds Ophelia.*

[162] **arras** *covering or tapestry hung upon walls. The most famous tapestries were woven at Arras in France.*

[164] **thereon** *as a result. Hamlet has fallen from his reason on to his love for Ophelia.*

[166] **try** *attempt*

And my young mistress thus I did bespeak:
'Lord Hamlet is a prince out of thy star,   140
This must not be'. And then I prescripts
   gave her,
That she should lock herself from his resort,
Admit no messengers, receive no tokens.
Which done, she took the fruits of my advice
And he repelled – a short tale to make –
Fell into a sadness, then into a fast,
Thence to a watch, thence into a weakness,
Thence to a lightness, and, by this declension,
Into the madness wherein now he raves
And we all mourn for.

KING   Do you think 'tis this?   150
QUEEN It may be, very like.
POLONIUS Hath there been such a time (I would fain
   know that)
   That I have positively said, ' 'Tis so',
   When it proved otherwise?
KING   Not that I know.
POLONIUS Take this from this, if this be otherwise.
   If circumstances lead me, I will find
   Where truth is hid, though it were hid indeed
   Within the centre.
KING   How may we try it further?
POLONIUS You know sometimes he walks four hours
   together,
   Here in the lobby?
QUEEN   So he does indeed.   160
POLONIUS At such a time I'll loose my daughter to
   him.
   Be you and I behind an arras then,
   Mark the encounter. If he love her not,
   And be not from his reason fall'n thereon,
   Let me be no assistant for a state
   But keep a farm and carters.
KING   We will try it.

[167] **sadly** *seriously, mournfully, in melancholy fashion. The entry of the melancholy and satirical scholar with his book is a long-enduring convention of Renaissance drama.*

[169] **board him presently** *encounter him instantly. The metaphor is from a sea-fight where two ships encounter each other, grapple and the crew of one attacks or boards the other vessel.*

[173] **fishmonger** *a) a dealer in fish, b) possibly a pimp owing to the association between fish, especially cod, and the male sexual organ, c) since fish were caught on hooks or snared in nets there is another possible sense of cunning betrayer*

[175] **honest a man** *when applied to the female sex, 'honest' also means chaste. Again the emphasis is part of the ambiguous pattern of sexual imagery which surrounds the family of Polonius.*

[180] **if the sun . . .** *It was believed that maggots and worms were actually created by the sun shining on dead flesh. If the sun can breed maggots by kissing the carrion flesh of a dead dog is it not even more likely to kiss Ophelia (since she, too, possesses flesh good for kissing) and make her pregnant.*

[183] **Conception** *Another train of thought is introduced by the pun on conception which means both pregnancy and the power of thought or understanding. Hamlet is aware that Ophelia has been prevented from seeing him. He therefore tells Polonius that if he wishes to prevent his daughter from becoming pregnant he had better see that she follows the truly contemplative life and, like the melancholic scholar, avoid the sun.*

It is notable that this is the same pun as I. 2. 67 and it carries the same meaning. The sun is the sun of court favour, or indeed the King himself. If Polonius is worried about Ophelia he ought to observe that Claudius, and not Hamlet, is the most lecherous member of the Danish court. His kiss is indeed the kiss of death – implications which are more fully developed in the graveyard scene.

[193] **matter** *subject-matter. Hamlet takes him to mean quarrel, trouble.*

[198] **purging** *discharging*

  amber *yellowish fossil resin found along south shores of the Baltic. Hamlet means that the substance discharged from the eyes is of roughly this colour and consistency.*

[198–9] **plum-tree gum** *sap oozing from a plum tree*

Enter HAMLET *reading on a book*

QUEEN But look where sadly the poor wretch comes
    reading.

POLONIUS Away, I do beseech you, both away:
    I'll board him presently. O, give me leave.
                    [*Exeunt* KING *and* QUEEN
    How does my good Lord Hamlet?   170

HAMLET Well, God-a-mercy.

POLONIUS Do you know me, my lord?

HAMLET Excellent well; you are a fishmonger.

POLONIUS Not I, my lord.

HAMLET Then I would you were so honest a man.

POLONIUS Honest, my lord?

HAMLET Ay sir, to be honest – as this world goes – is
    to be one man picked out of ten thousand.

POLONIUS That's very true, my lord.

HAMLET For if the sun breed maggots in a dead dog – 180
    being a good kissing carrion – Have you a daughter?

POLONIUS I have, my lord.

HAMLET Let her not walk i'th'sun. Conception is a
    blessing. But as your daughter may conceive –
    friend, look to't.

POLONIUS [*Aside*] How say you by that? Still harping
    on my daughter. Yet he knew me not at first. He
    said I was a fishmonger. He is far gone, far gone.
    And truly in my youth I suffered much extremity
    for love. Very near this. I'll speak to him again. 190
    [*Aloud*] What do you read, my lord?

HAMLET Words, words, words.

POLONIUS What is the matter, my lord?

HAMLET Between who?

POLONIUS I mean, the matter that you read, my lord.

HAMLET Slanders sir; for the satirical rogue says here
    that old men have grey beards, that their faces are
    wrinkled, their eyes purging thick amber and plum-
    tree gum, and that they have a plentiful lack of wit,

[200] hams   *back of the knee – hence, thighs and buttocks*

[202] hold it not honesty   *believe it to be indecent*

[203] old as I am   *Polonius treats Hamlet's sudden assumption of age as madness but Hamlet has been giving him a satirical view of old age as foolish and old age ought, like Saturn, god of old age and melancholy, to be wise. Hamlet claims the wisdom of the crab.*

crab   *Its sideways movement and tendency to back away when touched made early observers think it walked backwards. This strange motion seemed irregular and unnatural. If it is a sign of Hamlet's madness to believe himself a crab and walk backwards it is also a wise posture of defence to adopt in Elsinore, and Hamlet's madness may be the only sane course to follow amid the mad folly of murder and lust. If the rest of the court walks forward, then Hamlet resembles the crab since he moves in the opposite direction.*

[206–7] out of the air   *One treatment of madness was to confine the patient in a small space, preferably dark. Compare the comic treatment of Malvolio in* Twelfth Night.

[210] pregnant   *compelling, cogent, clear, full of meaning*
       happiness   *aptness, fitness of expression*

[212] delivered of   *a) express in speech, b) give birth to the pregnant thoughts of line 210*

[228] indifferent   *neither good nor bad in quality or fortune*

[230] button   *at the highest point of fortune*

together with most weak hams. All of which, sir, 200
though I most powerfully and potently believe, yet
I hold it not honesty to have it thus set down – for
yourself, sir, shall grow old as I am if, like a crab,
you could go backward.

POLONIUS [Aside] Though this be madness, yet there
is method in't. [To HAMLET] Will you walk out of the
air, my lord?

HAMLET Into my grave?

POLONIUS Indeed, that's out of the air. [Aside] How
pregnant sometimes his replies are – a happiness 210
that often madness hits on, which reason and sanity
could not so prosperously be delivered of. I will
leave him and suddenly contrive the means of meeting between him and my daughter. [To HAMLET]
My lord, I will take my leave of you.

HAMLET You cannot, sir, take from me anything that I
will more willingly part withal – except my life,
except my life, except my life.

Enter ROSENCRANTZ *and* GUILDENSTERN

POLONIUS Fare you well, my lord.

HAMLET These tedious old fools! 220

POLONIUS You go to seek the Lord Hamlet, there he is.

ROSENCRANTZ [To POLONIUS] God save you, sir.

GUILDENSTERN My honoured lord!

ROSENCRANTZ My most dear lord!

HAMLET My excellent good friends! How dost thou,
Guildenstern? Ah, Rosencrantz! Good lads, how
do you both?

ROSENCRANTZ As the indifferent children of the earth.

GUILDENSTERN Happy in that we are not over happy;
On fortune's cap we are not the very button. 230

HAMLET Nor the soles of her shoe?

ROSENCRANTZ Neither, my lord.

HAMLET Then you live about her waist, or in the
middle of her favours?

[235] privates *private persons – but Hamlet has been driving them to the comparison of living in the private parts or sexual organs of fortune*

[237] strumpet *whore. Fortune is traditionally a whore because she gives her favours to all men and is constant to none.*

[240] doomsday *Those who were to survive the day of judgement were marked or sealed as honest men according to the Revelation of St John.*

[247–8] confines *places of confinement*
[248] wards *separate divisions or areas of a prison*

[252] thinking makes it so *it is human thought which distinguishes degrees and determines value*

[254] ambition *recognised as one of the chief causes of melancholy*

[256] bounded *confined within the limits of*

[258] bad dreams *another traditional symptom of melancholy*

[260–1] substance . . . dream *the object desired by ambitious people is even less solid or important than a dream – as if a dream could cast a shadow*

[262] shadow *an unreal appearance, delusive image*
[265–7] beggars bodies . . . shadows *then beggars (who have no ambition) are solid, real people with bodies, and kings and heroes who strain or reach beyond the limits of mankind (as a result of ambition) are the beggars' shadows*
Rosencrantz and Guildenstern preach humility to Hamlet but, as he is about to demonstrate, are themselves ambitious shadows or reflections of the King employed to act as shadows or parasites on Hamlet.
[270] sort you *place you, class you*

GUILDENSTERN Faith, her privates we.

HAMLET In the secret parts of Fortune? O most true –
she is a strumpet. What news?

ROSENCRANTZ None, my lord, but that the world's
grown honest.

HAMLET Then is doomsday near, but your news is not 240
true. Let me question more in particular. What have
you, my good friends, deserved at the hands of
Fortune, that she sends you to prison hither?

GUILDENSTERN Prison, my lord?

HAMLET Denmark's a prison.

ROSENCRANTZ Then is the world one.

HAMLET A goodly one; in which there are many confines, wards, and dungeons, Denmark being one
o'th'worst.

ROSENCRANTZ We think not so, my lord. 250

HAMLET Why then, 'tis none to you, for there is nothing either good or bad but thinking makes it so. To
me it is a prison.

ROSENCRANTZ Why, then your ambition makes it one;
'tis too narrow for your mind.

HAMLET O God, I could be bounded in a nutshell, and
count myself a king of infinite space – were it not
that I have bad dreams.

GUILDENSTERN Which dreams indeed are ambition.
For the very substance of the ambitious is merely 260
the shadow of a dream.

HAMLET A dream itself is but a shadow.

ROSENCRANTZ Truly, and I hold ambition of so airy
and light a quality that it is but a shadow's shadow.

HAMLET Then are our beggars bodies, and our mon-
archs and outstretched heroes, the beggars'
shadows. Shall we to the court? For, by my fey,
I cannot reason.

BOTH We'll wait upon you.

HAMLET No such matter. I will not sort you with the 270
rest of my servants; for, to speak to you like an

[273] in the beaten way of friendship   *according to the well-worn path of our friendship*

[283] to th'purpose   *let us come to the point*

[285] modesties   *powers of self-control*

[286] colour   *conceal*

[289] conjure you   *ask you in a way that compels you to answer. Hamlet uses their youth as a spell or invocation in the way that a necromancer, often called a conjurer, would compel spirits to answer his questions.*

[290–1] consonancy   *similar upbringing*

[292–3] what more dear . . . charge you withal   *what is more precious or sacred to you that a more skilled constructor of questions could command you by*

[293] even   *straightforward*

[296] an eye of you   *I shall watch you – because I am suspicious of you now*

[299] anticipation   *forestalling of your answer*

[300] discovery   *disclosure (of what they had presumably sworn not to reveal)*

[301] moult   *drop, lose – they can keep the full plumage or fine feathers of their sworn secrecy*

[302] mirth   *cheerfulness*

[303] custom of exercise   *usual or habitual sports and pastimes*

[303–4] goes . . . disposition   *my temperament, spirits, are so weighed down and depressed*

[304] frame   *structure*

[305] sterile promontory   *unfertile piece of rocky land surrounded by water. Shakespeare evidently thought of the castle of Elsinore as being on a promontory. It is evident that this speech also treats the theatre where the play is being performed as an emblem of the world. Since the actors called the theatre 'The Globe' they were obviously aware of such implications. Hamlet and his fellow actors are standing on the promontory of the stage jutting out into the audience.*

[306] canopy   *ceremonial cloth or cover supported on poles over a bed, a throne, or the person of the King on a royal procession; the cover over the stage*

brave   *splendid*

[307] firmament   *vault or arch of the sky*

[307–8] fretted with golden fire   *adorned with interlaced work of gold (from the sun or stars)*

honest man, I am most dreadfully attended. But,
in the beaten way of friendship, what make you at
Elsinore?

ROSENCRANTZ To visit you, my lord. No other occasion.

HAMLET Beggar that I am, I am even poor in thanks;
but I thank you – and sure, dear friends, my thanks
are too dear a half-penny. Were you not sent for?
Is it your own inclining? Is it a free visitation? 280
Come, deal justly with me. Come, come; nay, speak.

GUILDENSTERN What should we say, my lord?

HAMLET Why, anything! But to th'purpose: you were
sent for, and there is a kind of confession in your
looks which your modesties have not craft enough
to colour. I know the good King and Queen have
sent for you.

ROSENCRANTZ To what end, my lord?

HAMLET That you must teach me. But let me conjure
you, by the rights of our fellowship, by the con- 290
sonancy of our youth, by the obligation of our ever-
preserved love, and by what more dear a better
proposer can charge you withal, be even and direct
with me, whether you were sent for or no?

ROSENCRANTZ [*Aside to* GUILDENSTERN] What say you?

HAMLET [*Aside*] Nay, then, I have an eye of you.
[*Aloud*] If you love me, hold not off.

GUILDENSTERN My lord, we were sent for.

HAMLET I will tell you why. So shall my anticipation
prevent your discovery – and your secrecy to the 300
King and Queen moult no feather. I have of late –
but wherefore I know not – lost all my mirth, for-
gone all custom of exercises; and indeed it goes so
heavily with my disposition that this goodly frame
the earth seems to me a sterile promontory. This
most excellent canopy the air – look you, this brave
o'er-hanging firmament, this majestical roof fretted
with golden fire – why, it appeareth no other thing

[310] vapours *mist or fog – also gases usually thought of as coming from the stomach and affecting the head causing depression, melancholia and similar diseases*

[311] faculties *powers, abilities, aptitudes: man's reason is noble and his power to translate that reason into action, infinite*

express *exact, fitted to its purpose*

[313] apprehension *faculty of learning, understanding, perceiving. The description insists that man is excellent both in the power of his reason and in his ability to act. Both his mind and his body are therefore involved to make him the model and touchstone of perfection for the animal kingdom. For Hamlet the intellect alone is not enough.*

[314] paragon *touchstone, model of perfection*

[315] quintessence *the most essential substance – what was left once the four elements of earth, air, fire and water had been extracted*

[323] lenten entertainment *food and welcome suitable to Lent – the time of fasting before Easter which begins on Ash Wednesday in the Christian calendar*

[324] coted *passed by, overtook*

[327] tribute *a) tax paid to a king acknowledging submission, b) praise and payment given to the actor for playing the king*

[331] tickle a'th'sere *made to laugh very easily. The 'sear' is the catch in the lock of a gun or pistol which holds the hammer cocked. If it is 'tickle', easily moved, then the gun is liable to fire suddenly.*

[332] freely *openly*

[335] the tragedians of the city *In terms of the plot the players ought to come from Wittenberg or one of the main towns in Denmark but they are treated as being Shakespeare's company – the Lord Chamberlain's Men – hence the joke about their ill reception by Polonius.*

[336–7] Their residence . . . ways *If they stayed or resided in the city they did better both for their estimation and their cash takings than as a touring company*

[338] inhibition *a court order (presumably prohibiting playing)*

[339] innovation *change, new style, new fashion. The phrase is deliberately obscure. There were many reasons why the court or government might exercise censorship on the London theatres and Shakespeare is careful not to be too specific about them. The audience might see an allusion to some recent theatrical case. The childrens' companies in particular tended to present dangerously satirical plays.*

[345] eyrie *nest*

to me than a foul and pestilent congregation of
vapours. What a piece of work is a man. How noble 310
in reason, how infinite in faculties. In form and
moving how express and admirable, in action how
like an angel, in apprehension how like a god. The
beauty of the world. The paragon of animals. And
yet, to me what is this quintessence of dust? Man
delights not me – no, nor woman neither, though
by your smiling you seem to say so.

ROSENCRANTZ My lord, there was no such stuff in my
thoughts.

HAMLET Why did ye laugh, then, when I said 'Man 320
delights not me'?

ROSENCRANTZ To think, my lord, if you delight not in
man, what lenten entertainment the players shall
receive from you. We coted them on the way; and
hither are they coming to offer you service.

HAMLET He that plays the king – shall be welcome.
His Majesty shall have tribute of me. The adven-
turous knight shall use his foil and target; the lover
shall not sigh gratis; the humorous man shall end
his part in peace; the clown shall make those laugh 330
whose lungs are tickle a'th' sere; and the lady shall
say her mind freely, or the blank verse shall halt
for't. What players are they?

ROSENCRANTZ Even those you were wont to take such
delight in – the tragedians of the city.

HAMLET How chances it they travel? Their residence,
both in reputation and profit, was better both ways.

ROSENCRANTZ I think their inhibition comes by the
means of the late innovation.

HAMLET Do they hold the same estimation they did 340
when I was in the city? Are they so followed?

ROSENCRANTZ No, indeed, they are not.

HAMLET How comes it? Do they grow rusty?

ROSENCRANTZ Nay, their endeavour keeps in the
wonted pace, but there is, sir, an eyrie of children,

[346] eyases *young hawks*

cry out *give tongue like a pack of hounds. The metaphor appears to change abruptly from hawking to hunting.*

on the top of question *A double metaphor seems to be involved. A 'question' is a controversy or argument, here probably of a public nature. A 'quest', however, is the peculiar noise made by a pack of hounds when in sight of the quarry. The voices of these children are shrill enough to be distinguished, therefore, at the 'top' of the noise of the 'quest' of a pack of hounds who are in pursuit of some 'question' or controversy of the day. The sense of shrillness is perhaps intensified by the fact that 'pitch' is used of voices and of the highest point reached by a hawk or eyas at the top of its flight.*

[347] tyrannically *excessively – the kind of ironic applause that greets a stage tyrant's passion (compare Bottom in* A Midsummer Night's Dream, *I. 2. 28–40)*

[348] berattle *rattle away at, assail with noise*

common stages *public playhouses – described by the children as common or vulgar*

[352] escoted *paid for*

[353] quality *profession of acting*

[359] tar *provoke, incite*

[360–1] no money . . . argument *no money offered for the theme or plot of a play*

[366] carry it away *gain the advantage, victory*

[367–8] Hercules and his load *In Greek mythology the eleventh labour of Hercules was to obtain the golden apples of the sun from the garden of the Hesperides. Hercules persuaded Atlas to obtain them for him and took over Atlas's task of supporting the globe on his shoulders while he did so. The reference to Hercules and his load means that the boys gained the advantage over the company at the Globe theatre.*

[370] mows *grimaces*

[372] picture in little *miniature*

[374] natural *a) normal, in accordance with nature, b) foolish,*

[377] appurtenance *that which naturally and fitly belongs to* welcome'

[378] fashion *customary outward show*

comply *observe the formalities of courtesy and politeness*

[379] garb *style, manner – continuing the clothes motif suggested by* fashion

extent *the extent of my welcome*

little eyases, that cry out on the top of question and
are most tyrannically clapped for't. These are now
the fashion, and so berattle the common stages (so
they call them) that many wearing rapiers are afraid
of goosequills and dare scarce come thither.   350

HAMLET What, are they children? Who maintains
'em? How are they escoted? Will they pursue the
quality no longer than they can sing? Will they not
say afterwards, if they should grow themselves to
common players (as it is most like, if their means
are no better), their writers do them wrong to make
them exclaim against their own succession?

ROSENCRANTZ Faith, there has been much to-do on
both sides, and the nation holds it no sin to tar them
to controversy. There was, for a while, no money   360
bid for argument unless the poet and the player
went to cuffs in the question.

HAMLET Is't possible?

GUILDENSTERN O, there has been much throwing
about of brains.

HAMLET Do the boys carry it away?

ROSENCRANTZ Ay, that they do, my lord – Hercules
and his load too.

HAMLET It is not very strange; for my uncle is King of
Denmark, and those that would make mows at him   370
while my father lived give twenty, forty, fifty, a
hundred ducats apiece for his picture in little.
'Sblood, there is something in this more than
natural, if philosophy could find it out.

Flourish for the Players

GUILDENSTERN There are the players.

HAMLET Gentlemen, you are welcome to Elsinore.
Your hands – come then. Th'appurtenance of welcome is fashion and ceremony; let me comply with
you in this garb, lest my extent to the players (which
I tell you must show fairly outwards) should more   380

[385] north-north-west *when the wind is from the north or north-west. Timothy Bright in* A Treatise of Melancholy *(1586) says that winds from the south or south-east provide a soothing climate which helps to cure melancholy.*

[386] a hawk from a handsaw *In distinguishing the various parts of the soul in the same treatise Bright makes an analogy with a hawk, which has a life and character of its own, but can be trained to obey commands; a hand, which has no life of its own but is yet alive, and a saw which is not alive but simply an instrument for performing tasks. Hamlet is thus warning Rosencrantz and Guildenstern that his melancholy does not prevent him from distinguishing between true independent friends and those who are merely the King's instruments. Alternatively 'handsaw' may be a misprint for 'harnsa' or 'heyrn-sew' = heron shaw. Herons were often the game hawked after because they supplied such good sport. Hamlet can tell hunter from hunted.*

[391] Happily *Perhaps*

[398] Roscius *Gallus Quintus Roscius was perhaps the most famous of Roman actors. Cicero took lessons in delivery from him.*

[400] Buzz, buzz *derogatory noise made when what is reported is believed to be rumour, not fact. A 'buzz' can still mean a rumour.*

[406] individible *not divided, indivisible – i.e. the best actors for a single scene or for an epic with any number of scenes*

[407] Seneca *Roman tragedian*

[408] Plautus *Roman comedian*

[408–9] law of writ and the liberty *plays written according to classical rules of writing and plays which are free from them. A legal pun is involved. Plays at the Globe were performed within the Liberty of the Clink, a special area where the Sheriff's writ or authority did not run. The Lord of the Liberty could therefore permit the building of a theatre.*

[410] Jephthah *One of the Judges or leaders of Israel who fought for the liberty of his people but found himself fatally bound by a law of his own making. He promised to sacrifice to God the first thing he met after his victory. On his return his daughter came out of the city to meet him.*

appear like entertainment than yours. You are
welcome – but my uncle-father and aunt-mother
are deceived.

GUILDENSTERN In what, my dear lord?

HAMLET I am but mad north-north-west. When the
wind is southerly, I know a hawk from a handsaw.

Enter POLONIUS

POLONIUS Well be with you, gentlemen.

HAMLET Hark you, Guildenstern, and you too, at each
ear a hearer: that great baby you see there is not yet
out of his swaddling clouts.   390

ROSENCRANTZ Happily he is the second time come to
them, for they say an old man is twice a child.

HAMLET I will prophesy he comes to tell me of the
players, mark it. You say right, sir – a Monday
morning – 'twas then indeed.

POLONIUS My lord, I have news to tell you.

HAMLET My lord, I have news to tell you.

When Roscius was an actor at Rome –

POLONIUS The actors are come hither, my lord.

HAMLET Buzz, buzz.   400

POLONIUS Upon my honour –

HAMLET Then came each actor on his ass –

POLONIUS The best actors in the world, either for
tragedy, comedy, history, pastoral, pastoral-comical,
historical-pastoral, tragical-historical, tragical-
comical-historical-pastoral, scene individable or
poem unlimited. Seneca cannot be too heavy nor
Plautus too light. For the law of writ and the
liberty, these are the only men.

HAMLET O Jephthah, judge of Israel, what a treasure 410
had'st thou!

POLONIUS What a treasure had he, my lord?

HAMLET Why –

'One fair daughter, and no more,
The which he loved passing well.'

[426] first row   *first line*

pious chanson   *religious ballad*

Hamlet appears to be quoting a ballad on Jephtah. Its first line is 'I read that many year ago'; the line immediately following Hamlet's quotation is 'Great wars there should be'.

[427] abridgement   *that which will shorten my time and labour*

[430] valanced   *covered with a beard. M. Bradbrook has suggested that in Shakespeare's company Burbage would be playing Hamlet and the first Player is made up to look like Burbage with a pointed beard as in the Dulwich portrait.*

[431] beard   *outwit, outface, set at defiance – from the idea of taking a lion by the beard. Hamlet is being ironically courteous and Shakespeare is again referring to his company of fellow-actors.*

[434] altitude of a chopine   *grown by the height of a high-heeled shoe. The chopine was made of cork and leather and worn under the normal shoe. In fashionable Venice it could be as much as a foot and a half high.*

[435] cracked   *broken. The parts of women were taken by boy players who also sang. Once their voices broke, both roles could no longer be performed.*

within the ring   *A gold coin had the King's head surrounded by a circle stamped on it. If a crack at the edge of the metal reached within this ring the coin was no longer legal tender – 'uncurrent' – and need not be accepted.*

[437] fly at   *set our falcons or hawks to attack. Hamlet suggests that French falconers were impatient and liable to free their hawks at the first bird seen instead of waiting for a bird, such as a heron, that would provide good sport.*

[438] straight   *immediately*

[439] quality   *profession*

[444] caviare to the general   *too delicate for most people. Caviare is the roe of the sturgeon and is an acquired taste – since it is scarce and expensive it is not a taste likely to be shared by many. Hamlet implies that the popular taste was mistaken.*

[444–5] received it   *heard and understood it*

[446] cried in the top of mine   *were heard (and deserved to be heard) above mine – because their judgements were better*

[446–7] well digested   *well-shaped, composed*

[449] sallets   *spicey, obscene, words. Salads were spiced with herbs and vinegar to make them sharp or 'savory'.*

POLONIUS [*Aside*] Still on my daughter.

HAMLET Am I not i'th'right, old Jephthah?

POLONIUS If you call me Jephthah, my lord, I have a
daughter that I love passing well.

HAMLET Nay, that follows not.   420

POLONIUS What follows then, my lord?

HAMLET Why –
    'As by lot, God wot'
and then, you know,
    'It came to pass, as most like it was'.
The first row of the pious chanson will show you
more; for look where my abridgement comes.

Enter the PLAYERS

You are welcome, masters, welcome all. I am glad
to see thee well – welcome, good friends. O, my old
friend, why, thy face is valanced since I saw thee   430
last! Com'st thou to beard me in Denmark? What,
my young lady and mistress. By'r lady, your lady-
ship is nearer to heaven than when I saw you last by
the altitude of a chopine. Pray God your voice, like
a piece of uncurrent gold, be not cracked within the
ring. Masters, you are all welcome. We'll e'en to it
like French falconers, fly at anything we see. We'll
have a speech straight. Come, give us a taste of your
quality; come, a passionate speech.

I PLAYER What speech, my good lord?   440

HAMLET I heard thee speak me a speech once, but it
was never acted – or if it was, not above once – for
the play, I remember, pleased not the million;
'twas caviare to the general. But it was, as I received
it, and others whose judgements in such matters
cried in the top of mine, an excellent play, well
digested in the scenes, set down with as much
modesty as cunning. I remember one said 'there
were no sallets in the lines, to make the matter
savoury, nor no matter in the phrase that might   450

[452] honest method   *proper design*

[453] more handsome than fine   *more appropriate and pleasantly useful than artful, subtle and intricate*

[454] Aeneas' tale to Dido   *For the importance of the story of Troy see Introduction p.* 19.

[458] rugged   *covered in hair, rough, cruel*

Hyrcanian beast   *tiger. Hyrcania was a district of Asia, south of the Caspian sea mentioned by Virgil (Aeneid IV. 367) as famous for its tigers.*

[460] sable   *black – the heraldic term, and so refers to his armour and the arms or device on his shield. The speech is full of heraldic terms as Shakespeare is using it as an emblematic device.*

[462] couchèd   *hidden, concealed*

ominous   *ill-omened*

[464] dismal   *evil, unlucky, terrible*

[465] gules   *red*

tricked   *covered – another heraldic term meaning to draw a coat of arms in outline. Pyrrhus is now outlined in blood.*

[467] impasted   *made into a paste or crust. The blood has congealed and has been baked, and is now cracking in the dry heat of the streets of the burning city.*

[470] o'ersizèd   *covered over. Size is a kind of clear glue used to prepare rough surfaces for colouring.*

[471] carbuncles   *red precious stones. They were supposed to give out light in the dark.*

[475] discretion   *understanding*

[477] too short   *Priam's arm is too weak to lift his sword so his blows fall short.*

[479] Repugnant   *Contrary to command, resisting command*

[480] drives   *strikes*

[481] whiff   *gust*

fell   *cruel*

[482] unnervèd   *weak – since his nerves or sinews were old*

senseless   *without the five senses – yet it reacted as if it felt this blow*

[483] top   *highest point, pinnacle. The towers of Troy were famous.*

[486] declining   *falling*

milky   *grey, white-haired*

indict the author of affection' but called it 'an
honest method, as wholesome as sweet, and by very
much more handsome than fine'. One speech in it
I chiefly loved. 'Twas Aeneas' tale to Dido; and
thereabout of it especially where he speaks of
Priam's slaughter. If it live in your memory, begin
at this line – let me see, let me see:

> *The rugged Pyrrhus, like th'Hyrcanian best*

'Tis not so. It begins with Pyrrhus –

> *The rugged Pyrrhus, he whose sable arms,*   460
> *Black as his purpose, did the night resemble*
> *When he lay couchèd in the ominous horse,*
> *Hath now this dread and black complexion*
>   *smeared*
> *With heraldry more dismal; head to foot*
> *Now is he total gules, horridly tricked*
> *With blood of fathers, mothers, daughters, sons,*
> *Baked and impasted with the parching streets,*
> *That lend a tyrannous and damned light*
> *To their lord's murder. Roasted in wrath and fire,*
> *And thus o'ersizèd with coagulate gore,*   470
> *With eyes like carbuncles, the hellish Pyrrhus*
> *Old grandsire Priam seeks –*

So proceed you.

POLONIUS Fore God, my lord, well spoken, with good
accent and good discretion.

I PLAYER   *Anon he finds him*
> *Striking too short at Greeks; his antique sword,*
> *Rebellious to his arm, lies where it falls,*
> *Repugnant to command. Unequal matched,*
> *Pyrrhus at Priam drives, in rage strikes wide,*   480
> *But with the whiff and wind of his fell sword*
> *Th'unnervèd father falls. Then senseless Ilium,*
> *Seeming to feel this blow, with flaming top*
> *Stoops to his base, and with a hideous crash*
> *Takes prisoner Pyrrhus' ear. For lo! his sword,*
> *Which was declining on the milky head*

[488] painted tyrant   *like a picture of a tyrant, fixed and immovable in one posture*

[489] like a neutral to his will and matter   *as if he were indifferent to his intention, 'will' and task, 'matter'*

[491] against   *before*

[492] wrack   *a) a mass of clouds driven before the wind in the upper air, b) revenge – a different word altogether but a possible meaning in this spelling*

[495] region   *upper or highest part of the sky*

[496] rousèd vengeance   *provoked, active, awakened vengeance – the 'wrack' begins to move again*

[497] Cyclops'   *In Greek mythology a race of one-eyed giants who worked in the forge of Hephaistos/Vulcan, metal worker to the gods. As well as making the armour of Ares/Mars, the god of war, they also made the thunderbolts of Zeus/Jove.*

[498] proof eterne   *forged hard enough to withstand blows for ever*

[501] Out   *Away!*

strumpet   *whore*

[502] synod   *council*

[503] fellies   *pieces of curved wood which form the rim of a wheel. Fortune is supposed to have a wheel which turns, raising some men to good fortune and lowering others to bad. This wheel never stops turning.*

[504] nave   *central hub of the wheel*

[505] fiends   *devils in hell. The mixture of classical and Christian mythology is common in the Renaissance.*

[508] jig   *a) a dance, b) a joke*

[510] mobled   *muffled*

[514] bisson rheum   *blinding tears*

[516] o'er teemèd   *worn out with childbearing*

[518] in venom steeped   *dipped in poison*

[519] state   *rule, empire*

Of reverend Priam, seemed i'th'air to stick.
So, as a painted tyrant, Pyrrhus stood
And, like a neutral to his will and matter,
Did nothing.   490
But as we often see, against some storm,
A silence in the heavens, the wrack stand still,
The bold winds speechless, and the orb below
As hush as death, anon the dreadful thunder
Doth rend the region; so, after Pyrrhus' pause,
A rousèd vengeance sets him new a-work;
And never did the Cyclops' hammers fall
On Mars's armour, forged for proof eterne,
With less remorse than Pyrrhus' bleeding sword
Now falls on Priam.   500
Out, out thou strumpet Fortune! All you gods,
In general synod, take away her power.
Break all the spokes and fellies from her wheel
And bowl the round nave down the hill of heaven
As low as to the fiends.

POLONIUS This is too long.

HAMLET It shall to the barber's – with your beard.
   Prithee say on. He's for a jig, or a tale of bawdry, or
   he sleeps. Say on – come to Hecuba.

I PLAYER *But who, ah who, had seen the mobled queen –*   510

HAMLET 'The mobled queen'?

POLONIUS That's good; 'mobled queen' is good.

I PLAYER *Run barefoot up and down, threat'ning the*
          flames
       With bisson rheum; a clout upon that head
       Where late the diadem stood, and for a robe,
       About her lank and all o'er teemèd loins,
       A blanket in the alarm of fear caught up –
       Who this had seen, with tongue in venom steeped
       'Gainst Fortune's state would treason have
          pronounced.
       But if the gods themselves did see her then,   520
       When she saw Pyrrhus make malicious sport

[525] milch *capable of giving milk – would have moved the gods so much that their rage would turn from blood to milk and cause the sun, moon and stars to weep tears like the milk of human kindness, or pity*

[531] bestowed *lodged and provided with food*

[532] abstract and brief chronicles *short and condensed accounts*

[536] desert *as they deserve*

[537] God's bodykins *by God's small body – i.e. the sacramental wafer used in the communion service*

[539] after *according to*

      honour and dignity *It was an important part of Renaissance courtesy and manners to treat people in a way suitable to the worth and position of the giver, not the receiver. A court official who would maltreat players would not be truly gentle or courteous.*

[548] study *learn*

[549] set down *write*

In mincing with his sword her husband's limbs,
The instant burst of clamour that she made,
(Unless things mortal move them not at all)
Would have made milch the burning eyes of
   heaven
   And passion in the gods.

POLONIUS Look whe'er he has not turned his colour, and has tears in's eyes. Prithee no more.

HAMLET 'Tis well. I'll have thee speak out the rest of this soon. Good my lord, will you see the players 530 well bestowed? Do you hear: let them be well used; for they are the abstract and brief chronicles of the time. After your death you were better have a bad epitaph than their ill report while you live.

POLONIUS My lord, I will use them according to their desert.

HAMLET God's bodykins man! much better. Use every man after his desert, and who shall scape whipping? Use them after your own honour and dignity – the less they deserve, the more merit is in your bounty. 540 Take them in.

POLONIUS Come, sirs.

HAMLET Follow him friends. We'll hear a play to-morrow. Dost thou hear me old friend – can you play *The Murder of Gonzago?*

I PLAYER Ay, my lord.

HAMLET We'll ha't tomorrow night. You could, for a need, study a speech of some dozen or sixteen lines which I would set down and insert in't, could you not? 550

I PLAYER Ay, my lord.

HAMLET Very well. Follow that lord – and look you mock him not.

           [*Exeunt* POLONIUS *and* PLAYERS
My good friends, I'll leave you till night. You are welcome to Elsinore.

ROSENCRANTZ Good my lord.

[560] **dream of passion**   *display of emotion only as real as a dream*

[561] **force his soul**   *compel his soul to agree with his imagination or spoken thoughts to such an extent that . . .*

[562] **her working**   *the operation of his soul*

wanned   *turned pale*

[563] **distraction in's aspect**   *grief in his face*

[564–5] **function suiting . . . conceit**   *adapting the whole action of his body to convey his thought in expressive gestures – he suits 'the action to the word, the word to the action' (III. 2. 18)*

[571] **cleave**   *split wide open*

general ear   *the ear of the body politic – the ears of all the people*

[572] **free**   *those with free or guiltless souls*

[573] **Confound**   *Confuse, silence*

[573–4] **amaze . . . ears**   *astonish, dazzle the senses of sight and hearing*

[576] **muddy mettled**   *dull spirited*

peak   *droop, waste away*

[577] **unpregnant . . . cause**   *not ready to deliver, or perform, my revenge*

[580] **defeat**   *act of destruction*

[581] **pate**   *head*

[583] **lie i'th'throat**   *accuse of complete and utter deceit and bad aith*

[586] **take it**   *accept it – without challenging the person to a duel. These are all standard provocations for a duel.*

[587] **pigeon livered**   *cowardly. The liver was regarded as the seat of the passions and doves or pigeons were gentle birds of peace.*

gall   *bitter bile – which inflamed the liver*

[589] **region kites**   *birds of prey soaring in the upper air*

[*Exeunt* ROSENCRANTZ *and* GUILDENSTERN

HAMLET Ay, so God buy to you. Now I am alone.
O, what a rogue and peasant slave am I.
Is it not monstrous that this player here,
But in a fiction, in a dream of passion,   560
Could force his soul so to his own conceit
That from her working all his visage wanned;
Tears in his eyes, distraction in's aspect,
A broken voice and his whole function suiting
With forms to his conceit? And all for nothing.
For Hecuba!
What's Hecuba to him, or he to Hecuba
That he should weep for her? What would
   he do
Had he the motive and the cue for passion
That I have? He would drown the stage with
   tears   570
And cleave the general ear with horrid speech;
Make mad the guilty and appal the free,
Confound the ignorant, and amaze indeed
The very faculties of eyes and ears.
Yet I –
A dull and muddy mettled rascal – peak
Like John-a-dreams unpregnant of my cause
And can say nothing; no, not for a king
Upon whose property and most dear life
A damned defeat was made. Am I a coward?   580
Who calls me villain breaks my pate across
Plucks off my beard and blows it in my face;
Tweaks me by the nose, gives me the lie
   i'th'throat
As deep as to the lungs? Who does me this?
Ha!
'Swounds I should take it. For it cannot be
But I am pigeon livered and lack gall
To make oppression bitter, or ere this
I should 'a fatted all the region kites

[591] kindless *unnatural*

[593] brave *noble, courageous*

[597] drab *whore*
[598] scullion *kitchen maid*
[599] About *Turn about, start thinking*

[601] cunning *close approximation to reality*
[602] presently *instantly*

[608] tent him to the quick *probe the deepest part of his wound where the flesh is tender and therefore healthy*
        blench *turn pale*

[613] potent *powerful*

[615] relative *pertinent*

With this slave's offal. Bloody, bawdy villain. 590
Remorseless, treacherous, lecherous kindless
    villain.
O vengeance!
Why, what an ass am I. This is most brave
That I, the son of a dear father murdered,
Prompted to my revenge by heaven and hell,
Must, like a whore, unpack my heart with
    words
And fall a-cursing like a very drab,
A scullion. Fie upon it, foh.
About my brains. Hum, I have heard
That guilty creatures, sitting at a play, 600
Have by the very cunning of the scene
Been struck so to the soul that presently
They have proclaimed their malefactions;
For murder, though it have no tongue, will
    speak
With most miraculous organ. I'll have these
    players
Play something like the murder of my father
Before mine uncle. I'll observe his looks,
I'll tent him to the quick. If he do blench,
I know my course. The spirit that I have seen
May be a devil; and the devil hath power 610
T'assume a pleasing shape. Yea and perhaps,
Out of my weakness and my melancholy,
(As he is very potent with such spirits)
Abuses me to damn me. I'll have grounds
More relative than this. The play's the thing
Wherein I'll catch the conscience of the King.
                              [*Exit*

ACT THREE, scene 1

[1] drift of conference   *aim, direction in your conversation*
[2] puts on   *clothes himself with*
[3] Grating   *Disturbing, irritating*

[5] distracted   *disordered, divided, perplexed*

[7] forward   *ready, inclined to have his depth charted, be examined*
[8] crafty madness   *cunning insanity – they take the same view as Polonius, that there is method in the madness. This cunning observed in the insane was treated as another symptom of lunacy or melancholy.*

[12] disposition   *mood, inclination. Hamlet evidently had to force or compel himself to be polite to them.*
[13] Niggard   *Sparing, economical – in asking questions, but fully prepared to answer ours*
[14] assay him ... pastime   *attempt to make him take part in any sport, test his desire for amusement*

[17] o'er-raught   *overtook*

ACT THREE

Scene 1. *Enter* KING, QUEEN, POLONIUS, OPHELIA, ROSEN-
CRANTZ, GUILDENSTERN, LORDS

KING And can you by no drift of conference
    Get from him why he puts on this confusion,
    Grating so harshly all his days of quiet
    With turbulent and dangerous lunacy?
ROSENCRANTZ He does confess he feels himself
        distracted,
    But from what cause he will by no means
        speak.
GUILDENSTERN Nor do we find him forward to be
        sounded;
    But, with a crafty madness, keeps aloof
    When we would bring him on to some
        confession
    Of his true state.
QUEEN   Did he receive you well?   10
ROSENCRANTZ Most like a gentleman.
GUILDENSTERN But with much forcing of his
        disposition.
ROSENCRANTZ Niggard of question; but of our
        demands
    Most free in his reply.
QUEEN   Did you assay him
    To any pastime?
ROSENCRANTZ Madam, it so fell out that certain
        players
    We o'er-raught on the way. Of these we told
        him;
    And there did seem in him a kind of joy
    To hear of it. They are here about the court,
    And, as I think, they have already order   20
    This night to play before him.

[23] matter *argument, plot, play*

[26] further edge *encourage – sharpen him as you would a knife*

[29] closely *secretly, privately*

[31] Affront *Confront, meet face to face*
[32] lawful espials *acting as spies in a lawful and proper fashion. It would be proper for Ophelia's father and the King to learn Hamlet's feelings and intentions towards Ophelia.*
[34] frankly *openly, plainly*

[39] happy cause *lucky cause*
[41] wonted way *accustomed behaviour. Gertrude's kindness to Ophelia at this point has a particularly striking effect. She is prepared to trust Ophelia to behave in a chaste yet kind manner which will restore Hamlet to sanity.*
[44] bestow *place ourselves*
　　　book *evidently a prayer-book, bible or missal*
[45] show of such an exercise *the appearance of performing some religious rite, task or devotion*
　　　colour *disguise, excuse. Ophelia would not normally be left unattended except in her own closet.*
[47] too much *too often, frequently*
　　　devotion's visage *a face calm and composed in the act of prayer*
[48] pious action *actions appropriate to a religious ceremony – like reading a prayer-book or bible*
　　　sugar o'er *cover with sugar to make appear sweet and palatable*

POLONIUS 'Tis most true,
And he beseeched me to entreat your Majesties
To hear and see the matter.

KING With all my heart; and it doth much content me
To hear him so inclined.
Good gentlemen, give him a further edge,
And drive his purpose into these delights.

ROSENCRANTZ We shall, my lord.

[Exeunt ROSENCRANTZ *and* GUILDENSTERN

KING Sweet Gertrude, leave us too;
For we have closely sent for Hamlet hither,
That he (as 'twere by accident) may here   30
Affront Ophelia.
Her father and myself – lawful espials –
Will so bestow ourselves that, seeing unseen,
We may of their encounter frankly judge,
And gather by him, as he is behaved,
If't be th'affliction of his love or no
That thus he suffers for.

QUEEN I shall obey you.
And for your part, Ophelia, I do wish
That your good beauties be the happy cause
Of Hamlet's wildness. So shall I hope your
virtues   40
Will bring him to his wonted way again,
To both your honours.

OPHELIA Madam, I wish it may

[Exit QUEEN

POLONIUS Ophelia walk you here. Gracious, so please
you,
We will bestow ourselves. Read on this book,
That show of such an exercise may colour
Your loneliness – We are oft to blame in this,
'Tis too much proved, that with devotion's
visage
And pious action we do sugar o'er
The devil himself.

[51] **beautied with plast'ring art** *made beautiful by the art of covering it with a face-pack or plaster to hide the wrinkles and then painted with rouge*

[56] **To be or not to be** *The phrase is one of the fundamental distinctions of Aristotelian philosophy adopted by Thomas Aquinas. The distinction is between essence (to be) and matter (not to be). Essence is immaterial, eternal and the real substance of anything. Matter is material, changeable and impermanent and determines the accidents of appearance. God is essence and intelligence. The natural objects of the world are a combination of essence and matter. Man is like natural substance in that he is composed of matter, he is like God in having a divine, and immortal, intelligence. 'To be' is therefore to follow the reason and soul, 'not to be', to follow the passions of the material body. Hamlet uses this distinction between soul and body, reason and passion to debate his own continued existence and apparent lack of action. Shakespeare uses the scholastic terms of debate to make Hamlet question, in the tradition of melancholy, whether human life is worth living.*

[60] **opposing end them** *end the troubles by taking bodily action against them with arms. The military metaphors are strangely mixed. Suffering or endurance belongs to the soul but while a sea of troubles might be endured, it is more difficult to endure arrows without dying. It might be possible to resist arrows by arms, it is hopeless to engage the sea in this way. Both the active and the contemplative way end in death.*

[63] **That flesh is heir to** *The troubles that human beings naturally inherit because they have bodies of flesh subject to passion*

       consumation *climax, final settlement*

[65] **rub** *impediment*

[67] **shuffled off** *got rid of – with a sense of cheating or evasion*

       mortal coil *noise, tumult, confusion of mortal existence*

[68] **give us pause** *cause us to hesitate*

       respect *consideration*

[69] **calamity of so long life** *makes calamity so long-lived*

[71] **contumely** *offensive or contemptuous language*

[73] **insolence of office** *arrogant behaviour of those in official positions of authority*

       spurns *rejections, insults*

[74] **takes** *receives, accepts*

[75] **quietus** *freedom, discharge, acquittal from an account*

KING [*Aside*]   O 'tis too true!
How smart a lash that speech doth give my
    conscience   50
The harlot's cheek, beautied with plast'ring
    art,
Is not more ugly to the thing that helps it
Than is my deed to my most painted word.
O heavy burden.

POLONIUS I hear him coming; let's withdraw, my lord.
[*Exeunt* KING *and* POLONIUS

Enter HAMLET

HAMLET To be, or not to be – that is the question.
Whether 'tis nobler in the mind to suffer
The slings and arrows of outrageous fortune
Or to take arms against a sea of troubles
And by opposing end them? To die, to sleep;   60
No more? And by a sleep, to say we end
The heart-ache and the thousand natural
    shocks
That flesh is heir to. 'Tis a consumation
Devoutly to be wished. To die, to sleep.
To sleep – perchance to dream. Ay, there's
    the rub.
For in that sleep of death, what dreams may
    come
When we have shuffled off this mortal coil
Must give us pause. There's the respect
That makes calamity of so long life.
For who would bear the whips and scorns of
    time,   70
Th'oppressor's wrong, the proud man's
    contumely,
The pangs of despisèd love, the law's delay,
The insolence of office, and the spurns
That patient merit of th'unworthy takes,
When he himself might his quietus make

[76] bodkin *dagger. It is also an instrument with a short blade used by printing compositors. Hamlet could mean that a man might 'make', write or print, his own 'quietus' by using the printer's tool to kill himself.*

fardels *bundles, burdens*

[79] bourn *boundary, frontier*

[80] puzzles the will *confuses, paralyses the power to act*

[83] conscience *a) consciousness, power of thought, b) power of distinguishing between good and evil*

[84] native hue *natural colour*

[85] sicklied o'er *turned white or pale*

cast *tinge, hue, colour*

The normal red healthy colour of the face associated with action is made to look sick or pale by the pale colour caused by thought and contemplation.

[86] pitch and moment *of the highest possible importance. 'Pitch' is the highest point reached by a hawk.*

[87] regard *look, aspect*

currents *course of events*

awry *away from the proper course*

[88] name *reputation*

action *a) activity, b) a battle*

These lines develop the contrast between thought and action established by 'cowards' and 'the native hue of resolution'. An enterprise of such importance would require the highest pitch of resolution. This, however, has been 'sicklied o'er' and it is this 'regard' or aspect of fear and cowardice which causes the main course of the venture to turn aside and lose the reputation of a true military engagement. The enterprise is described rather as a sling or arrow which reaches the highest point of its flight and then inexplicably changes course.

[89] orisons *prayers*

[93] remembrances *love tokens, gifts to cause her to remember their love*

[99] Their perfume lost *The gifts have lost their perfume since they are no longer accompanied by words of such sweet breath.*

[101] wax *grow*

[103] honest *chaste. Ophelia appears with her prayer-book as the emblem of the contemplative life, yet her first act is to deny the power of memory by returning Hamlet's gifts. His reaction is sudden and violent as he identifies Ophelia with all that he loathes in the court.*

With a bare bodkin? Who would these
    fardels bear,
To grunt and sweat under a weary life,
But that the dread of something after death –
The undiscovered country, from whose bourn
No traveller returns – puzzles the will,   80
And makes us rather bear those ills we have
Than fly to others that we know not of?
Thus conscience does make cowards of us all.
And thus the native hue of resolution
Is sicklied o'er with the pale cast of thought,
And enterprises of great pitch and moment
With this regard their currents turn awry
And lose the name of action. – Soft you now,
The fair Ophelia – Nymph, in thy orisons
Be all my sins remembered?

OPHELIA   Good my lord,   90
    How does your honour for this many a day?

HAMLET I humbly thank you; well, well, well.

OPHELIA My lord, I have remembrances of yours
    That I have longèd long to re-deliver.
    I pray you now receive them.

HAMLET   No, not I.
    I never gave you aught.

OPHELIA My honoured lord, you know right well
    you did.
    And with them words of so sweet breath
        composed
    As made the things more rich. Their perfume
        lost
    Take these again; for to the noble mind   100
    Rich gifts wax poor when givers prove unkind.
    There my lord.

HAMLET Ha, ha. Are you honest?

OPHELIA My lord?

HAMLET Are you fair?

OPHELIA What means your lordship?

[108] admit no discourse *permit no communication*

[111] the power of beauty *Beauty will change Chastity into a whore more easily than Chastity can keep Beauty, like herself, chaste. Hamlet is punning upon the names of the three Graces, Chastity, Beauty and Passion – Castitas, Pulchritudo, Voluptas. They are usually shown as linked together in a dance in which Beauty leads Chastity towards Passion or Love. Passion has a double aspect, united to Beauty and Chastity she is the passion of love, separated from them she could become lust. Hamlet asserts that Beauty always converts Chastity into a passionate whore.*

[115] gives it proof *proves it true. His mother's conduct has shown that the paradox is fact.*

[118] innoculate *bud one plant upon another, engraft*
        stock *stem, trunk*

[119] relish *have a taste, tinge or trace of*

[121] nunnery *a community of nuns where she would have the grace of chastity and follow the life of contemplation*

[122] indifferent *fairly*

[126] beck *command*

[129] arrant *notorious*

[133] shut upon him *the idea that madmen should, for their own health be confined in a small space*

[136] plague *affliction, calamity*

[138] calumny *false report which will destroy your reputation*

[139] if thou . . . marry *if you must marry*

[141] monsters *a man with horns, a cuckold*

HAMLET That if you be honest and fair – your honesty should admit no discourse to your beauty.

OPHELIA Could beauty, my lord, have better commerce than with honesty? 110

HAMLET Ay, truly. For the power of beauty will sooner transform honesty from what it is to a bawd, than the force of honesty can translate beauty into his likeness. This was sometime a paradox – but now the time gives it proof. I did love you once.

OPHELIA Indeed, my lord, you made me believe so.

HAMLET You should not have believed me. For virtue cannot so innoculate our old stock but we shall relish of it. I loved you not.

OPHELIA I was the more deceived. 120

HAMLET Get thee to a nunnery. Why wouldst thou be a breeder of sinners? I am myself indifferent honest, but yet I could accuse me of such things that it were better my mother had not borne me. I am very proud, revengeful, ambitious – with more offences at my beck than I have thoughts to put them in, imagination to give them shape, or time to act them in. What should such fellows as I do crawling between earth and heaven? We are arrant knaves, all. Believe none of us. Go thy ways to a nunnery. 130 Where's your father?

OPHELIA At home, my lord.

HAMLET Let the doors be shut upon him, that he may play the fool nowhere but in's own house. Farewell.

OPHELIA O help him you sweet heavens!

HAMLET If thou dost marry, I'll give thee this plague for thy dowry: be thou as chaste as ice, as pure as snow, thou shalt not escape calumny. Get thee to a nunnery – go, farewell. Or, if thou wilt needs marry, marry a fool; for wise men know well enough what 140 monsters you make of them. To a nunnery go; and quickly too, farewell.

OPHELIA O heavenly powers, restore him!

[144] paintings *face painting*

[146] jig *dance, move quickly with a jerky motion*
amble *move slowly with an artificial or acquired walk*
lisp *speak in an affected fashion*
[147] nickname *call by other than its proper name, miscall*
[148] wantonness *lasciviousness, affectation*
ignorance *sin caused by lack of knowledge*
  As descriptions of Ophelia these words are madness – but
what Hamlet describes is the figure of lust with its painted face,
provocative walk and air of unthinking sexuality. It fits, he believes,
all women.

[154] eye, tongue, sword *The sword belongs to the soldier, the*
tongue to the courtier and the eye to the scholar. The Renaissance ideal
of the complete man was one who took part in the active, contemplative
and passionate life. He ought, therefore, to be a courtier, a scholar
and a soldier.
[155] expectancy *hope for the future*
[156] glass of fashion *a mirror which showed people how they*
should behave
  mould of form *an influence of people's behaviour, they*
are made to copy him, the shaper of conduct
[157] observed of all observers *the object of attention of all who*
wanted to note or mark the proper forms of courtesy and behaviour
[161] jangled *not rung as a peal of bells in order but sounded at*
random. The harmony which governs music was frequently used as a
comparison for the harmony of the laws which governed the universe.
The harmony of reason and the harmony of love are thus particularly
musical subjects.
[162] blown *in full bloom*
[165] affections *feelings*
[166] form *shape, order*
[168] sits on brood *sits on to hatch, like a bird sitting on eggs*
[169] hatch and disclose *the birth or hatching and bringing to*
light of that 'something' which he has been brooding over
  doubt *suspect*

HAMLET I have heard of your paintings too, well
enough. God hath given you one face, and you make
yourselves another. You jig and amble, and you lisp,
and nickname God's creatures, and make your
wantonness your ignorance. Go to, I'll no more
on't; it hath made me mad. I say we will have no
more marriage. Those that are married already, all   150
but one, shall live. The rest shall keep as they are.
To a nunnery, go.

[*Exit*

OPHELIA O, what a noble mind is here o'erthrown.
  The courtier's, soldier's, scholar's, eye,
   tongue, sword;
  Th'expectancy and rose of the fair state,
  The glass of fashion and the mould of form,
  Th'observed of all observers – quite, quite
   down.
  And I of ladies most deject and wretched
  That sucked the honey of his music vows,
  Now see that noble and most sovereign reason,   160
  Like sweet bells jangled, out of time and harsh;
  That unmatched form and feature of blown
   youth
  Blasted with ecstasy. O woe is me
  T'have seen what I have seen, see what I see!

Enter KING *and* POLONIUS

KING Love! His affections do not that way tend.
  Nor what he spake, though it lacked form a
   little,
  Was not like madness. There's something in
   his soul
  O'er which his melancholy sits on brood,
  And I do doubt the hatch and disclose
  Will be some danger; which to prevent   170
  I have in quick determination

[174] seas   *Sea voyages were considered a cure for melancholy.*

[176] something-settled matter   *a disease, or melancholy, which has somewhat fixed itself in his heart*

[186] show his grief   *reveal his cause of sorrow*
       round   *blunt*
[187] in the ear   *within the hearing of*
[188] find him not   *does not discover what is the matter with him*

ACT THREE, scene 2

[1] speech   *Hamlet is evidently rehearsing the speech which he has inserted.*

[2] trippingly   *quickly and lightly*

[2–3] mouth it   *speak with unnecessarily wide mouth movements for emphasis*

[3] had as lief   *I should be as well pleased as if . . .*

[4] saw   *make frequent jerky movements as if sawing*

[7–8] acquire and beget   *obtain and achieve*

[9] robustious   *noisy, violent*

[10] periwig-pated   *wearing a wig. Periwigs, later abbreviated to 'wigs', might be part of an actor's costume but only became fashionable dress after the restoration of Charles II (1660).*

[11] groundlings   *spectators who occupied the standing space in the open yard of the theatre*

Thus set it down: he shall with speed to
  England
For the demand of our neglected tribute.
Haply the seas and countries different
With variable objects, shall expel
This something-settled matter in his heart
Whereon his brains still beating puts him thus
From fashion of himself. What think you on't?

POLONIUS It shall do well. But yet I do believe
    The origin and commencement of his grief   180
    Sprung from neglected love. How now
      Ophelia,
    You need not tell us what Lord Hamlet said,
    We heard it all. My lord, do as you please;
    But if you hold it fit, after the play,
    Let his queen mother all alone entreat him
    To show his grief. Let her be round with him;
    And I'll be placed, so please you, in the ear
    Of all their conference. If she find him not,
    To England send him – or confine him where
    Your wisdom best shall think.

KING   It shall be so.   190
    Madness in great ones must not unwatched go.
                        [*Exeunt*

Scene 2. *Enter* HAMLET *and* THREE OF THE PLAYERS

HAMLET Speak the speech I pray you as I pronounced
it to you, trippingly on the tongue. But if you mouth
it, as many of our players do, I had as lief the town
crier spoke my lines. Nor do not saw the air too
much with your hand – thus – but use all gently.
For in the very torrent, tempest, and (as I may say)
whirlwind of your passion, you must acquire and
beget a temperance that may give it smoothness.
O it offends me to the soul to hear a robustious
periwig-pated fellow tear a passion to tatters, to very   10
rags, to split the ears of the groundlings – who for

[12] capable of *able to understand, appreciate*

[12–13] inexplicable dumb shows *performances carried on simply by gesture which do not have any significance that can be explained or understood. Hamlet evidently disapproves of dumb shows and is therefore surprised when the actors perform one.*

[14–15] Termagant . . . Herod *characters from the old cycles of religious mystery plays. Termagant is a mythical god supposedly worshipped by the Saracens.*

Herod the tyrannical King of Israel who ordered the massacre of all first-born male children – which caused Joseph and Mary to escape to Egypt with the child Jesus. Both parts are a temptation to the 'robustious' style of acting.

[18] discretion *judgement*

[18–19] Suit the action to the word . . . action *The gestures must express and interpret the lines, as the lines must be used to give point to the gestures. Hamlet, and Shakespeare, insist upon the vital combination of words and gesture that make the stage picture and impress the scene upon the mind of the audience.*

[20] modesty *moderation*

[21] from the purpose *away from, contrary to the purpose*

[23] the mirror up to nature *reveal the truth about nature. The point about mirrors, for the Elizabethans, was that they gave you a true reflection of yourself. Thus in the 'mirror' of the play Claudius will see himself not as king but as a murderer. The phrase, therefore, does not mean that art must simply imitate life.*

[25] age and body of the time *the present generation and the whole state of society at this time*

[26] form and pressure *shape and impression, image*

[26–7] come tardy off *not well executed*

[27] unskilful *those lacking in knowledge or judgement*

[28] censure *judgement*

[29] allowance *reckoning, consideration*

[35–6] Nature's journeymen *Since the actors strutted in a fashion that was not Christian they could not have been made by God or Nature but by some day labourer hired by Nature who had performed his task unskilfully, producing poor imitations.*

[38] indifferently *fairly well*

[41] clowns *actors taking comic roles*

[43] barren *barren of wits – some stupid members of the audience*

[44–5] necessary question *important part of the plot*

the most part are capable of nothing but inexplicable dumb shows and noise. I would have such a fellow whipped for o'erdoing Termagant – it out-Herod's Herod. Pray you, avoid it.

1 PLAYER I warrant your honour.

HAMLET Be not too tame neither, but let your own discretion be your tutor. Suit the action to the word, the word to the action – with this special observance; that you o'erstep not the modesty of nature. 20 For anything so o'erdone is from the purpose of playing; whose end, both at the first and now, was and is to hold, as 'twere, the mirror up to nature – to show virtue her own feature, scorn her own image, and the very age and body of the time his form and pressure. Now this overdone or come tardy off, though it makes the unskilful laugh, cannot but make the judicious grieve; the censure of the which one must, in your allowance, o'erweigh a whole theatre of others. O there be players that 30 I have seen play (and heard others praise and that highly) not to speak it profanely, that, neither having th'accent of Christians, nor the gait of Christian, pagan, nor man, have so strutted and bellowed that I have thought some of Nature's journeymen had made men, and not made them well, they imitated humanity so abominably.

1 PLAYER I hope we have reformed that indifferently with us, sir.

HAMLET O reform it altogether. And let those that 40 play your clowns speak no more than is set down for them. For there be of them that will themselves laugh, to set on some quantity of barren spectators to laugh too, though in the meantime some necessary question of the play be then to be considered. That's villainous – and shows a most pitiful ambition in the fool that uses it. Go, make you ready.

[*Exeunt* PLAYERS

[50] presently   *immediately*

[57] conversation   *society, act of meeting other people*
    coped   *encountered: you are the most upright man I have
ever encountered in all my dealings with other people*
[59] advancement   *preferment, advantage*
[60] revenue   *return, yield, profit from any lands or property,
income*
[62] candied tongue   *sugared tongue, candied over with flattery
and sweet sayings*
    absurd pomp   *unharmonious, illogical display – with perhaps
a hint of the baptismal formula renouncing 'pompae diaboli', the
displays, processions of the devil, the vanities of the world*
[63] crook   *bend – the tongue has now become the whole man*
    pregnant   *ready to move*
[64] thrift   *advantage, profit*
    fawning   *abject behaviour – licking or caressing like a dog*
[65] my dear soul   *my soul which is dear, precious, to me*
    mistress of her choice   *was in command of her choice, ob-
tained the power of judgement, discrimination*
[66] distinguish   *separate, classify, perceive clearly*
    election   *exercise of deliberate choice or preference*
[67] sealed   *place a seal upon as a mark of approval, give solemn
pledges of good faith, mark out, choose*
    *The image is very strong. As soon as Hamlet's soul was free to make
her choice and able to pick out her own preference among men, she
put her seal upon you as a solemn pledge that you are hers. The
marriage of souls or minds is implied.*
[68] in suff'ring all . . . nothing   *as a man that undergoes every
kind of pain and distress and yet appears to endure nothing*
[71] blood   *passion*
    judgement   *reason*
    comeddled   *mixed, mingled, in harmony*
[72] pipe   *musical instrument*

Enter POLONIUS, ROSENCRANTZ *and* GUILDENSTERN

[*to* POLONIUS] How now, my lord. Will the King
hear this piece of work?

POLONIUS And the Queen too, and that presently. 50
HAMLET Bid the Players make haste.

[*Exit* POLONIUS

Will you two help to hasten them?
ROSENCRANTZ Ay, my lord.

[*Exeunt* ROSENCRANTZ *and* GUILDENSTERN

HAMLET What ho, Horatio!

Enter HORATIO

HORATIO Here, sweet lord, at your service.
HAMLET Horatio, thou art e'en as just a man
    As e'er my conversation coped withal.
HORATIO O my dear lord!
HAMLET   Nay, do not think I flatter;
    For what advancement may I hope from thee
    That no revenue hast but thy good spirits   60
    To feed and clothe thee? Why should the
        poor be flattered?
    No, let the candied tongue lick absurd pomp,
    And crook the pregnant hinges of the knee
    Where thrift may follow fawning. Dost thou
        hear?
    Since my dear soul was mistress of her choice
    And could of men distinguish her election,
    Sh'hath sealed thee for herself. For thou
        hast been
    As one, in suff'ring all, that suffers nothing.
    A man that Fortune's buffets and rewards
    Hast ta'en with equal thanks – and blest are
        those   70
    Whose blood and judgement are so well
        comeddled
    That they are not a pipe for Fortune's finger

155

[73] sound what stop *cover the holes or stops with the fingers in order to play a note. Horatio's soul is already so well balanced in reason and passion, so much in harmony, that Fortune (often thought of as a tempest or wind) cannot blow through him like an instrument to create her own music, i.e. Horatio cannot be made to change his tune by circumstances.*

[74] passion's slave *enslaved to his senses and therefore completely at the mercy of his emotions, entirely unrestrained by reason*

[76] Something *Somewhat. Hamlet checks both himself and Horatio's answering protestation.*

[80] act afoot *that action, the representation of my father's murder, being performed*

[81] very comment of thy soul *most critical observation*

[82] occulted *hidden*

[83] unkennel *reveal – used of a fox leaving or being driven out of his lair*

[86] stithy *an anvil, forge. In Roman mythology Vulcan was the metal-worker of the gods. Since his forge was underground he became associated with the metal-working gods of Northern mythology and thus connected with the idea of hell.*

[89] censure of his seeming *judgement of his appearance or false seeming*

[92] idle *void of sense, foolish, incoherent, mad*

[94] cousin *address used by a king for other kings, his own relatives and his own nobles*

How . . . fares? *How is your condition, how are you? Hamlet interprets it to mean 'how do you eat?' and replies specifically to that question.*

[95] chameleon's dish *I eat the same food as a chameleon – a lizard which changes its colour to match its surroundings and was believed to live on air*

[96] promise crammed *the air is filled with the King's promises*

[97] capons *castrated cocks reared for food – a capon that was 'crammed' would be fattened for table. Hamlet suggests that the King crams him with promises before killing him.*

[98] have nothing *have nothing to do with, no responsibility for – your answer has nothing to do with my words*

[101] university *Plays were frequently performed in the halls of the colleges of Oxford and Cambridge. Their shape is that of the hall of an Elizabethan manor house and therefore similar to the shape of the Elizabethan stage itself.*

To sound what stop she please. Give me that
   man
That is not passion's slave and I will wear him
In my heart's core, Ay in my heart of heart,
As I do thee. Something too much of this.
There is a play tonight before the King,
One scene of it comes near the circumstance
Which I have told thee of my father's death.
I prithee, when thou seest that act afoot,   80
Even with the very comment of thy soul
Observe my uncle. If his occulted guilt
Do not itself unkennel in one speech,
It is a damnèd ghost that we have seen,
And my imaginations are as foul
As Vulcan's stithy. Give him heedful note,
For I mine eyes will rivet to his face;
And, after, we will both our judgements join
In censure of his seeming.

HORATIO   Well, my lord,
   If he steal aught the whilst this play is playing   90
   And scape detecting, I will pay the theft.

Enter trumpets and kettledrums. Danish march.
Sound a flourish

Enter KING, QUEEN, POLONIUS, OPHELIA,
ROSENCRANTZ, GUILDENSTERN, *and other* LORDS
attendant, with his GUARD *carrying torches*

HAMLET They are coming to the play. I must be idle.
   Get you a place.

KING How fares our cousin Hamlet?

HAMLET Excellent i'faith – of the chameleon's dish.
   I eat the air, promise crammed. You cannot feed
   capons so.

KING I have nothing with this answer, Hamlet. These
   words are not mine.

HAMLET No, nor mine now. [*To* POLONIUS] My lord,   100
   you played once i'th'university you say?

[106] Capitol *Polonius may have been killed in a stage Capitol but Caesar was actually assassinated in the Curia Pompeii near the theatre of Pompey in the Campus Martius.*

[107] brute part *a) a cruel part, b) a stupid part, wanting in reason like a lower animal. The word could also mean 'heroic', from Brutus the great-grandson of Aeneas, the legendary founder of Britain.*

[107–8] capital a calf *a) such a first-rate calf, b) such an extremely stupid fool. Hamlet's words can therefore be taken as regretting the brutality of the death or praising Brutus for removing such a tedious fool.*

[109] stay upon your patience *wait for your indulgence, permission*

[111] metal *material, precious metal*

[114] lie in your lap *It was customary for young men to sit at ladies' feet with their head in their laps. Ophelia misunderstands Hamlet's request as a lunatic demand for instant sexual intercourse.*

[118] country matters *matters as performed in the country, sexual intercourse – with a clear pun on 'cunt', the female sexual organ*

[120] fair thought *a) suitable idea – but it may also mean, b) beautiful remembrance, or c) female cause for anxiety. It is suitable for a maid or virgin to have no thought of a thing between her legs but it is also a token of love and its total absence may be a cause of anxiety. Hamlet's sexual puns, like his words in the nunnery scene, have both a bitter and a loving sense. See Introduction p. 22.*

[122] Nothing *Hamlet puns on 'no thing' – sexual organ.*

[123] merry *happy, gay, amusing*

[126] jig-maker *writer of light theatrical afterpieces designed to follow tragedies*

[128–9] two hours *Hamlet is talking apparent madness but Shakespeare uses the traditional time of a stage performance deliberately. The audience are about to see Hamlet's father die on stage.*

[132] suit of sables *gown trimmed with the fur of the sable, a species of marten with brown silky fur. 'Sable' is also the heraldic name for black and colours of mourning. Hamlet proposes to abandon mourning and remembrance for the most luxurious and expensive clothing.*

[135] build churches *a man who wishes his memory to last longer than half a year must build a church where prayers may be said for his soul. Before the Reformation it was common to endow chantry chapels for this purpose.*

POLONIUS That did I, my lord, and was accounted a good actor.

HAMLET What did you enact?

POLONIUS I did enact Julius Caesar. I was killed i'th'Capitol. Brutus killed me.

HAMLET It was a brute part of him to kill so capital a calf there. Be the players ready?

ROSENCRANTZ Ay, my lord. They stay upon your patience.

QUEEN Come hither, my dear Hamlet, sit by me.   110

HAMLET No, good mother. Here's metal more attractive.

POLONIUS [*Aside to* KING] O, ho! Do you mark that?

HAMLET Lady, shall I lie in your lap?

OPHELIA No my lord.

HAMLET I mean, my head upon your lap?

OPHELIA Ay, my lord.

HAMLET Do you think I meant country matters?

OPHELIA I think nothing, my lord.

HAMLET That's a fair thought to lie between maids' legs.   120

OPHELIA What is my lord?

HAMLET Nothing.

OPHELIA You are merry, my lord.

HAMLET Who, I?

OPHELIA Ay my lord.

HAMLET O God your only jig-maker, what should a man do but be merry? For look you how cheerfully my mother looks, and my father died within's two hours.

OPHELIA Nay, 'tis twice two months, my lord.   130

HAMLET So long? Nay then, let the devil wear black for I'll have a suit of sables. O heavens, die two months ago and not forgotten yet? Then there's hope a great man's memory may outlive his life half a year; but by'r Lady he must build churches then – or else shall he suffer not thinking on, with the

[137] hobby-horse   *figure of a horse strapped round a dancer at waist height in the morris dance. Puritan authorities were attempting to suppress it as obscene and profane.*

Hautboys   *wooden double-reeded instrument of high pitch forming a treble to the basoon and oboe*

The Dumb Show   *See Introduction p.* 17.

takes her up   *raises her from her knees*

declines   *lays*

[140] miching mallecho   *As Hamlet says, it means 'mischief' but the phrase is otherwise obscure. Some connection with the Spanish 'malhecho' – 'wickedness' is usually assumed.*

[142] argument   *plot*

[145] cannot keep counsel   *cannot keep their purpose secret – it is not the business of actors to keep their play a secret, they are bound to tell all. Some editors treat this as an aside by Hamlet accusing the actors of giving away his scheme by performing the dumb show.*

[146] show   *dumb show*

[147] show   *appearance, display – sight, spectacle, exhibition to public view. Hamlet asserts that the actor will not be ashamed to tell her the meaning of any exhibition of herself which she would not be ashamed to make in public – presumably by taking her clothes off.*

[150] naught   *good for nothing, wicked, obscene*

hobby-horse, whose epitaph is 'For O, for O, the hobby-horse is forgot'

The trumpet sounds. Hautboys play.
The Dumb Show enters

Enter a KING *and* QUEEN *very lovingly, the* QUEEN *embracing him. She kneels and makes show of protestation unto him. He takes her up and declines his head upon her neck; lays him down upon a bank of flowers. She, seeing him asleep, leaves him. Anon comes in a* FELLOW, *takes off his crown, kisses it, and pours poison in the* KING'S *ears and exits. The* QUEEN *returns, finds the* KING *dead, and makes passionate action. The* POISONER, *with some two or three mutes, comes in again seeming to lament with her. The dead body is carried away. The* POISONER *woos the* QUEEN *with gifts. She seems loath and unwilling awhile, but in the end accepts his love.*

[Exeunt

OPHELIA What means this, my lord?

HAMLET Marry, this is miching mallecho; it means mischief.

OPHELIA Belike this show imports the argument of the 140 play?

Enter PROLOGUE

HAMLET We shall know by this fellow: the players cannot keep counsel; they'll tell all.

OPHELIA Will he tell us what this show meant?

HAMLET Ay, or any show that you will show him. Be not you ashamed to show, he'll not shame to tell you what it means.

OPHELIA You are naught, you are naught. 150 I'll mark the play.

PROLOGUE *For us, and for our tragedy,*
Here stooping to your clemency,
We beg your hearing patiently.

[Exit

161

[155] posy   *a motto, usually in verse, engraved on the inside of a ring*

[158] Phoebus' cart   *the sun. In Greek mythology Phoebus Apollo was god of the sun which he drove like a chariot through the sky.*

[159] Neptune's salt wash   *the sea. Neptune is the Roman name for the sea-god.*

Tellus' orbed ground   *the earth, globe. Tellus is a personified figure of an earth goddess.*

[162] Hymen   *Greek spirit of marriage – from the sacred song at marriages and certain religious mysteries*

[163] commutual   *mutually, together*

[167] cheer   *good health*

[168] distrust you   *I am full of anxiety on your account*

[169] Discomfort   *Distress, depress*

[170] hold quantity   *keep a relative proportion*

[171] In neither . . . extremity   *Either both are nothing at all or they exist to an extreme degree*

[172] proof   *sufficient evidence, testing, experience*

[173] sized   *my fear is the same size or quantity as my love*

[177] operant powers   *active powers – the powers which give the human being motion and therefore life*

leave   *cease*

[180] confound the rest   *may God destroy what you were about to say*

[183] None wed the second . . . first   *Only wives who kill their first husbands marry again. This play is not only an attack on Claudius, it accuses Gertrude of complicity in the murder.*

[184] wormwood   *a herb proverbial for its bitter taste. It was thought to be a cure for worms in the ear or in the womb. Hamlet's play is designed to cure the ear of Denmark and disinfect Gertrude. 'Wormwood' is also used of anything that is bitter to the soul.*

HAMLET Is this a prologue – or the posy of a ring?
OPHELIA 'Tis brief, my lord.
HAMLET As woman's love.

      Enter KING *and his* QUEEN
PLAYER KING *Full thirty times hath Phoebus' cart
      gone round
      Neptune's salt wash and Tellus' orbed ground,
      And thirty dozen moons with borrowed sheen*   160
      *About the world have times twelve thirties been,
      Since love our hearts, and Hymen did our hands,
      Unite commutual in most sacred bands.*
PLAYER QUEEN *So many journeys may the sun and
      moon
      Make us again count o'er, ere love be done.
      But, woe is me, you are so sick of late,
      So far from cheer and from your former state,
      That I distrust you. Yet, though I distrust,
      Discomfort you, my lord, it nothing must.
      For women's fear and love hold quantity,*   170
      *In neither aught, or in extremity.
      Now, what my love is, proof has made you know;
      And as my love is sized, my fear is so.
      Where love is great, the littlest doubts are fears;
      Where little fears grow great, great love grows
      there*
PLAYER KING *Faith I must leave thee love, and shortly
      too.
      My operant powers their functions leave to do;
      And thou shalt live in this fair world behind,
      Honoured, beloved, and haply one as kind
      For husband shalt thou –*
PLAYER QUEEN   *O confound the rest!*   180
      *Such love must needs be treason in my breast.
      In second husband let me be accurst –
      None wed the second but who killed the first.*
HAMLET That's wormwood, wormwood.

[185] instances *examples*

move *urge, encourage*

[186] respects *considerations*

[187–8] a second time . . . bed *I kill my dead husband a second time when my second husband kisses me, i.e. every act of love with a second husband is the equivalent of murder*

[190] determine *intend to perform*

[191] Purpose *Intention, resolution, determination*

[192] validity *strong, sound*

[195] necessary *inevitable, determined, compelled by practical necessity – our purposes are debts that we owe only to ourselves and it is inevitable that we should omit to pay debts to ourselves*

[197] passion *It is significant that the Player King believes passion to be a much stronger force than memory.*

[200] enactures *fulfilment, climax, carrying out an act – translating joy or grief into action is such a violent process that its very fulfilment destroys the passion*

[202] accident *chance, occasion*

[205] prove *try, determine*

[206] love lead fortune . . . love *whether fortune follows love or love follows fortune. Although the Player King says that the matter is still to be determined, all his examples show love following fortune.*

lead *guide the course of – whether love guides the course of fortune or fortune guides love. Although it is still to be determined all the Player King's examples show love following the course of a man's fortunes.*

[207] down *fallen, dismissed from office*

[210] not needs *does not require assistance or money*

[211] try *test, experiment with. The result of the experiment is to 'season' him.*

[212] seasons *mixes, adds to – changes him into an enemy*

[213] orderly *in orderly, logical fashion. A good rhetorical speech ought to return to its first starting point.*

[214] wills *desires, determinations, intentions*

run *run on – proceed in such opposite directions*

Will is the active power of the soul concerned with translating desires and intentions into fact. The operation of fate often brings about the exact contrary of our intentions as we try and realise them.

[215] devices *plans, stratagems*

[216] ends *results*

PLAYER QUEEN *The instances that second marriage*
    move
    Are base respects of thrift, but none of love.
    A second time I kill my husband dead,
    When second husband kisses me in bed.

PLAYER KING *I do believe you think what now you*
    speak;
    But what we do determine oft we break.   190
    Purpose is but the slave to memory,
    Of violent birth, but poor validity;
    Which now, the fruit unripe, sticks on the tree,
    But fall unshaken when they mellow be.
    Most necessary 'tis that we forget
    To pay ourselves what to ourselves is debt.
    What to ourselves in passion we propose
    The passion ending, doth the purpose lose.
    The violence of either grief or joy
    Their own enactures with themselves destroy.   200
    Where joy most revels grief doth most lament;
    Grief joys, joy grieves, on slender accident.
    This world is not for aye; nor 'tis not strange
    That even our loves should with our fortunes
    change;
    For 'tis a question left us yet to prove,
    Whether love lead fortune, or else fortune love.
    The great man down, you mark his favourite flies;
    The poor advanced makes friends of enemies.
    And hitherto doth love on fortune tend,
    For who not needs shall never lack a friend,   210
    And who in want a hollow friend doth try,
    Directly seasons him his enemy.
    But, orderly to end where I begun,
    Our wills and fates do so contrary run
    That our devices still are overthrown —
    Our thoughts are ours, their ends none of our own.
    So think thou wilt no second husband wed,
    But die thy thoughts when thy first lord is dead.

[220] Sport *Leisure, entertainment*

[222] anchor's cheer *the food of an anchorite or religious hermit*
[223] opposite *contrary, reverse, diametrically opposed*
blanks *makes void, empty*
[225] hence *in life after death*
[228] deeply *intensely, earnestly*

[229] beguile *while away the time*

[233] protest *promise*
[234] word *promise*
[235] argument *account of the plot. The King, having seen the dumb show, is anxious to discover if the play is suitable for court performance, or if Hamlet knows how offensive it is.*
[236] offence *anything causing annoyance or disgust*
[238] offence *crime. It is no crime to poison in jest or play.*
[240] 'The Mouse-trap' *The audience knows very well that it is called 'The Murder of Gonzago'. It has two titles because it is both a murder and a trap. Hamlet calls it 'The Mouse-trap' because he has cast Claudius for the major role of mouse.*
Tropically *As a trope or figure, figuratively, emblematically*
[241] image *representation*
[243] knavish *vulgar, obscene, unprincipled*
[245] free *free from guilt. Hamlet's words can mean a) your Majesty and the rest of us who are all guiltless, or b) your Majesty, who is guilty, and we who are guiltless.*
touches us not *makes no impression on us, does not affect us*
gallèd *chafed, rubbed, made sore – by saddle or harness*
jade *a broken down or worthless horse – it can mean a whore*
[246] withers *the ridge between the shoulder bones on a horse*
unwrung *not twisted, strained*
[247] nephew to the King *as Hamlet is nephew to Claudius*

166

PLAYER QUEEN *Nor earth to me give food, nor heaven*
light,
Sport and repose lock from me day and night, 220
To desperation turn my trust and hope,
An anchor's cheer in prison be my scope,
Each opposite that blanks the face of joy
Meet what I would have well, and it destroy.
Both here and hence pursue me lasting strife,
If, once a widow, ever I be wife!

HAMLET If she should break it now!

PLAYER KING *'Tis deeply sworn. Sweet, leave me here*
awhile;
My spirits grow dull, and fain I would beguile
The tedious day with sleep

          [Sleeps

PLAYER QUEEN   *Sleep rock thy brain,* 230
And never come mischance between us twain.

          [Exit

HAMLET Madam, how like you this play?

QUEEN The lady doth protest too much, methinks.

HAMLET O, but she'll keep her word.

KING Have you heard the argument? Is there no offence in't?

HAMLET No, no, they do but jest – poison in jest – no offence i'th'world.

KING What do you call the play?

HAMLET 'The Mouse-trap'. Marry, how? Tropically. 240 This play is the image of a murder done in Vienna: Gonzago is the Duke's name; his wife, Baptista. You shall see anon. 'Tis a knavish piece of work, but what of that? Your Majesty, and we that have free souls, it touches us not. Let the gallèd jade wince, our withers are unwrung.

Enter LUCIANUS

This is one Lucianus – nephew to the King.

OPHELIA You are as good as a chorus, my lord.

[249] interpret *explain, act as interpreter. The interpreter was the actor who spoke the lines of the play at a puppet show.*

[250] dallying *playing, flirting*

Hamlet would act as interpreter and provide the dialogue between Ophelia and her lover if he could observe the puppets or actors performing that passion. These lines are usually described as insulting, but what Hamlet is saying is that he could insert a better speech for the dumb show of love if he and Ophelia were the actors.

[251] keen *sharp, witty*

[252] groaning . . . off mine edge *it would require a great deal of effort on your part to blunt the edge of my wit. But 'edge' also means edge of sexual desire which it would cost Ophelia the groaning of losing her virginity to blunt.*

[254] better *more witty*

worse *more obscene*

[255] mis-take *take by mistake, deceive – with a pun upon the marriage vows of the Church of England, 'for better or worse'*

[257–8] croaking raven . . . revenge *Hamlet is misquoting two lines of Richard III in an old play called* The True Tragedy of Richard III *as a parody of the absurd style of revenge:*

The skreeking raven sits croaking for revenge
Whole herds of beasts come bellowing for revenge . . .

[260] Confederate season *Time conspiring to assist the murderer*

[261] rank *evil smelling*

[262] Hecat's ban *made three times damnable by the curse of Hecate – a goddess of the moon associated with witchcraft*

[264] usurps *replaces the functions of healthy life immediately*

[265] estate *kingdom, commonwealth*

[266] extant *in existence, not destroyed or lost*

[270] false fire *a blank discharge of firearms. Hamlet jeers at the King for being frightened by the mere noise of a shot.*

[275] strucken deer *A deer struck or wounded to death was supposed to leave the herd and weep. It is frequently used as a symbol for melancholy and a guilty conscience.*

[277] watch *stay awake, remain on guard*

[280] turn Turk *become infidel and faithless – change completely for the worse*

[281] Provincial roses *either a) roses from Provins – the damask rose, or b) roses from Provence*

raced shoes *shoes slashed in patterns*

HAMLET I could interpret between you and your love,
if I could see the puppets dallying.   250

OPHELIA You are keen, my lord, you are keen.

HAMLET It would cost you a groaning to take off mine
edge.

OPHELIA Still better – and worse.

HAMLET So you mis-take your husbands. – Begin,
murderer. Pox, leave thy damnable faces and begin.
Come, 'The croaking raven doth bellow for revenge'.

LUCIANUS *Thoughts black, hands apt, drugs fit, and*
            time agreeing,
        Confederate season else no creature seeing,   260
        Thou mixture rank, of midnight weeds collected,
        With Hecat's ban thrice blasted, thrice infected.
        Thy natural magic and dire property
        On wholesome life usurps immediately.
            [*Pours the poison in the* KING'*s ear*]

HAMLET He poisons him i'th'garden for his estate. His
name's Gonzago. The story is extant, and written
in very choice Italian. You shall see anon how the
murderer gets the love of Gonzago's wife.

OPHELIA The King rises.

HAMLET What, frighted with false fire?   270

QUEEN How fares my lord?

POLONIUS Give oe'r the play.

KING Give me some lights. Away!

POLONIUS Lights, lights, lights!
                    [*Exeunt all but* HAMLET *and* HORATIO

HAMLET Why, let the strucken deer go weep,
                The hart ungallèd play,
            For some must watch, while some must
                sleep,
                Thus runs the world away.
Would not this, sir, and a forest of feathers – if the
rest of my fortunes turn Turk with me – with two 280
Provincial roses on my raced shoes, get me a

[282] fellowship *partnership*

     cry *company*

[283] Half a share *The partners in a theatrical company were called 'shareres' because they shared the profits. Lesser members of the company would be 'half-sharers', hired men and apprentices. Horatio thinks Hamlet's performance worth only a half share.*

[285] Damon dear *my dear friend*

[286] dismantled *uncovered, left unprotected*

[287] Jove *in Roman mythology the ruler of the Olympian gods*

[288] peacock *was thought to be a vain, showy and lecherous bird*

[297] comedy *Hamlet is parodying some famous lines from Kyd's* The Spanish Tragedy, *IV. 1. 197 –*

        And if the world like not this tragedy

        Hard is the hap of old Hieronimo . . .

– where the play is the instrument of Hieronimo's revenge.

[300] vouchsafe *grant*

[305] retirement *the King has retired to his private apartments in a great rage*

     distempered *out of temper. Hamlet uses its other meaning of diseased, unbalanced in temperament.*

[308] choler *anger. Hamlet ironically recommends a doctor since purging, to clear out the impure humours, was regular treatment once excess choler had been diagnosed. In fact the play changes the King's temper from sanguine to melancholy.*

[314] frame *order*

     start *shy away like a frightened horse. Unable to follow the logic of Hamlet's train of thought Guildenstern thinks it madness.*

fellowship in a cry of players, sir?

HORATIO Half a share.

HAMLET A whole one, I!

> For thou dost know, O Damon dear,
> This realm dismantled was
> Of Jove himself, and now reigns here
> A very very – peacock!

HORATIO You might have rhymed.

HAMLET O good Horatio I'll take the Ghost's word for 290 a thousand pound. Did'st perceive?

HORATIO Very well, my lord.

HAMLET Upon the talk of the poisoning?

HORATIO I did very well note him.

Enter ROSENCRANTZ *and* GUILDENSTERN

HAMLET Ah, ha! Come, some music! Come, the recorders.

> For if the King like not the comedy
> Why then, he likes it not, perdy!

Come, some music.

GUILDENSTERN Good my lord, vouchsafe me a word 300 with you.

HAMLET Sir, a whole history.

GUILDENSTERN The King, sir –

HAMLET Ay sir, what of him?

GUILDENSTERN Is, in his retirement, marvellous distempered.

HAMLET With drink, sir?

GUILDENSTERN No, my lord, rather with choler.

HAMLET Your wisdom should show itself more richer to signify this to his doctor – for for me to put him 310 to his purgation would perhaps plunge him into far more choler.

GUILDENSTERN Good my lord, put your discourse into some frame, and start not so wildly from my affair.

HAMLET I am tame, sir. Pronounce.

[320] breed   *kind. Guildenstern is still thinking in terms of horses.*
[321] wholesome   *sensible*

[328] command   *have at your disposa*

[332] amazement   *perturbation, shocked anger*
       admiration   *wonder, astonishment*

[337] closet   *private apartment*
[339] trade   *business*
[341] pickers and stealers   *hands. 'By this hand' was a common form of oath and a 'picker' is a thief. The catechism uses the phrase, 'Keep my hands from picking and stealing'. Hamlet's oath suggests that he does not trust Rosencrantz's love.*
[343] distemper   *disorder of mind*
[344] liberty   *freedom – from disease. But perhaps he means that Hamlet will be restrained or confined*
       deny your griefs   *refuse to tell, share, your griefs. Grief or melancholy could only be cured if it could be opened, uttered or spoken.*
[345] advancement   *promotion, preferment – as Rosencrantz and Guildenstern understand it. Hamlet means he has not completed his task.*
[347] voice   *vote, support*
       succession   *to the throne of Denmark*
[349] grass grows   *'while the grass grows the horse starves'*
[350] musty   *old, stale*

GUILDENSTERN The Queen your mother, in most great affliction of spirit, hath sent me to you.

HAMLET You are welcome

GUILDENSTERN Nay, good my lord, this courtesy is not of the right breed. If it shall please you to make me 320 a wholesome answer, I will do your mother's commandment. If not, your pardon and my return shall be the end of my business.

HAMLET Sir, I cannot.

ROSENCRANTZ What, my lord?

HAMLET Make you a wholesome answer. My wit's diseased. But, sir, such answer as I can make, you shall command – or rather (as you say) my mother. Therefore no more, but to the matter. My mother, you say? 330

ROSENCRANTZ Then thus she says: your behaviour hath struck her into amazement and admiration.

HAMLET O wonderful son that can so stonish a mother! But is there no sequel at the heels of this mother's admiration? Impart.

ROSENCRANTZ She desires to speak with you in her closet ere you go to bed.

HAMLET We shall obey, were she ten times our mother. Have you any further trade with us?

ROSENCRANTZ My lord, you once did love me. 340

HAMLET And do still – by these pickers and stealers.

ROSENCRANTZ Good my lord, what is the cause of your distemper? You do surely bar the door upon your own liberty if you deny your griefs to your friend.

HAMLET Sir, I lack advancement.

ROSENCRANTZ How can that be, when you have the voice of the King himself for your succession in Denmark?

HAMLET Ay sir, but 'While the grass grows' – the proverb is something musty. 350

Enter the PLAYERS *with recorders*

[351] withdraw   *retire in order to speak privately*

[352–3] recover the wind of me   *move so that the direction of the wind blows from you to me. The wind blows the scent of the hunter to the hunted animal and, seeking to escape, it is driven into the trap down-wind.*

[353] toil   *net, snare, trap*

[354–5] duty be too bold . . . unmannerly   *if I appear rude or too bold in my attempt to serve you it is because my love for you makes me forget my manners*

[357] pipe   *recorder*

[362] touch   *fingering necessary to produce a note*

[363] lying   *telling untruths – and since Guildenstern is so good at that he ought to have no difficulty playing the recorder*

Govern   *Control*

ventages *finger holes*

[366] stops   *the closing of the finger holes to alter the pitch. Hamlet is showing Guildenstern how to play a scale. In doing so he uses the well-known emblem of musical harmony to show that it is the King and his court who are disordered in mind since they have broken the harmony and proportion of the universe by being slaves of passion and pipes for Fortune's finger (cf. III. 2. 72).*

[372] mystery   *a) hidden truth, b) difficult technical accomplishment such as the art of music*

[373] compass   *the range of notes which the instrument is capable of reaching*

[374] organ   *the recorder. The transition from music to man is made by the Pythagorean concept that the intervals between the concentric spheres of the universe were in the same proportion as the eight notes of a musical scale. A man's ideal figure ought to fit into a sphere or circle so that his body (the microcosm) forms part of the general order and harmony of the universe (the macrocosm). A man's soul ought to be in tune with the music of the spheres.*

[377] fret   *a) vex, irritate, b) fit with a fret – small bars of wire or wood to guide the fingering on a lute or other stringed instrument*

O, the recorders! Let me see one. To withdraw with you – why do you go about to recover the wind of me, as if you would drive me into a toil?

GUILDENSTERN O my lord, if my duty be too bold, my love is too unmannerly.

HAMLET I do not well understand that. Will you play upon this pipe?

GUILDENSTERN My lord, I cannot.

HAMLET I pray you.

GUILDENSTERN Believe me, I cannot. 360

HAMLET I do beseech you.

GUILDENSTERN I know no touch of it, my lord.

HAMLET It is as easy as lying. Govern these ventages with your fingers and thumb, give it breath with your mouth, and it will discourse most eloquent music. Look you, these are the stops.

GUILDENSTERN But these cannot I command to any utterance of harmony, I have not the skill.

HAMLET Why look you now how unworthy a thing you make of me! You would play upon me, you 370 would seem to know my stops, you would pluck out the heart of my mystery. You would sound me from my lowest note to the top of my compass, and there is much music, excellent voice, in this little organ – yet cannot you make it speak. 'Sblood, do you think I am easier to be played on than a pipe? Call me what instrument you will, though you can fret me, yet you cannot play upon me.

Enter POLONIUS

God bless you, sir.

POLONIUS My lord, the Queen would speak with you, 380 and presently.

HAMLET Do you see yonder cloud that's almost in shape of a camel?

POLONIUS By th'mass, and 'tis like a camel indeed.

HAMLET Methinks it is like a weasel.

[389] by and by   *soon*

[390] bent   *extent to which a bow may be bent – the limit, inclination*

[395] witching time   *the time of night when witches are most active and their charms likely to be most effective*

[396] yawn   *open wide*

[397] Contagion   *Evil which, like disease, is infectious and liable to spread. The night air was thought particularly unhealthy.*

drink hot blood   *one of the ceremonies of the black mass where blood is substituted for wine*

[398] bitter   *cruel, severe, unpleasant – like the taste of blood*

[400] nature   *natural qualities – of kindness and love*

[401] Nero   *Roman Emperor A.D. 54–68 caused his mother Agrippina to be murdered at the instigation of Poppaea Sabina*

[404] hypocrites   *A hypocrite is one who deliberately does not express his true feelings. Hamlet's tongue is about to express the daggers to his mother which his soul will not permit him to use.*

[405] shent   *put to shame*

[406] seals   *turn the words into deeds by putting a seal on them*

ACT THREE, scene 3

[1] like him   *I do not like his conduct*

stands it safe   *nor is it the case that we are safe to allow*

[3] commission   *the legal warrant giving them power to act as the King's representatives*

dispatch   *prepare with speed*

[5] terms of our estate   *the condition of being a king*

endure   *permit*

[7] brows   *face, appearance, melancholic disposition*

POLONIUS It is backed like a weasel

HAMLET Or like a whale?

POLONIUS Very like a whale.

HAMLET Then I will come to my mother by and by.
[*Aside*] They fool me to the top of my bent. [*To* 390
POLONIUS] I will come by and by.

POLONIUS I will say so.

HAMLET 'By and by' is easily said.

> [*Exit* POLONIUS
> Leave me, friends.
> [*Exeunt all but* HAMLET

'Tis now the very witching time of night,
When churchyards yawn, and hell itself
    breathes out
Contagion to this world. Now could I drink
    hot blood
And do such bitter business as the day.
Would quake to look on. Soft, now to my
    mother.
O heart lose not thy nature. Let not ever   400
The soul of Nero enter this firm bosom.
Let me be cruel, not unnatural.
I will speak daggers to her – but use none.
My tongue and soul in this be hypocrites,
How in my words somever she be shent,
To give them seals – never my soul consent.

> [*Exit*

Scene 3. *Enter* KING, ROSENCRANTZ *and* GUILDENSTERN

KING I like him not, nor stands it safe with us
    To let his madness range. Therefore prepare
        you,
    I your commission will forthwith dispatch,
    And he to England shall along with you.
    The terms of our estate may not endure
    Hazard so near's as doth hourly grow
    Out of his brows.

[7] ourselves provide *prepare ourselves, make ready*

[8] holy and religious *The King's anxiety is religious because he has a sacred duty to his people and their safety depends on his.*

[10] upon *by means of*

[11] peculiar *individual – who is responsible only for his own life*

[13] noyance *harm*

[15] cease *end, death – in death the King does not die alone*

[16] gulf *whirlpool, abyss*

[17] massy *heavy*

[20] mortised and adjoined *fitted together so that they are attached. A mortise is a join between two pieces of wood fitted into each other without the use of nails.*

[21] small annexment *small thing joined on to, minor subordinate*

    petty consequence *unimportant result, unimportant follower*

As the things joined to the wheel follow it to ruin so the minor court officials who wait upon the King also attend his ruin.

[24] Arm you *Make yourselves ready*

[25] fetters *iron bands round the legs joined by a chain to prevent movement*

[27] closet *private apartment*

[28] arras *tapestry fixed to the wall cf. II. 2. 162*

    convey *conceal – but also to transfer by deed or legal process*

[29] process *what is said, the conversation – but also legal proceedings, mandate, deed. The legal terms form a submerged metaphor.*

    tax him home *reproach him directly, effectively*

[31] meet *suitable*

[33] of vantage *with profit*

GUILDENSTERN   We will ourselves provide.
     Most holy and religious fear it is
     To keep those many many bodies safe
     That live and feed upon your Majesty.   10
ROSENCRANTZ The single and peculiar life is bound
     With all the strength and armour of the mind
     To keep itself from noyance; but much more
     That spirit upon whose weal depends and rests
     The lives of many. The cease of majesty
     Dies not alone, but like a gulf doth draw
     What's near it with it. It is a massy wheel,
     Fixed on the summit of the highest mount,
     To whose huge spokes ten thousand lesser
        things
     Are mortised and adjoined; which when it falls,   20
     Each small annexment, petty consequence,
     Attends the boist'rous ruin. Never alone
     Did the king sigh, but with a general groan.
KING Arm you, I pray you, to this speedy voyage,
     For we will fetters put about this fear
     Which now goes too free-footed.
ROSENCRANTZ   We will haste us.
       [*Exeunt* ROSENCRANTZ *and* GUILDENSTERN

Enter POLONIUS

POLONIUS My lord, he's going to his mother's closet.
     Behind the arras I'll convey myself
     To hear the process. I'll warrant she'll tax
       him home,
     And, as you said, and wisely was it said,   30
     'Tis meet that some more audience than a
       mother
     (Since nature makes them partial) should
       o'erhear
     The speech, of vantage. Fare you well, my
       liege.
     I'll call upon you ere you go to bed,

[37] primal   *original*

eldest   *oldest. Having murdered his brother Abel, Cain was cursed by God and cast out of human society (Genesis 4. 10–12).*

[39] inclination   *disposition, leaning towards – though the disposition to pray is as keen as the actual power of converting that desire into action. Claudius finds that the power of conscience and thought, his sense of his own guilt, paralyses his power of action and prevents him praying.*

[41] bound   *compelled, by oath or duty, to perform two actions at the same time.*

[42] in pause   *hesitating*

[45] rain enough   *Rain is a sign of God's mercy since a) it is connected with the idea of the sky weeping tears of pity, b) as an agent of growth it suggests rebirth and forgiveness.*

[46] Whereto   *What is the purpose of*

[47] confront   *come face to face with*

[48] twofold force   *as in the Lord's Prayer that one may not be led into temptation and delivered from the evil one has been tempted to commit*

[52] serve my turn   *fit my circumstances, occasion, help me*

[56] retain th'offence   *retain the advantage gained by the crime*

[57] corrupted currents   *courses of events which have been made rotten, untruthful, open to bribery, or otherwise turned awry, out of their course cf. III. 1. 87*

[58] gilded   *a) covered in gold to conceal its guiltiness – and capable of dispensing gold as a bribe, b) covered in blood*

[59–60] wicked prize . . . law   *the reward or position obtained by wickedness is sufficient to obtain complete possession of (buy out) the forces of law and order*

[61] There   *In heaven – before the court of God*

shuffling   *deceit, trickery, treachery*

action   *a) deed, b) legal prosecution which is now placed before the court with complete and true details – with no possibility of deceit or bribery*

lies   *is admissable, sustainable*

[63] teeth and forehead   *in the hostile presence of. The faults are on trial and the soul or conscience, formerly their accomplice, is forced to give evidence for the prosecution.*

[64] rests   *remains*

[65] can   *can perform*

And tell you what I know.

KING   Thanks, dear my lord.

                              [Exit POLONIUS

O, my offence is rank, it smells to heaven.
It hath the primal eldest curse upon't –
A brother's murder. Pray can I not,
Though inclination be as sharp as will.
My stronger guilt defeats my strong intent   40
And (like a man to double business bound)
I stand in pause where I shall first begin
And both neglect. What if this cursed hand
Were thicker than itself with brother's blood?
Is there not rain enough in the sweet heavens
To wash it white as snow? Whereto serves
   mercy
But to confront the visage of offence?
And what's in prayer but this twofold force,
To be forestallèd ere we come to fall,
Or pardoned being down? Then I'll look up   50
My fault is past. But O, what form of prayer
Can serve my turn. 'Forgive me my foul
   murder'?
That cannot be, since I am still possessed
Of those effects for which I did the murder –
My crown, mine own ambition, and my queen.
May one be pardoned and retain th' offence?
In the corrupted currents of this world
Offence's gilded hand may shove by justice;
And oft 'tis seen the wicked prize itself
Buys out the law. But 'tis not so above.   60
There is no shuffling, there the action lies
In his true nature – and we ourselves
   compelled
Even to the teeth and forehead of our faults
To give in evidence. What then? What rests?
Try what repentance can. What can it not?
Yet what can it when one can not repént?

[67] bosom   *breast, seat of the emotions – thoughts*

[68] limèd   *trapped. Birds were trapped by twigs covered with bird lime; the more they struggled the more they stuck to the twig.*

[69] assay   *attempt*

[73] pat   *immediately, without delay*

[74] heaven   *The fact that Claudius is praying causes Hamlet to assume that his soul is in a state of grace and therefore ready to go to heaven.*

[75] scanned   *examined*

[79] hire and salary   *wages and fees – employment and payment for it*

[80] grossly   *coarsely, flagrantly, shamefully*

   full of bread   *full fed – filled that is with food which indulges the senses and is damnable, not filled, as he ought to be with the bread and wine of the Christian sacrament*

[81] broad blown   *in full blossom*

   flush   *full of life, spirit – like flowers in May, hence proud*

[82] audit   *the account of his sins which must be given before he is judged in heaven*

[83] in our circumstance   *in our situation – as mortals*

   course of thought   *progress, direction of thought – the way we, with our mortal finite knowledge, are bound to consider these matters*

[84] heavy   *grievous, troublesome – with the idea that he may be weighed down with sin which will tip the scale of justice against him*

[86] seasoned   *ready*

[88] hent   *may mean a) grip – and so a stroke, b) occasion, opportunity*

[92] relish   *trace*

[93] heels may kick at heaven   *he may be upset, trapped killed. 'To turn up a person's heels' is to kill them.*

[95] stays   *waits for me*

[96] physic   *purge, medicine. Prayer is the purge of the soul but this prayer can only prolong life, not cure the disease.*

O wretched state, O bosom black as death.
O limèd soul that struggling to be free
Art more engaged! Help, angels. Make assay.
Bow stubborn knees, and heart with strings
   of steel   70
Be soft as sinews of the new born babe.
All may be well.

Enter HAMLET

HAMLET Now might I do it, pat; now he is a-praying.
And now I'll do't. And so he goes to heaven –
And so am I revenged? That would be scanned.
A villain kills my father; and for that,
I, his sole son, do this same villain send
To heaven.
Why, this is hire and salary – not revenge.
He took my father grossly, full of bread,   80
With all his crimes broad blown, as flush as
   May.
And how his audit stands who knows save
   heaven?
But in our circumstance and course of thought
'Tis heavy with him. And am I then revenged
To take him in the purging of his soul
When he is fit and seasoned for his passage?
No.
Up sword, and know thou a more horrid hent.
When he is drunk asleep, or in his rage,
Or in th'incestuous pleasure of his bed,   90
At game, a-swearing, or about some act
That has no relish of salvation in't –
Then trip him, that his heels may kick at
   heaven,
And that his soul may be as damned and black
As hell, whereto it goes. My mother stays.
This physic but prolongs thy sickly days.
                           [Exit

ACT THREE, scene 4

[1] lay home to him *touch the root of the matter, affect him strongly, fix the accusation of him*
[2] broad *unrestrained, open*

[4] heat *anger, choler – which heats the blood*
      silence *keep silent and watch*
[5] round *plain spoken*
[7] warrant *promise*

[10] thy father *the King, Claudius*
[11] my father *King Hamlet*

[15] rood *cross of Christ*
[18] set those to you *cause people to come and deal with you, influence you*
      can speak *can exert authority over you, persuade you*
[20] glass *mirror*
[21] inmost part of you *your soul*
      Hamlet is about to hold up a mirror of words to his mother's nature so that she can see and understand her soul. She interprets 'inmost part' to mean heart and organs, and fears lunatic violence and murder.

KING My words fly up, my thoughts remain below.
      Words without thoughts never to heaven go.
                              [*Exit*

Scene 4. *Enter* QUEEN *and* POLONIUS

POLONIUS He will come straight. Look you lay home
      to him.
      Tell him his pranks have been too broad to
      bear with,
      And that your Grace hath screened and stood
      between
      Much heat and him. I'll silence me even here.
      Pray you be round with him.
HAMLET [*Within*] Mother, mother, mother!
QUEEN I'll warrant you. Fear me not.
      Withdraw, I hear him coming.

Enter HAMLET

HAMLET Now mother, what's the matter?
QUEEN Hamlet, thou hast thy father much offended.   10
HAMLET Mother, you have my father much offended.
QUEEN Come, come. You answer with an idle tongue.
HAMLET Go, go. You question with a wicked tongue.
QUEEN Why, how now, Hamlet!
HAMLET   What's the matter now?
QUEEN Have you forgot me?
HAMLET   No, by the rood, not so;
      You are the Queen, your husband's brother's
      wife;
      And (would it were not so) you are my mother!
QUEEN Nay then, I'll set those to you that can speak.
HAMLET Come! Come and sit you down. You shall
      not budge.
      You go not till I set you up a glass   20
      Where you may see the inmost part of you.

[24] a rat   *spy, traitor*

[25] Dead for a ducat   *For a certainty – I bet a ducat I will kill this rat*

[28] King   *Hamlet evidently thinks his mother has been used as a decoy to give Claudius the opportunity to murder him.*

[31] As kill a king   *Hamlet has assumed that his mother is guilty of murder. It now appears that she was at least ignorant of the crime.*

[34] better   *better in rank, the King*

[40] proof and bulwark   *tempered and fortified against natural feeling*

[41] wag   *move briskly – with the implication of foolish or indiscreet speech*

[42] rude   *harsh, unkind, violent*

[43] blurs   *stains, disfigures, defiles*

[44] rose   *the emblem of beauty and chastity*

[46] blister   *a blister raised by the burn of a branding iron. Prostitutes were sometimes branded.*

[48] contraction   *the pledging of mutual faith in the marriage service*

[50] rhapsody of words   *the sacred vows of the marriage service become merely an actor's rhetoric. 'Rhapsody' comes from the Greek word meaning a recital of poetry.*

  Heaven's face   *the sun*

  glow   *burn or blush with shame*

[51] solidity and compound mass   *solid body composed of various elements. It could either refer to the sun or, as most editors assume, to the earth.*

QUEEN What wilt thou do? Thou wilt not murder me?
　　　Help, help ho!
POLONIUS　　　What ho! help, help, help!
HAMLET How now, a rat?
　　　Dead for a ducat, dead.

　　　　　　　　　　　　[*Kills* POLONIUS

POLONIUS O, I am slain.
QUEEN O me, what hast thou done?
HAMLET　　　　　　　Nay, I know not.
　　　Is it the King?
QUEEN O, what a rash and bloody deed is this.
HAMLET A bloody deed? Almost as bad, good mother,　30
　　　As kill a king and marry with his brother.
QUEEN As kill a king?
HAMLET　　　　　Ay lady, it was my word.
　　　Thou wretched, rash, intruding fool, farewell.
　　　I took thee for thy better. Take thy fortune.
　　　Thou find'st to be too busy is some danger.
　　　Leave wringing of your hands. Peace, sit you
　　　　down
　　　And let me wring your heart – for so I shall,
　　　If it be made of penetrable stuff,
　　　If damnèd custom have not brazed it so
　　　That it be proof and bulwark against sense.　　40
QUEEN What have I done, that thou dar'st wag thy
　　　　tongue
　　　In noise so rude against me?
HAMLET　　　　　　　Such an act
　　　That blurs the grace and blush of modesty;
　　　Calls virtue hypocrite; takes off the rose
　　　From the fair forehead of an innocent love
　　　And sets a blister there; makes marriage vows
　　　As false as dicers' oaths. O, such a deed
　　　As from the body of contraction plucks
　　　The very soul, and sweet religion makes
　　　A rhapsody of words. Heaven's face doth glow;　50
　　　Yea this solidity and compound mass

187

[52] against the doom   *before the day of judgement*

[53] thought sick   *melancholy*

[56] counterfeit presentment   *portrait – a picture which counterfeits or looks like real life*

[58] Hyperion's curls   *hair like the sun's – see I. 2. 140*

Jove   *in classical mythology the ruler of the Olympian gods*

[59] Mars   *the god of war*

[60] station   *way of standing, carriage of the body*

Mercury   *the messenger of the gods, and hence the god who goes between heaven and earth*

[62] combination   *union of virtues in the mind*

form   *physical body*

The gods set their seals on him to indicate that he has the qualities of majesty, strength, swiftness which the gods represent. The description of the picture is a character sketch of the man.

[63] set his seal   *marked his virtues as genuine and authentic*

[66] mildewed ear   *an ear of grain suffering from rot or mildew which infects and destroys the others round it*

[68] leave to   *leave off, cease*

[69] batten   *fatten yourself. Eating grass or pasture is here both an image of sexuality (cf. I. 2. 144) and of the lost sheep who have strayed from the steep way to heaven and are lost on the moor.*

[70] call it love   *That, of course, is exactly what Gertrude did call it.*

[71] heyday   *high noon, high point of excitement, sexuality*

[72] judgement   *reason – the same opposition between blood (passion) and judgement (reason) found in Hamlet's speech to Horatio (III. 2. 69–75). Gertrude's blood and judgement are clearly not well 'commeddled' and she is passion's slave.*

[73] Sense   *a) The five senses which, according to Aristotle, are necessary for movement, b) good sense, reason, judgement*

[75] apoplexed   *paralysed*

[76] ecstasy   *madness*

thralled   *enslaved*

[77] reserved   *retained*

quantity   *small amount, element*

[78] serve   *be used*

such   *so great*

[79] cozened   *cheated*

hoodman blind   *blind man's buff – a game in which a blindfolded person attempts to catch and identify the other players*

With heated visage, as against the doom,
Is thought sick at the act.

QUEEN   Ay me, what act,
That roars so loud and thunders in the index?

HAMLET Look here upon this picture and on this,
The counterfeit presentment of two brothers.
See what a grace was seated on this brow,
Hyperion's curls, the front of Jove himself,
An eye like Mars, to threaten and command,
A station like the herald Mercury   60
New lighted on a heaven-kissing hill –
A combination and a form indeed
Where every god did seem to set his seal
To give the world assurance of a man.
This was your husband. Look you now what
   follows –
Here is your husband, like a mildewed ear
Blasting his wholesome brother. Have you
   eyes?
Could you on this fair mountain leave to feed
And batten on this moor? Ha, have you eyes?
You cannot call it love, for at your age   70
The heyday in the blood is tame, it's humble,
And waits upon the judgement; and what
   judgement
Would step from this to this? Sense, sure,
   you have,
Else could you not have motion; but sure
   that sense
Is apoplexed – for madness would not err,
Nor sense to ecstasy was ne'er so thralled
But it reserved some quantity of choice
To serve in such a difference. What devil was't
That thus hath cozened you at hoodman blind?
Eyes without feeling, feeling without sight,   80
Ears without hands or eyes, smelling sans all,
Or but a sickly part of one true sense

[83] mope   *be so foolish, mistaken. Gertrude could not have made such a mistake given sight without touch, touch without sight, hearing without touch or sight, smell without anything else. Even if she had the partial but weak use of one sense she could not have made such an error.*

[85] mutine   *mutiny, rebel*

matron's bones   *body of a married woman – a person of dignity and sober social habits who has borne children*

[86] To flaming youth . . . fire   *Let virtue be as the wax of a candle or sealing wax and melt in the fire of youth which exists as a flame by burning the wax*

[88] compulsive ardour   *compelling fire of passion*

gives the charge   *causes a loaded fire-arm to go off, creates an explosion*

[90] panders   *reason, which should control the will or sexual drive, now acts as its bawd, procurer or pander*

[92] grained   *dyed with grain dye, indelibly dyed*

[93] leave   *lose*

tinct   *colour*

[94] rank   *evil smelling*

enseamed   *a) loaded with grease, b) marked as with a seam, crushed*

[95] Stewed   *Soaked, steeped, heated. The word is particularly strong since a 'stews' meant a brothel, after the use of hot bath houses as places of prostitution.*

honeying   *using terms of endearment, covering with sweetness*

[96] nasty   *filthy*

sty   *place of human habitation which resembles a pig sty. The phrase carries the sense of a) covering over the filthy corrupt sty with the appearance of sweetness and love, b) using endearments and making love over and over until the bed resembles a sty.*

[100] precedent   *former*

vice of kings   *a king like a Vice in a morality play, a stage jester, a buffoon*

[101] cutpurse   *thief, pickpocket – except that he cuts the pocket*

[105] shreds and patches   *The costume of the Vice was a coat made out of odd scraps of cloth.*

[109] tardy   *slow moving, delaying*

[110] lapsed in time and passion   *sunk in delay and melancholy – or, possibly, having let slip the opportunity and desire for revenge*

Could not so mope. O shame, where is thy
    blush?
Rebellious hell,
If thou can'st mutine in a matron's bones,
To flaming youth let virtue be as wax
And melt in her own fire. Proclaim no shame
When the compulsive ardour gives the charge,
Since frost itself as actively doth burn,
And reason panders will.

QUEEN   O Hamlet, speak no more.   90
Thou turn'st my eyes into my very soul,
And there I see such black and grained spots
As will not leave their tinct.

HAMLET   Nay, but to live
In the rank sweat of an enseamèd bed,
Stewed in corruption, honeying and making
    love
Over the nasty sty!

QUEEN   O, speak to me no more!
These words like daggers enter in my ears.
No more, sweet Hamlet.

HAMLET   A murderer and a villain.
A slave that is not twentieth part the tithe
Of your precedent lord. A vice of kings,   100
A cutpurse of the empire and the rule,
That from a shelf the precious diadem stole
And put it in his pocket.

QUEEN No more!

Enter GHOST

HAMLET A King of shreds and patches –
Save me, and hover o'er me with your wings
You heavenly guards. What would your
    gracious figure?

QUEEN Alas, he's mad.

HAMLET Do you not come your tardy son to chide,
That, lapsed in time and passion, lets go by   110

[111] important   *urgent*

[114] whet   *sharpen*
     almost blunted   *It is strange that the Ghost should describe Hamlet's purpose as blunted when he has been talking of damning the King in the previous scene. The audience are, therefore, clearly not expected to take the soliloquy at face value.*
[115] amazement   *distraction, overwhelming fear*
[116] fighting soul   *Gertrude is imagined as fighting a duel with her soul. To reconcile her body and soul, Hamlet must stop the duel by stepping between the combatants.*
[117] Conceit   *Imagination*
[120] bend   *turn*
[121] incorporal   *lacking a body, insubstantial*
[123] as the sleeping . . . alarm   *like soldiers leaping up from sleep during a night attack*
[124] bedded hairs   *hair lying flat on your head*
     like life in excrements   *as if these outgrowths were alive*
[126] distemper   *illness, madness*

[129] form and cause conjoined   *his appearance, and the reason which makes him appear, together would move stones to action if he preached to them*

[131] piteous   *merciful, tender*
     convert   *turn aside from, reverse, change – often used of turning the eyes, here it is the eyes which cause the turn*
[132] effects   *purposes*
[133] tears . . . blood   *Hamlet fears that he may again substitute the pale colour of thought, pity and mercy for the red of blood and revenge.*

[140] habit   *clothes, gown – the nightgown which was his casual dress in the evening for his own private apartments*

Th'important acting of your dread command?
O say!

GHOST Do not forget. This visitation
Is but to whet thy almost blunted purpose.
But look, amazement on thy mother sits.
O, step between her and her fighting soul.
Conceit in weakest bodies strongest works.
Speak to her, Hamlet.

HAMLET How is it with you, lady?

QUEEN   Alas, how is't with you?
That you do bend your eye on vacancy,   120
And with th'incorporal air do hold discourse?
Forth at your eyes your spirits wildly peep,
And, as the sleeping soldiers in th'alarm,
Your bedded hairs like life in excrements
Start up and stand on end. O gentle son,
Upon the heat and flame of thy distemper
Sprinkle cool patience. Whereon do you look?

HAMLET On him, on him! Look you how pale he
    glares.
His form and cause conjoined, preaching to
    stones,
Would make them capable. Do not look upon
    me,   130
Lest with this piteous action you convert
My stern effects. Then what I have to do
Will want true colour – tears perchance for
    blood.

QUEEN To whom do you speak this?

HAMLET Do you see nothing there?

QUEEN Nothing at all – yet all that is I see.

HAMLET Nor did you nothing hear?

QUEEN No, nothing but ourselves.

HAMLET Why, look you there. Look how it steals away.
My father in his habit as he lived.   140
Look where he goes even now out at the portal.
          [*Exit* GHOST

[142] coinage   *creation – with the sense of false creation, forgery*

[143] ecstasy   *madness*

[148] the matter will reword   *will repeat the substance of what I have said*

[149] gambol from   *shy away from, spring from*

[150] unction   *oil or ointment used to heal a wound or applied in a religious ritual of consecration and purification*

[151] trespass   *trespass against the law of God, sin*

[152] skin and film   *cover with a thin layer (of ointment) like a skin but without healing it*

[153] rank corruption   *evil-smelling putrefaction, suppuration*

   mining   *working beneath the surface to destroy*

[156] compost   *manure or decayed vegetable matter spread on plants to make them grow*

[157] ranker   *wilder, bigger – also, more evil smelling*

   Forgive   *Hamlet asks forgiveness for the apparent sanctimonious tone of his words since, in these times grown fat with self-indulgence, it is necessary for virtue to beg vice's pardon and ask permission to do him good. It is partly an apology for a lecture and partly a reminder that she ought, for her own good, to pay attention to it.*

[158] pursy   *fat, corpulent – like a swollen purse or bag*

[160] curb   *bow, bend*

[161] cleft   *split*

[166] monster custom   *the monstrous repetition of bad habits*

   all sense doth eat   *that devours all reason and good sense*

[167] of habits devil   *the devil of addiction to anything*

[169] frock or livery   *clothing or uniform – which can be worn again as a custom and is readily identifiable*

[170] aptly is put on   *that is easy to put on*

[173] use   *constant use, custom*

   stamp of nature   *natural character*

[174] throw   *twist, cast (as of metal), defeat (as in wrestling). A word has evidently here dropped out of the line of type. Q2 reads: 'And either the devil, or throw him out'. I assume that the line was somehow displaced, the obvious 'cast' omitted and 'throw' transposed in the correction.*

QUEEN This is the very coinage of your brain.
This bodiless creation ecstasy
Is very cunning in.

HAMLET   Ecstasy?
My pulse as yours doth temperately keep time,
And makes as healthful music. It is not
    madness
That I have uttered. Bring me to the test,
And I the matter will reword which madness
Would gambol from. Mother, for love of grace,
Lay not that flattering unction to your soul,   150
That not your trespass but my madness
    speaks.
It will but skin and film the ulcerous place,
Whiles rank corruption, mining all within,
Infects unseen. Confess yourself to heaven.
Repent what's past. Avoid what is to come.
And do not spread the compost on the weeds
To make them ranker. Forgive me this my
    virtue,
For in the fatness of these pursy times
Virtue itself of vice must pardon beg,
Yea, curb and woo for leave to do him good.   160

QUEEN O Hamlet, thou hast cleft my heart in twain.

HAMLET O, throw away the worser part of it
And live the purer with the other half.
Good night – but go not to my uncle's bed.
Assume a virtue, if you have it not.
That monster custom, who all sense doth eat,
Of habits devil, is angel yet in this,
That to the use of actions fair and good
He likewise gives a frock or livery
That aptly is put on. Refrain tonight,   170
And that shall lend a kind of easiness
To the next abstinence; the next more easy,
For use almost can change the stamp of nature,
And either throw the devil, or cast him out,

195

[176] desirous to be blest *anxious to obtain God's blessing through repentance*

[177] blessing beg *ask your blessing, as my mother*

[180] their *Heaven is treated as a plural.*

scourge and minister *whip and the person who administers it – the instrument and the agent of God's punishment*

[181] bestow *stow, hide*

answer well *account for, acknowledge responsibility for*

[184] behind *behind the beginning, to come, in the future*

[187] bloat *fat, bloated with drinking and self-indulgence*

[189] reechy *filthy, greasy*

[193] in craft *by design*

[194] that's but a queen *The tone is heavily sarcastic – you are only a queen and so of course you can't be expected to conceal; a queen should have more self-control than others.*

[195] paddock *toad*

gib *cat. These are all animals associated with witchcraft. She cannot conceal a secret from her familiar spirit.*

[196] dear concernings *important matters which affect one closely*

[199] famous ape *The story is lost: it must be about an ape who let some birds out of a basket and assumed that they could fly because they came out of the basket and broke his own neck, thus putting his theory into practice. It is a warning against the fallacy of the undistributed middle in a logical argument.*

[200] try conclusions *test the result*

[203] breathe *speak, utter*

With wondrous potency. Once more, good
   night,
And when you are desirous to be blest,
I'll blessing beg of you. For this same lord
I do repent — but Heaven hath pleased it so,
To punish me with this, and this with me,
That I must be their scourge and minister.   180
I will bestow him, and will answer well
The death I gave him. So, again, good night.
I must be cruel only to be kind;
Thus bad begins and worse remains behind.
One word more, good lady.

QUEEN   What shall I do?

HAMLET Not this, by no means, that I bid you do.
Let the bloat King tempt you again to bed,
Pinch wanton on your cheek, call you his
   mouse,
And let him, for a pair of reechy kisses,
Or paddling in your neck with his damned
   fingers,   190
Make you to ravel all this matter out,
That I essentially am not in madness,
But mad in craft. 'Twere good you let him
   know,
For who that's but a queen, fair, sober, wise,
Would from a paddock, from a bat, a gib,
Such dear concernings hide? Who would do
   so?
No, in despite of sense and secrecy,
Unpeg the basket on the house's top,
Let the birds fly, and, like the famous ape,
To try conclusions, in the basket creep   200
And break your own neck down.

QUEEN Be thou assured, if words be made of breath
And breath of life, I have no life to breathe
What thou hast said to me.

HAMLET I must to England; you know that?

[208] adders fanged   *snakes with poisonous fangs*

[209] mandate   *royal commission*

   sweep my way   *In ceremonial or festival processions it was common for the road in front of the main characters to be swept as they walked.*

[210] marshal me   *act as marshals, guides, controllers*

[211] engineer   *pioneer, military engineer*

[212] Hoist   *Raised up, blown up*

   petar   *mine, charge, bomb*

   In siege operations it was common for engineers to dig a mine or underground gallery under the defences and blow them up with a charge. The defence was to dig a counter-mine under it and set off a charge which would blow up the men and the explosives in the original mine. The method was still in use in trench warfare in 1917.

[215] in one line   *on one level*

   two crafts   *two concealed underground operations meet head on*

[216] set me packing   *a) send me away in haste, b) start me plotting (to devise a counter-mine)*

[221] draw toward an end with you   *to come to an end of my business with you – a common phrase but with an added pun here since life too is said to draw to an end and the body is drawn or dragged across the stage. The pun is visual as well as verbal.*

QUEEN   Alack,
    I had forgot. 'Tis so concluded on.
HAMLET There's letters sealed, and my two
        school-fellows
    (Whom I will trust as I will adders fanged)
    They bear the mandate. They must sweep my
        way
    And marshal me to knavery. Let it work;   210
    For 'tis the sport to have the engineer
    Hoist with his own petar; and't shall go hard
    But I will delve one yard below their mines
    And blow them at the moon. O, 'tis most sweet
    When in one line two crafts directly meet.
    This man shall set me packing.
    I'll lug the guts into the neighbour room.
    Mother, good night. Indeed, this counsellor
    Is now most still, most secret, and most grave,
    Who was in life a foolish prating knave.   220
    Come sir, to draw toward an end with you.
    Good night, mother.
                [*Exeunt;* HAMLET *tugging in* POLONIUS

ACT FOUR, scene 1

[1] matter in *cause, reason for*

heaves *of the breast, sighs*

[2] translate *explain*

fit *proper suitable*

[4] Bestow *Give us this place – i.e. leave us*

[7] contend *Storms are frequently described as a battle between the elements.*

[11] brainish apprehension *mad illusion. The phrase is deliberately awkward, drawing attention to Gertrude's deception of Claudius.*

[16] answered *accounted for, how will we answer the accusation of*

[17] laid *put upon us – we shall be held responsible for*

providence *foresight*

[18] kept short *controlled – kept on a short lead or chain like an animal*

out of haunt *out of the haunts, society, of men*

[22] divulging *being disclosed, made known*

[23] pith *central core, spinal cord, essence*

[25] ore *gold – from the Latin 'aurum'*

[26] mineral *substance obtained by mining – normally called ore. Gertrude says that Hamlet's purity of heart shines through his madness like specks of gold in an ore of base metal. Her description is again deliberately false.*

ACT FOUR

Scene 1. *Enter* KING *and* QUEEN *with* ROSENCRANTZ *and* GUILDENSTERN

KING   There's matter in these sighs, these profound heaves
You must translate; 'tis fit we understand them.
Where is your son?

QUEEN   Bestow this place on us a little while.
           [*Exeunt* ROSENCRANTZ *and* GUILDENSTERN
Ah, mine own lord, what have I seen tonight!

KING   What, Gertrude? How does Hamlet?

QUEEN   Mad as the sea and wind, when both contend
Which is the mightier. In his lawless fit,
Behind the arras hearing something stir,
Whips out his rapier, cries, 'A rat, a rat!'   10
And in this brainish apprehension kills
The unseen good old man.

KING   O heavy deed!
It had been so with us had we been there.
His liberty is full of threats to all –
To you yourself, to us, to every one.
Alas, how shall this bloody deed be answered?
It will be laid to us, whose providence
Should have kept short, restrained, and out of haunt
This mad young man. But so much was our love
We would not understand what was most fit,   20
But, like the owner of a foul disease,
To keep it from divulging, let it feed
Even on the pith of life. Where is he gone?

QUEEN   To draw apart the body he hath killed,
O'er whom his very madness, like some ore
Among a mineral of metals base,

[32] countenance *lend our countenance to, support. The King appears to promise royal protection for Hamlet despite his crime.*

[33] further aid *more people to help you*

[40] untimely *unseasonable, prematurely, unfortunately*
     So haply slander *There is a gap here in all the early texts. The general sense must be something like the words supplied.*
[41] diameter *whole extent from side to side*
[42] level *direct*
     blank *target*

ACT FOUR, scene 2

[1] stowed *hidden*

Shows itself pure. He weeps for what is done.
KING O Gertrude come away!
    The sun no sooner shall the mountains touch
    But we will ship him hence; and this vile deed   30
    We must with all our majesty and skill
    Both countenance and excuse. Ho,
      Guildenstern!

Enter ROSENCRANTZ *and* GUILDENSTERN

    Friends both, go join you with some further
      aid.
    Hamlet in madness hath Polonius slain,
    And from his mother's closet hath he dragged
      him.
    Go seek him out. Speak fair, and bring the
      body
    Into the chapel. I pray you haste in this.
        [*Exeunt* ROSENCRANTZ *and* GUILDENSTERN
    Come Gertrude, we'll call up our wisest
      friends
    And let them know both what we mean to do
    And what's untimely done. So haply slander –   40
    Whose whisper o'er the world's diameter
    As level as the cannon to his blank,
    Transports his poisoned shot – may miss our
      name,
    And hit the woundless air. O, come away,
    My soul is full of discord and dismay!
                [*Exeunt*

Scene 2. *Enter* HAMLET

HAMLET Safely stowed.
GENTLEMEN [*Within*] Hamlet! Lord Hamlet!
HAMLET But soft, what noise? Who calls on Hamlet?
  O, here they come.

[7] **Compounded it**   *Mixed it with*
    kin   *related – according to Genesis 3. 19, man is made from dust*

[12] **keep your counsel**   *keep what you have told me secret*

[14] **replication**   *reply, answer, rejoinder*

[16–7] **countenance**   *favour*

[17] **authorities**   *positions of authority – and therefore of profit*

[18] **best service**   *There is a play upon meaning: a) do their best duty as servants, b) fulfil the King's needs best as a 'service' or course at table which he eats. By acting as the King's best servants they will inevitably be used by him as a 'service' and devoured or destroyed when he has no further need of them.*

[19] **an ape an apple**   *The text is corrupt at this point. Q2 reads, 'like an apple in the corner', F reads, 'like an ape in the corner', Q1, 'as an ape doth nuts in the corner'.*

[21] **gleaned**   *gathered, picked up, scraped together*

[28–9] **The body is with the King . . . body**   *Rosencrantz and Guildenstern regard this as madness. Hamlet is using the concept of the King having two bodies – a body natural (his own) and a body politic (the state). Claudius has a body natural, 'the body is with the King', but since he is not the true King of Denmark he cannot possess the body politic, 'the King is not with the body'.*

[29] **a thing**   *To call the King a thing is treason.*

[31] **Of nothing**   *Hamlet again uses the pun on 'no thing' – the King is without body or political substance.*

Hide fox   *Hamlet escapes with a tag which suggests that the courtiers are the King's dogs or hounds.*

Enter ROSENCRANTZ *and* GUILDENSTERN

ROSENCRANTZ What have you done, my lord, with the
    dead body?

HAMLET Compounded it with dust, whereto 'tis kin.

ROSENCRANTZ Tell us where 'tis, that we may take it
    thence,
    And bear it to the chapel.

HAMLET Do not believe it.   10

ROSENCRANTZ Believe what?

HAMLET That I can keep your counsel, and not mine
    own. Besides, to be demanded of a sponge – what
    replication should be made by the son of a king?

ROSENCRANTZ Take you me for a sponge, my lord?

HAMLET Ay, sir; that soaks up the King's counten-
    ance, his rewards, his authorities. But such officers
    do the King best service in the end – he keeps them
    like an ape an apple in the corner of his jaw; first
    mouthed to be last swallowed. When he needs what   20
    you have gleaned it is but squeezing you and,
    sponge, you shall be dry again.

ROSENCRANTZ I understand you not, my lord.

HAMLET I am glad of it – a knavish speech sleeps in a
    foolish ear.

ROSENCRANTZ My lord, you must tell us where the
    body is, and go with us to the King.

HAMLET The body is with the King, but the King is
    not with the body. The King is a thing –

GUILDENSTERN A thing, my lord!   30

HAMLET Of nothing. Bring me to him. Hide fox, and
    all after.

                                        [Exeunt

Scene 3. *Enter* KING *and two or three*

KING I have sent to seek him, and to find the body.
    How dangerous is it that this man goes loose.

ACT FOUR, scene 3

[3] put the strong law upon him *place the restraints, fetters, of the extreme or cruel forms of law upon him*

[4] distracted *confused – by contradictory feelings and emotions, easily swayed one way or another*

[6] scourge *punishment*
    weighed *considered*

[7] bear *maintain, carry*

[9] Deliberate pause *The result of very careful consideration*

[10] appliance *that which is applied, remedy*

[14] Without *Outside*
    pleasure *will, determination*

[21] convocation *assembly*
    politic *skilled in politics or policy – with the suggestion that policy is Machiavellian and a matter of deceit. There is a possible pun upon the Diet of Worms at which, in 1521, Martin Luther appeared to defend his doctrines in the presence of the Emperor Charles V.*

[25] variable service *different courses served at the same meal*

Yet must not we put the strong law on him,
He's loved of the distracted multitude,
Who like not in their judgement but their eyes.
And where 'tis so, th'offender's scourge is
    weighed,
But never the offence. To bear all smooth
    and even
This sudden sending him away must seem
Deliberate pause. Diseases desperate grown
By desperate appliance are relieved,   10
Or not at all.

Enter ROSENCRANTZ

How now, what hath befallen?
ROSENCRANTZ Where the dead body is bestowed, my
        lord,
    We cannot get from him.
KING   But where is he?
ROSENCRANTZ Without, my lord; guarded, to know
    your pleasure.
KING Bring him before us.
ROSENCRANTZ Ho, Guildenstern! Bring in the lord.

Enter HAMLET *and* GUILDENSTERN

KING Now, Hamlet, where's Polonius?
HAMLET At supper.
KING At supper? Where?
HAMLET Not where he eats, but where he is eaten. A   20
    certain convocation of politic worms are e'en at
    him. Your worm is your only emperor for diet. We
    fat all creatures else to fat us, and we fat ourselves
    for maggots. Your fat king and your lean beggar is
    but variable service – two dishes, but to one table.
    That's the end.
KING Alas, alas!
HAMLET A man may fish with the worm that hath eat of

[32] progress *a formal state journey made by the King round his kingdom*

[35] other place *hell*

[37] nose *smell*

[42] tender *care for*

[45] at help *helpful, favourable*

[46] Th'associates *Those associated with you in the royal commission*

      tend *attend upon, wait for you*

      bent *prepared, directed towards*

[49] cherub *angel. The idea that no secrets were hidden from the cherubim perhaps comes from Ezekiel 28.*

[50] dear mother *Hamlet apparently addresses the King as 'mother'.*

[55] at foot *at heel, close behind his steps*

a king and eat of the fish that hath fed of that worm.

KING What dost thou mean by this?   30

HAMLET Nothing but to show you how a king may go
a progress through the guts of a beggar.

KING Where is Polonius?

HAMLET In heaven, send thither to see. If your messenger find him not there, seek him i'th'other place
yourself. But if, indeed, you find him not within
this month, you shall nóse him as you go up the
stairs into the lobby.

KING Go seek him there.

> [*Exeunt* ATTENDANTS

HAMLET He will stay till you come.   40

KING Hamlet, this deed, for thine especial safety –
  Which we do tender, as we dearly grieve
  For that which thou hast done – must send
   thee hence
  With fiery quickness. Therefore prepare
   thyself;
  The bark is ready, and the wind at help,
  Th'associates tend, and everything is
   bent
  For England.

HAMLET   For England!

KING   Ay, Hamlet.

HAMLET   Good.

KING So is it, if thou knew'st our purposes.

HAMLET I see a cherub that sees them. But come, for
England. Farewell, dear mother.   50

KING Thy loving father, Hamlet.

HAMLET My mother: father and mother is man and
wife; man and wife is one flesh; and so, my mother.
Come, for England.   [*Exit*

KING Follow him at foot, tempt him with speed
  aboard.
  Delay it not, I'll have him hence tonight.
  Away, for everything is sealed and done

[58] leans on *rests upon, depends on*

[59] England *the King of England*
     at aught *at any value*
[60] give thee sense *my great power should give you some idea of how you ought to value my good will*
[61] cicatrice *scar*
[62] free awe *unconstrained respect – the King of England continues to pay tribute to Denmark of his own free will. The idea is based upon the Viking occupation of north-east England.*
[63] coldly set *estimate lightly*
[64] sovereign process *royal commission*
     imports at full *signifies exactly, completely*
[65] congruing *agreeing – the mandate or commission commands the King of England to open the sealed letter which orders the death of Hamlet. Rosencrantz and Guildenstern may know the terms of their commission but they merely carry the letter.*
[67] hectic *continuing fever*
[69] haps *whatever may happen by chance or fortune*

ACT FOUR, scene 4

[2] licence *permission*
[3] conveyance *safe conduct*

[5] would aught *has any business with us*
[6] in his eye *in his presence*

[11] How purposed . . . ? *What is the purpose or object of the expedition?*

That else leans on th'affair. Pray you make
   haste.
                  [Exeunt all but the KING
And, England, if my love thou hold'st at
   aught –
As my great power thereof may give thee sense,   60
Since yet thy cicatrice looks raw and red
After the Danish sword, and thy free awe
Pays homage to us – thou mayest not coldly set
Our sovereign process, which imports at full,
By letters congruing to that effect,
The present death of Hamlet. Do it, England:
For like the hectic in my blood he rages,
And thou must cure me. Till I know 'tis done,
Howe'er my haps, my joys were ne'er begun.
                       [Exit

Scene 4. *Enter* FORTINBRAS *with his army over the stage*

FORTINBRAS Go, Captain, from me greet the Danish
   king.
Tell him that by his licence Fortinbras
Craves the conveyance of a promised march
Over his kingdom. You know the rendezvous.
If that his Majesty would aught with us,
We shall express our duty in his eye;
And let him know so.
CAPTAIN   I will do't, my lord.
FORTINBRAS Go softly on.
               [Exeunt all but the CAPTAIN

Enter HAMLET, ROSENCRANTZ,
GUILDENSTERN *and* OTHERS

HAMLET Good sir, whose powers are these?
CAPTAIN They are of Norway, sir.   10
HAMLET How purposed, sir, I pray you?

[15] main *main land, main area of the country*

[17] addition *exaggeration*

[20] five ducats, five *only five ducats*

[22] ranker *richer, higher*
sold in fee *sold in fee-simple, freehold, giving absolute possession*
[23] Polack *King of Poland*

[26] debate the question of this straw *bring the contention about this unimportant matter to a conclusion*
[27] imposthume *abcess, ulcer – since even the death of two thousand men will not settle the question it will remain as a festering sore until it destroys the body politic*
[28] inward breaks *bursts inside*
no cause without *no visible sign or cause*

[32] all occasions *every chance event*
inform against *lay accusations against, tell against*
[34] chief good and market *main aim and business*
[36] large discourse *wide-ranging powers of understanding*
[37] Looking before and after *Examining the past and future. The exercise of memory and foresight is the virtue of prudence.*
[38] That capability *The power of prudence*
[39] fust *go mouldy*
[40] Bestial oblivion *An animal-like forgetfulness. Animals were in general not considered to have the power of memory.*
craven scruple *cowardly doubt, question, hesitation*
[41] too precisely *too exactly, rigorously, strictly*
th'event *the future result, consequence*
Hamlet blames himself either for lack of memory or too careful, and therefore cowardly, an exercise of foresight.

CAPTAIN Against some part of Poland.

HAMLET Who commands them, sir?

CAPTAIN The nephew to old Norway, Fortinbras.

HAMLET Goes it against the main of Poland, sir,
    Or for some frontier?

CAPTAIN Truly to speak, and with no addition,
    We go to gain a little patch of ground
    That hath in it no profit but the name.
    To pay five ducats, five, I would not farm it.   20
    Nor will it yield to Norway or the Pole
    A ranker rate should it be sold in fee.

HAMLET Why, then the Polack never will defend it.

CAPTAIN Yes, it is already garrison'd.

HAMLET Two thousand souls and twenty thousand
    ducats
    Will not debate the question of this straw.
    This is th'imposthume of much wealth and
    peace,
    That inward breaks, and shows no cause
    without
    Why the man dies. I humbly thank you, sir.

CAPTAIN God buy you, sir.

                             [*Exit*

ROSENCRANTZ   Will't please you go, my lord.   30

HAMLET I'll be with you straight. Go a little before.
               [*Exeunt all but* HAMLET
    How all occasions do inform against me,
    And spur my dull revenge. What is a man,
    If the chief good and market of his time
    Be but to sleep and feed? A beast, no more.
    Sure he that made us with such large
    discourse,
    Looking before and after, gave us not
    That capability and godlike reason
    To fust in us unused. Now, whether it be
    Bestial oblivion, or some craven scruple   40
    Of thinking too precisely on th'event –

[46] gross as earth   *as large, obvious as the earth*

[47] mass and charge   *a) numbers and great expense, b) weight (of a cannon ball) and force (of the explosive propelling charge)*

[48] delicate and tender prince   *a prince carefully brought up in delicate or courtly manners, a prince with a proper education*

[49] puffed   *swollen, made great*

[50] Makes mouths   *Makes faces, express defiance*
     invisible event   *unseen consequence, future*

[51] unsure   *uncertain, liable to chance or accident, not knowing the future*

[53] Rightly to be great   *To be truly great in mind or soul*

[54] stir   *move, take action*
     great argument   *many reasons, good cause*

[55] find quarrel in a straw   *accept a straw, or something unimportant, as the reason for action*

[56] honour's at the stake   *honour has been tied to a stake like a bear in bear baiting where it must fight and cannot escape. To be truly great is not to take action only when some important reason or cause of advantage can be found for it, but nobly to find great cause for action in an unimportant or trivial matter which involves one's honour.*

     How stand I, then...?   *What is my situation, how do I bear comparison?*

[57] stained   *defiled, dishonoured*

[58] Excitements   *Causes for moving my mind and passions to action*

[61] fantasy and trick of fame   *imaginary idea and illusion of fame. They have an illusion or 'trick' of fame and so are tricked or deceived by fame into giving up their lives for a 'trick' or trifle.*

[63] the numbers cannot try the cause   *the area fought for is too small even for the whole armies engaged to fight the battle on it. 'Try the cause' is a legal expression meaning conduct or determine the case — the trial in this case is a trial by battle.*

[64] continent   *not sufficient to contain the bodies of those killed*

ACT FOUR, scene 5

[2] importunate   *troublesomely persistent*
    distract   *mad, out of her senses*

A thought which, quartered, hath but one
    part wisdom
And ever three parts coward – I do not know
Why yet I live to say 'This thing's to do'
Sith I have cause, and will, and strength,
    and means,
To do't. Examples gross as earth exhort me:
Witness this army of such mass and charge
Led by a delicate and tender prince
Whose spirit, with divine ambition puffed,
Makes mouths at the invisible event   50
Exposing what is mortal and unsure
To all that fortune, death, and danger, dare,
Even for an egg-shell. Rightly to be great
Is not to stir without great argument,
But greatly to find quarrel in a straw
When honour's at the stake. How stand I, then,
That have a father killed, a mother stained,
Excitements of my reason and my blood,
And let all sleep, while to my shame I see
The imminent death of twenty thousand men   60
That, for a fantasy and trick of fame,
Go to their graves like beds, fight for a plot
Whereon the numbers cannot try the cause,
Which is not tomb enough and continent
To hide the slain? O, from this time forth,
My thoughts be bloody, or be nothing worth.
                                    [Exit

Scene 5. *Enter* QUEEN, HORATIO *and a* GENTLEMAN

QUEEN I will not speak with her.
GENTLEMAN She is importunate, indeed distract.
    Her mood will needs be pitied.
QUEEN   What would she have?
GENTLEMAN She speaks much of her father; says she
    hears

[5] tricks *stratagems, deceitful acts*
　　hems *the sound made in clearing the throat, hesitates,*
stammers

[6] Spurns *Kicks out*
　　enviously *angrily; reacts with scorn and anger to trifles*

[8] unshaped *unarranged, formless*

[9] collection *collect their thoughts, infer, deduce what she means*
　　yawn *gape, are astonished*

[10] botch *patch, fit together crudely*

[11] yield *furnish, produce*

[12] thought *process of rational thought, reason, substance*

[13] unhappily *in unhappy or distressed fashion – or the lines may
mean 'would make one think there might be an interpretation made,
though not a certain one, but a very unfortunate one'*

[15] ill-breeding minds *minds accustomed to produce ill or evil
thoughts*

[18] toy *trifle*
　　amiss *disaster*

[19] artless jealousy *ungovernable suspicion, not controlled or
concealed by art and therefore easily detected*

[20] spills itself . . . spilt *it gives itself away owing to its fear of
detection – or 'spill' may mean destroy*

[25] cockle hat *a hat with a cockle or scallop shell in it as a sign
that its wearer had been on a pilgrimage to the shrine of St James of
Compostella in Spain*
　　staff *pilgrim's staff*

[26] shoon *shoes*
　　*The cockle shell was used for baptism in the early church and
lovers who became love's pilgrims had also to be born again. The
famouse ballad 'Walsingham' bears some resemblance to Ophelia's
song and achieves its unusual tragic effect by the same method of
associating a love song with the imagery of a religious pilgrimage.*

[27] what imports this song? *what does this song mean?*

[28] mark *observe*

There's tricks i'th'world, and hems, and
    beats her heart;
Spurns enviously at straws, speaks things in
    doubt,
That carry but half sense. Her speech is
    nothing,
Yet the unshaped use of it doth move
The hearers to collection. They yawn at it,
And botch the words up fit to their own
    thoughts,   10
Which, as her winks and nods and gestures
    yield them,
Indeed would make one think there might be
    thought,
Though nothing sure, yet much unhappily.
HORATIO 'Twere good she were spoken with; for she
    may strew
Dangerous conjectures in ill-breeding minds.
QUEEN Let her come in.

                      [*Exit* GENTLEMAN
[*Aside*] To my sick soul, as sin's true nature is,
Each toy seems prologue to some great amiss.
So full of artless jealousy is guilt,
It spills itself in fearing to be spilt.   20

Enter OPHELIA *distracted*

OPHELIA Where is the beauteous majesty of Denmark?
QUEEN How now, Ophelia?

She sings

OPHELIA   How should I your true love know
        From another one?
      By his cockle hat and staff,
        And his sandal shoon.
QUEEN Alas, sweet lady, what imports this song?
OPHELIA Say you? Nay, pray you, mark.

[31] turf *a turf for a pillow, a stone on which to rest the feet. Burial customs tend to treat the corpse as somehow alive. The adaptations of these customs can still be seen on Elizabethan tomb sculpture.*

[35] shroud *White was the traditional colour for grave clothes at this time.*

[37] Larded *Covered, strewn*

[38] did not go *The metre requires 'did go'. Ophelia suddenly remembers that her father did not receive these traditional burial rites.*

[41] God dild you *may God reward you*

the owl *bird of Athena/Minerva and therefore a symbol of wisdom*

[41-2] a baker's daughter *a prostitute – another case in which reason panders will (cf. III. 4. 90)*

[43] God be at your table *may God bless the food at your table – may it be a banquet of reason and life like a rite and not a banquet of sense. The reason/passion and sense/sensuality contrasts of the play are painfully present in Ophelia's mad speeches.*

[44] Conceit upon her father *A thought about her father. But Ophelia's song is about a lost love and must remind the audience of Hamlet, father and son, as well as Polonius.*

[47] St Valentine's Day *14 February marks the end of winter and the day that animals and men choose their mates. The custom comes from the pagan festival of the Lupercalia at Rome held in mid-February. The tradition is that a man marries the first girl he sees on St Valentine's morning.*

[52] dupped *did up, opened*

Song

> He is dead and gone, lady,
>> He is dead and gone; 30
> At his head a grass green turf,
>> At his heels a stone.

O, Ho!

Enter KING

QUEEN Nay, but Ophelia –
OPHELIA   Pray you, mark.

Song

> White his shroud as the mountain snow,

QUEEN Alas, look here, my lord.
OPHELIA   Larded with sweet flowers;
>> Which bewept to the grave did not go
>> With true-love showers.

KING How do you, pretty lady? 40
OPHELIA Well, God dild you! They say the owl was a
   baker's daughter. Lord, we know what we are, but
   know not what we may be. God be at your table!
KING Conceit upon her father.
OPHELIA Pray let's have no words of this; but when
   they ask you what it means, say you this:

Song

> Tomorrow is St Valentine's day,
>> All in the morning betime,
> And I a maid at your window,
>> To be your Valentine. 50

> Then up he rose, and donned his clothes,
>> And dupped the chamber door;
> Let in the maid, that out a maid
>> Never departed more.

KING Pretty Ophelia!

[56] without an oath *The ballad she is singing evidently contains blasphemous oaths and Ophelia substitutes 'Gis' and 'Cock' for them.*

[57] Gis *by Jesus! – but the actual name is avoided*

Saint Charity *not a saint, but by saintly, Christian, charity*

[59] do't *copulate*

[60] By Cock *by God. Again the blasphemous word is avoided but another pun on the male sex is introduced.*

[61] tumbled *handled roughly, made love to. The St Valentine's song is about a girl seduced and abandoned, exactly the fate imagined for Ophelia by Polonius and Laertes. Ophelia's insanity is part of the price exacted by the passions of lust and revenge which riot through the court; her songs and speech unite them in a new and chilling combination.*

[67] cannot choose *I have no choice except to weep, cannot help weeping*

[76] single spies *individual scouts*

[77] battalions *large bodies of men in battle formation*

[79] remove *removal to England*

muddied *stirred up, clouded and confused – as mud is stirred up in a well or pool of drinking water*

[80] Thick and unwholesome *carries on the image of water muddied and therefore unfit to drink. The people have unfit thoughts.*

[81] greenly *stupidly – as if without experience*

[82] In hugger-mugger *In hasty, concealed and irregular fashion*

OPHELIA Indeed, la, without an oath, I'll make an end
on't.
    [*Sings*] By Gis, and by Saint Charity,
            Alack, and fie for shame!
        Young men will do't, if they come to't;
            By Cock, they are to blame.   60

        Quoth she 'Before you tumbled me
            You promised me to wed.'
He answers
        'So would I 'a done, by yonder sun,
            An thou hadst not come to my bed.'
KING How long hath she been thus?
OPHELIA I hope all will be well. We must be patient,
but I cannot choose but weep to think they would
lay him i'th'cold ground. My brother shall know of
it – and so I thank you for your good counsel. Come,
my coach! Good night, ladies; good night, sweet   70
ladies, good night, good night.
                                        [*Exit*
KING Follow her close, give her good watch, I pray
you.
                                    [*Exit* HORATIO
        O, this is the poison of deep grief; it springs
        All from her father's death. And now behold –
        O Gertrude, Gertrude!
        When sorrows come, they come not single
            spies
        But in battalions. First, her father slain,
        Next, your son gone, and he most violent
            author
        Of his own just remove. The people muddied,
        Thick and unwholesome in their thoughts
            and whispers   80
        For good Polonius' death. And we have done
            but greenly
        In hugger-mugger to inter him. Poor Ophelia

[84] pictures, or mere beasts *painted images or animals. Claudius agrees with Hamlet that without discourse of reason mankind is a painting or a beast – both vicious*

[85] as much containing   *containing as much trouble or sorrow in itself as all the other causes of sorrow mentioned*

[87] Feeds on   *Increases the growth of*

his wonder   *a) the object of his astonishment – his father's death, b) the result of his father's death – his own growing amazement and hatred*

in clouds   *hidden in clouds – before starting a storm*

[88] wants not   *does not lack*

buzzers   *those who buzz or spread rumours*

[89] pestilent speeches   *poisonous (because untrue) accounts*

[90] necessity   *the necessity of making up rumours*

of matter beggared   *being destitute of facts*

[91] nothing stick   *stops at nothing, even accusing the King*

[93] murdering piece   *cannon loaded with small shot (later called grape-shot) used against infantry at close quarters. It would inflict a number of terrible wounds, each capable of causing death – hence 'superfluous death'.*

[97] Switzers   *royal bodyguard of Swiss mercenaries considered more reliable than national troops. The Pope and the King of France had them. The Danish royal guard was not Swiss but was dressed like them and might be mistaken by travellers for a Swiss guard.*

[99] overpeering   *overflowing*

list   *boundaries*

[100] flats   *mudflats. The image is of the sea breaking dykes and devouring the mudflats behind them.*

impitious   *impetuous*

[101] riotous head   *violent insurrection. 'To make a head' is to advance in opposition against.*

[105] ratifiers and props   *that which makes valid and supports – i.e. antiquity and custom which guarantee every promise or declaration*

Divided from herself and her fair judgement,
Without the which we are pictures, or mere
  beasts.
Last, and as much containing as all these,
Her brother is in secret come from France,
Feeds on his wonder, keeps himself in clouds,
And wants not buzzers to infect his ear
With pestilent speeches of his father's death,
Wherein necessity, of matter beggared,   90
Will nothing stick our person to arraign
In ear and ear. O my dear Gertrude, this,
Like to a murdering piece, in many places
Gives me superfluous death.

A noise within

QUEEN Alack, what noise is this?
KING Attend!

Enter a MESSENGER

Where are my Switzers? Let them guard the
  door.
What is the matter?
MESSENGER   Save yourself, my lord.
The ocean, overpeering of his list,
Eats not the flats with more impitious haste   100
Than young Laertes, in a riotous head,
O'erbears your officers. The rabble call him
  'lord',
And, as the world were now but to begin,
Antiquity forgot, custom not known,
The ratifiers and props of every word,
They cry 'Choose we; Laertes shall be king'.
Caps, hands, and tongues, applaud it to the
  clouds,
'Laertes shall be king, Laertes king'.

A noise within

[110] counter   *Hounds run 'counter' when they follow a scent in the wrong direction – running towards the place the fox or animal has come from instead of pursuing it in its own direction.*

[118] drop . . . bastard   *if one drop of his blood was calm then it would prove that he had not inherited his father's blood and was a bastard*

[120] unsmirched   *clear, pale, unmarked by stain or blot*

[122] giant-like   *gigantic – with the added sense of presumptuous*
[123] fear   *be anxious about*
[124] divinity   *divine power*
      hedge   *guard, secure*
[125] peep   *a) make a small sound compared to what it would like to say, b) scarcely show itself, c) hardly look at what it would like to perform*
[126] Acts little of his will   *Performs only a small part of his (treason's) desires*
[127] Let him go   *Gertrude has interposed herself between Laertes and her husband, risking her own life for his.*

QUEEN How cheerfully on the false trail they cry!
     O, this is counter, you false Danish dogs!   110

Enter LAERTES *with* OTHERS

KING The doors are broke.
LAERTES Where is this King? Sirs, stand you all
     without.
ALL No, let's come in.
LAERTES I pray you, give me leave.
ALL We will, we will

                                 [*Exeunt*
LAERTES I thank you. Keep the door. O thou vile
     King,
     Give me my father.
QUEEN   Calmly, good Laertes.
LAERTES That drop of blood that's calm proclaims
     me bastard,
     Cries cuckold to my father, brands the
     harlot
     Even here, between the chaste unsmirched
     brow   120
     Of my true mother –
KING   What is the cause, Laertes,
     That thy rebellion looks so giant-like?
     Let him go, Gertrude. Do not fear our
     person.
     There's such divinity doth hedge a king
     That treason can but peep to what it would,
     Acts little of his will. Tell me, Laertes,
     Why thou art thus incensed. Let him go,
     Gertrude.
     Speak, man.
LAERTES Where is my father?
KING   Dead.
QUEEN   But not by him.
KING Let him demand his fill.   130

[131] juggled with   *a) deceived, cheated, beguiled by juggling or conjuring, b) used as a ball or other property juggled, manipulated*

[132] allegiance   *sworn loyalty to the King*

[134] dare   *am bold enough to risk, challenge, defy. Laertes is aware that his course of revenge is damnable and accepts it.*

To this point I stand   *I am resolved on this point, principle*

[135] both the worlds   *this world and the world after death*

[137] throughly   *thoroughly*

[138] stay   *hinder, prevent*

will   *my own desires or intention and nothing else, even if all the world attempted to hinder me*

[139] means   *resources*

husband   *cultivate, manage, save*

[141] certainty   *the truth, a proper account*

[143] swoopstake   *sweeping all the stakes off the gambling table, indiscriminately*

[147] kind   *natural*

[148] Repast   *Feed. It was thought that the pelican fed its young by allowing them to drink blood from its own breast.*

[151] most sensibly   *acutely, intensely*

[152] level   *plain*

[155] heat   *the heat of his anger is likely to dry up and paralyse his brain as his melancholy or grief is to burn out with hot tears the power of sight from his eye*

[156] sense and virtue   *power of sense perception and the element of sight*

LAERTES How came he dead? I'll not be juggled with.
　　　　To hell, allegiance! Vows, to the blackest devil!
　　　　Conscience and grace, to the profoundest pit!
　　　　I dare damnation. To this point I stand,
　　　　That both the worlds I give to negligence,
　　　　Let come what comes – only I'll be revenged
　　　　Most throughly for my father.
KING Who shall stay you?
LAERTES　　　　　My will, not all the world's.
　　　　And for my means, I'll husband them so well
　　　　They shall go far with little.
KING　　　　　　　　Good Laertes,　　140
　　　　If you desire to know the certainty
　　　　Of your dear father, is't writ in your revenge
　　　　That, swoopstake, you will draw both friend
　　　　　　and foe,
　　　　Winner and loser?
LAERTES　　　　　None but his enemies.
KING Will you know them, then?
LAERTES To his good friends thus wide I'll ope my
　　　　　　arms
　　　　And, like the kind life-rend'ring pelican,
　　　　Repast them with my blood.
KING　　　　　　　Why, now you speak
　　　　Like a good child and a true gentleman.
　　　　That I am guiltless of your father's death,　　150
　　　　And am most sensibly in grief for it,
　　　　It shall as level to your judgement 'pear
　　　　As day does to your eye.

　　　　　A noise within. 'Let her come in'

LAERTES How now, what noise is that?

　　　　　　Enter OPHELIA

　　　　O heat dry up my brains! Tears seven times
　　　　　　salt
　　　　Burn out the sense and virtue of mine eye.

[157] **paid with weight** *repaid, revenged in large measure.*

[162] **fine** *delicate, refined – the mortal body is made less solid or dense by love and is therefore able to make part of itself immaterial in order to follow the person loved*

[163] **instance** *presence, example, remembrance*

[165] **barefaced** *It was usual for the face of a corpse to be uncovered.*

[172] **wheel** *refrain of the ballad. Ophelia then uses it in its emblematic sense of the wheel of occasion, thrift or opportunity. The false steward who ought to have been thrifty for his master instead seized his opportunity and took his daughter. All the characters she addresses are in one sense false stewards of Denmark.*

[174] **nothing's more than matter** *nonsense has more meaning than sensible matter*

[175] **rosemary** *herb used at weddings and funerals as a symbol of remembrance*

[176] **pansies** *also called heartsease or love-in-idleness. A fanciful application of the Old French 'pensée' connected them with thought and melancholy.*

[179] **fitted** *connected*

[180] **fennel** *symbolic of flattery*

columbines *Its horned shape might suggest a cuckold, or a cuckold-maker who would inevitably use flattery.*

[181] **rue** *the herb of sorrow and repentance.*

[182–3] **you must wear your rue with a difference** *Gertrude must wear the herb of sorrow or repentance with a difference because she has already worn the clothes of sorrow with a difference – casting them off for her marriage with Claudius. Yet rue is the proper flower for her wedding since it will bring her to sorrow and repentance.*

[183] **a daisy** *Daisies and violets go together as flowers of spring and love. Cf. Love's Labour's Lost, V. 2. 881 'When daisies pied and violets blue . . .'*

Ophelia's flower symbolism is very exact since the flowers which she offers, themselves symbolic of the passionate life, distinguish the particular passions of the recipients – flattery and lechery for Claudius, grief and sorrow for Ophelia and Gertrude, the flowers of spring and love for Laertes and Ophelia – but only the daisy is left since death has withered the violets as it has blasted Ophelia herself.

[186] **bonny sweet Robin** *The funeral words suddenly give way to another, lost, fragment of love lyric.*

228

By heaven, thy madness shall be paid with
  weight
Till our scale turn the beam. O rose of May,
Dear maid, kind sister, sweet Ophelia,
O heavens, is't possible a young maid's wits   160
Should be as mortal as an old man's life?
Nature is fine in love; and where 'tis fine
It sends some precious instance of itself
After the thing it loves.

OPHELIA   *Song*

    They bore him barefaced on the bier;
    Hey non nonny, nonny, hey nonny;
    And in his grave rained many a tear –

Fare you well, my dove.

LAERTES Hadst thou thy wits, and didst persuade
  revenge,
  It could not move thus.   170

OPHELIA You must sing 'A-down, a-down', an you
call him a-down-a. O how the wheel becomes it! It
is the false steward, that stole his master's daughter.

LAERTES This nothing's more than matter.

OPHELIA There's rosemary, that's for remembrance.
Pray you, love, remember. And there is pansies,
that's for thoughts.

LAERTES A document in madness – thoughts and remembrance fitted.

OPHELIA There's fennel for you, and columbines. 180
There's rue for you; and here's some for me. We
may call it herb of grace a Sundays. O, you must
wear your rue with a difference. There's a daisy. I
would give you some violets, but they withered all
when my father died. They say he made a good end.
[*Sings*] For bonny sweet Robin is all my joy.

LAERTES Thought and affliction, passion, hell itself
    She turns to favour and to prettiness

[195] flaxen *white*
  poll *head*

[197] cast away *spend time mourning in vain, uselessly*

[201] commune *share, take a part in, participate*

[205] collateral *subordinate, indirect*
[206] touched *implicated – i.e. if the King had a direct or indirect hand in the death of Polonius*

[212] means *way, method*
[213] hatchment *diamond frame on which was painted the family coat of arms. This together with the trophy of funeral armour and the sword formed the achievement erected over important tombs.*
[214] formal ostentation *formal show or ceremony to show in how much honour the dead man was held*

OPHELIA   *Song*

> And will he not come again,
> And will he not come again.   190
>   No, no, he is dead,
>   Go to thy death-bed,
> He never will come again.
>
> His beard was as white as snow,
> All flaxen was his poll.
>   He is gone, he is gone,
>   And we cast away moan:
> God-a-mercy on his soul.

And of all Christian souls, I pray God. God
  buy you.

                             [Exit

LAERTES Do you see this, O God?   200
KING Laertes, I must commune with your grief,
  Or you deny me right. Go but apart,
  Make choice of whom your wisest friends
    you will,
  And they shall hear and judge 'twixt you and
    me.
  If by direct or by collateral hand
  They find us touched, we will our kingdom
    give,
  Our crown, our life, and all that we call
    ours,
  To you in satisfaction; but if not,
  Be you content to lend your patience to us,
  And we shall jointly labour with your soul   210
  To give it due content.
LAERTES   Let this be so.
  His means of death, his obscure funeral –
  No trophy, sword, nor hatchment, o'er his
    bones,
  No noble rite, nor formal ostentation –

[216] call't in question *challenge, examine, cast doubt upon it*
[217] great axe *the axe of execution*

ACT FOUR, scene 6

[1] What are they . . . ? *What kind of men, what profession . . . ?*

[11] let to know *told*

[13] means *means, method of access to*

[15] of very warlike appointment *very well equipped for fighting*

[17] put on a compelled valour *were compelled to adopt a courageous course of action*

grapple *two ships coming together and held by grappling irons – iron hooks attached to ropes or poles*

Cry to be heard, as 'twere from heaven to earth
That I must call't in question.

KING   So you shall,
And where th'offence is, let the great axe fall.
I pray you go with me.

                                [Exeunt

Scene 6. Enter HORATIO *with an* ATTENDANT

HORATIO What are they that would speak with me?
ATTENDANT Sea-faring men, sir. They say they have
   letters for you.
HORATIO Let them come in.

                         [Exit ATTENDANT
I do not know from what part of the world
I should be greeted, if not from Lord Hamlet.

Enter SAILOR

SAILOR God bless you, sir.
HORATIO Let Him bless thee too.
SAILOR He shall, sir, an't please Him. There's a letter
   for you, sir. It came from th'ambassador that was
   bound for England – if your name be Horatio, as I   10
   am let to know it is.

HORATIO   *Reads the Letter*

*Horatio, when thou shalt have overlooked this,
give these fellows some means to the King: they
have letters for him. Ere we were two days old
at sea, a pirate of very warlike appointment gave
us chase. Finding ourselves too slow of sail, we
put on a compelled valour; and in the grapple I
boarded them. On the instant they got clear of
our ship; so I alone became their prisoner. They
have dealt with me like thieves of mercy, but they*   20
*knew what they did, I am to do a good turn for
them. Let the King have the letters I have sent –*

[23] repair   *make your way to me*

[26] light for the bore of the matter   *too light for the calibre of gun which should fire them. Hamlet says that the matter is so explosive (so big a gun) that his words are too small to fit it.*

ACT FOUR, scene 7

[1] my acquittance seal   *confirm my innocence*
[2] put me   *accept me in your heart as a friend*
[3] knowing   *intelligent, perceptive*

[6] feats   *crimes, evil deeds*
[7] capital in nature   *of a kind punishable by death*

[9] stirred up   *roused, provoked*
[10] much unsinewed   *without many sinews, very weak. The King admits his reasons seem weak and draws the audience's attention to the fact that he cannot give his real reasons.*

[14] conjunctive   *closely joined, united. The marriage service describes the couple as 'those whom God hath conjoined'.*
[15] the star   *The star is fixed in its sphere and can only move as the sphere revolves round the earth.*

and repair thou to me with as much speed as thou
wouldest fly death. I have words to speak in thine
ear will make thee dumb; yet they are much too
light for the bore of the matter. These good fellows
will bring thee where I am. Rosencrantz and
Guildenstern hold their course for England; of
them I have much to tell thee. Farewell.

    He that thou knowest thine,

Hamlet. 30

Come, I will give you way for these your
   letters,
And do't the speedier that you may direct me
To him from whom you brought them.

[*Exeunt*

Scene 7. *Enter* KING *and* LAERTES

KING Now must your conscience my acquittance seal,
      And you must put me in your heart for friend,
      Sith you have heard, and with a knowing ear,
      That he which hath your noble father slain
      Pursued my life.

LAERTES   It well appears. But tell me,
      Why you proceeded not against these feats
      So crimeful and so capital in nature,
      As by your safety, wisdom, all thing's else,
      You mainly were stirred up.

KING   O, for two special reasons,
      Which may, perhaps, to you seem much
        unsinewed,   10
      But yet to me th'are strong. The Queen his
        mother
      Lives almost by his looks, and for myself
      (My virtue or my plague, be it either which)
      She is so conjunctive to my life and soul
      That, as the star moves not but in his sphere,
      I could not but by her. The other motive,

[17] count   *account, reckoning, legal indictment and declaration*

[18] general gender   *common race of men, the people*

[21] Convert   *Turn, change*
    gyves   *fetters – the crimes for which fetters are worn*
    graces   *honours, good or pleasing qualities*
    They would convert the fetters into honours and the crimes into good qualities.

[22] timbered   *constructed*
    loud   *strong, noisy, blusterous – conveys the sense of popular protest*

[23] reverted   *returned*

[26] driven   *who has been driven*
    desperate terms   *conditions of the utmost desperation, despair, madness*

[27] if praises may go back again   *if I may praise what she was*

[28] challenger on mount of all the age   *a) like a champion or challenger ready mounted on a horse waiting to do battle with the whole age, b) like a challenger on a mound – as in the coronation of the King of Hungary who stood on the mount of defiance and challenged the world to dispute his title to the crown*

[30] Break not your sleeps   *Lose no sleep over that*

[31] flat   *lacking in energy, stupid*
    dull   *lacking an edge, unintelligent*

[32] beard be shook with danger   *permit danger to shake my beard – danger must be very close to offer so personal an insult as shaking the beard*

[33] pastime   *a game, entertainment*

Why to a public count I might not go,
Is the great love the general gender bear him,
Who, dipping all his faults in their affection,
Work like the spring that turneth wood to
    stone,   20
Convert his gyves to graces. So that my
    arrows,
Too lightly timbered for so loud a wind,
Would have reverted to my bow again,
And not where I have aimed them.

LAERTES And so have I a noble father lost,
A sister driven into desperate terms,
Whose worth, if praises may go back again,
Stood challenger on mount of all the age
For her perfections. But my revenge will come.

KING Break not your sleeps for that. You must not
    think   30
That we are made of stuff so flat and dull
That we can let our beard be shook with
    danger,
And think it pastime. You shortly shall hear
    more.
I loved your father, and we love ourself,
And that, I hope, will teach you to imagine –

Enter a MESSENGER *with letters*

How now, what news?

MESSENGER Letters, my lord, from Hamlet:
These to your Majesty, this to the Queen.

KING From Hamlet? Who brought them?

MESSENGER Sailors, my lord, they say. I saw them not. 40
They were given me by Claudio, he received
    them
Of him that brought them.

KING   Laertes, you shall hear them.
Leave us.

                        [*Exit* MESSENGER

[44] naked   a) *without clothing,* b) *destitute of means or atten-dants,* c) *without concealment. The letter is ambiguous and ironically insulting.*

[50] abuse   *imposture, deceit, delusion*

[54] devise me   *resolve or guess for me what it means*
[55] lost   *bewildered, overwhelmed*

[60] ruled   *governed, guided*
[61] o'errule me to a peace   *command me, persuade me to reach a peaceful solution or agreement*
[63] checking at   *recoiling from, backing off from*

[65] ripe in my device   *ready in my invention, contriving mind*

[68] uncharge the practice   *acquit the plot of any evil intent*

[70] The rather   *More easily, readily*
[71] organ   *instrument*

[*Reads*] *High and Mighty. You shall know I am set naked*
    on your kingdom. Tomorrow shall I beg leave to
    see your kingly eyes; when I shall – first asking
    your pardon thereunto – recount the occasion of
    my sudden and more strange return.

                                   Hamlet.

    What should this mean? Are all the rest come
      back?
    Or is it some abuse and no such thing?   50
LAERTES Know you the hand?
KING 'Tis Hamlet's character. 'Naked'?
    And in a postscript here, he says, 'alone'.
    Can you devise me?
LAERTES I am lost in it, my lord. But let him come;
    It warms the very sickness in my heart
    That I shall live and tell him to his teeth,
    'Thus didest thou'.
KING   If it be so, Laertes –
    As how should it be so, how otherwise? –
    Will you be ruled by me?
LAERTES   Ay, my lord;   60
    So you will not o'errule me to a peace.
KING To thine own peace. If he be now returned,
    As checking at his voyage, and that he means
    No more to undertake it, I will work him
    To an exploit now ripe in my device,
    Under the which he shall not choose but fall;
    And for his death, no wind of blame shall
      breathe
    But even his mother shall uncharge the practice
    And call it accident.
LAERTES   My lord, I will be ruled;
    The rather if you could devise it so   70
    That I might be the organ.
KING   It falls right.
    You have been talked of since your travel
      much,

[74] sum of parts   *whole character and accomplishments*

[77] siege   *seat, and hence rank*
[78] riband in the cap ot youth   *ribbon, hence adornment suitable for youth*
[79] becomes   *suits*
[80] livery   *clothes*
[81] sables and his weeds   *furs and dark clothing*
[82] health and graveness   *mental or moral soundness or well-being and serious purpose*

[85] can well   *can perform well, ride well*

[88] incorpsed and demi-natured   *shared the horse's body and half its mind and spirit, been a centaur (half-man, half-horse)*
[89] brave   *splendid*
     topped my thought   *exceeded my expectation*
[90] forgery of shapes and tricks   *in imagining manoeuvres and tricks*
[93] Upon my life, Lamord   *The half-horse Norman, whom Laertes wagers his life on, also seems to be called 'Death'.*

[95–6] brooch indeed and gem   *chiefest and most precious ornament of*

[97] made confession of you   *acknowledged your character, brought it to attention with praise*
[99] art and exercise in your defence   *theory and practice of swordsmanship*
[100] rapier   *not the modern fencing foil but a light sword with double-edged blade and a sharp point*
[102] scrimers   *fencers, fencing masters*

And that in Hamlet's hearing, for a quality
Wherein they say you shine. Your sum of parts
Did not together pluck such envy from him
As did that one; and that, in my regard,
Of the unworthiest siege.

LAERTES   What part is that, my lord?

KING A very riband in the cap of youth,
Yet needful too, for youth no less becomes
The light and careless livery that it wears   80
Than settled age his sables and his weeds,
Importing health and graveness. Two months
    since
Here was a gentleman of Normandy.
I have seen myself, and served against, the
    French,
And they can well on horseback; but this
    gallant
Had witchcraft in't. He grew unto his seat,
And to such wondrous doing brought his horse,
As he had been incorpsed and demi-natured
With the brave beast. So far he topped my
    thought
That I, in forgery of shapes and tricks,   90
Come short of what he did.

LAERTES   A Norman was't?

KING A Norman.

LAERTES Upon my life, Lamord.

KING The very same.

LAERTES I know him well. He is the brooch indeed
And gem of all the nation.

KING He made confession of you
And gave you such a masterly report
For art and exercise in your defence,
And for your rapier most especial,   100
That he cried out 'twould be a sight indeed
If one could match you. The scrimers of
    their nation

[103] motion   *fencing stroke, position*

[105] envenom   *inflame*

[107] play   *engage in a fencing bout*

[110] painting of a sorrow   *This is the third time that Claudius has used the metaphor of painting for the contrast between the actions that a man might play and that which passes show.*

[113] love is begun by time   *the growth of love depends on time. In art and mythology, Venus goddess of love gave her son Cupid to Time to be brought up. Cf. the ceiling painted by Tiepolo, at the National Gallery, London.*

[114] passages of proof   *incidents which make good or prove, provide evidence for my opinion*

[115] qualifies   *moderates, reduces*

[117] A kind of wick or snuff   *Love is like a candle flame. It depends upon the wick to burn but the higher and brighter it burns the faster it uses up the wick and turns it into a burnt substance called snuff which, unless it is removed, is liable to put the flame out.*

abate   *make less, lower*

[119] pleurisy   *superabundance, excess*

[120] too much   *The fatal lung disease of pleurisy was thought to be caused by too much of the humour of blood.*

would do   *wish to do, intend*

[121] should do when we would   *ought to perform when we first desire it*

[123] are tongues . . . accidents   *every speech, action or chance event may delay or lessen the acting of a desire*

[124] spendthrift's sigh   *A sigh was supposed to drain the blood and harm the vital qualities. A person who sighed thus eased himself of pain but was a spendthrift of his own health and strength.*

[125] the quick of th'ulcer   *central, most tender part of the ulcer, most important part of this sore event*

[128] i'th'church   *This would be sacrilege and Laertes would certainly risk damnation for it.*

[129] sanctuarize   *give sanctuary, safety, mercy to. Murderers or other offenders could claim sanctuary at the altars of certain churches and be immune from arrest or punishment as long as they remained there. It is important that Claudius should declare that there are no limits to revenge and Laertes be prepared to violate sanctuary in order to achieve it. These are the ethics of blood revenge.*

He swore had neither motion, guard, nor eye,
If you opposed them. Sir, this report of his
Did Hamlet so envenom with his envy
That he could nothing do but wish and beg
Your sudden coming o'er, to play with you.
Now out of this –

LAERTES   What out of this, my lord?

KING Laertes, was your father dear to you?
    Or are you like the painting of a sorrow,   110
    A face without a heart?

LAERTES   Why ask you this?

KING Not that I think you did not love your father –
    But that I know love is begun by time,
    And that I see, in passages of proof,
    Time qualifies the spark and fire of it.
    There lives within the very flame of love
    A kind of wick or snuff that will abate it,
    And nothing is at a like goodness still,
    For goodness, growing to a pleurisy,
    Dies in his own too much. That we would
      do,   120
    We should do when we would, for this
      'would' changes
    And hath abatements and delays as many
    As there are tongues, are hands, are accidents;
    And then this 'should' is like a spendthrift's
      sigh
    That hurts by easing. But to the quick of
      th'ulcer:
    Hamlet comes back. What would you
      undertake
    To show yourself in deed your father's son
    More than in words?

LAERTES   To cut his throat i'th'church.

KING No place, indeed, should murder sanctuarize,
    Revenge should have no bounds. But, good
    Laertes,   130

[131] Keep close *Remain concealed*

[133] put on those *incite, impel some people to*

[135] in fine *in conclusion*

[136] remiss *careless, negligent*

[137] Most generous *Very magnanimous, high-spirited, courageous*

free from all contriving *free from all plotting*

[138] peruse *examine*

[139] shuffling *mixing, jumbling, changing the positions*

[140] unbated *not blunted, sharp. It was usual to bate or blunt the edges and points of rapiers used for practice.*

pass of practice *a) a practice bout, exercise, sporting engagement, b) a stratagem, plot, trick*

[143] unction *oil, ointment (see also note to line 162)*

mountebank *an unlicensed doctor or chemist, part conjuror, part charlatan and associated with illegal medicine of all kinds*

[145] cataplasm *a poultice, plaster*

rare *unusually excellent*

[146] simples *natural or organic medicinal remedies composed of a single substance*

[149] contagion *spreading poison*

gall *hurt, scratch*

[152] shape *arrangement, theatrical part, impersonation*

[153] drift *aim, intention – also the amount of deflection that a cannoneer has to allow for in sighting his cannon*

[155] back or second *a second (gun) to back up the first*

[156] blast in proof *blow up during test firing. All cannons had to be fired by their makers the first time in case they exploded under pressure.*

244

Will you do this? Keep close within your
    chamber.
Hamlet returned shall know you are come
    home.
We'll put on those shall praise your
    excellence,
And set a double varnish on the fame
The Frenchman gave you – bring you, in
    fine, together,
And wager on your heads. He, being remiss,
Most generous, and free from all contriving,
Will not peruse the foils. So that with ease
Or with a little shuffling, you may choose
A sword unbated, and, in a pass of practice,   140
Requite him for your father.
LAERTES   I will do't,
And for that purpose I'll anoint my sword.
I bought an unction of a mountebank,
So mortal that but dip a knife in it,
Where it draws blood no cataplasm so rare,
Collected from all simples that have virtue
Under the moon, can save the thing from
    death
That is but scratched withal. I'll touch my
    point
With this contagion, that, if I gall him slightly,
It may be death.
KING   Let's further think of this,   150
Weigh what convenience both of time and
    means
May fit us to our shape. If this should fail,
And that our drift look through our bad
    performance,
'Twere better not assayed. Therefore this
    project
Should have a back or second that might hold
If this did blast in proof. Soft, let me see.

[161] **preferred him**   *offered to him*

[162] **chalice for the nonce**   *a drinking cup or goblet for this occasion. As Laertes uses an 'unction' associated with the mass for poisoning, so Claudius now proposes to use a 'chalice' or religious cup.*

[163] **venomed stuck**   *poisoned stroke*

[168] **aslant**   *overhanging*

[169] **hoar**   *grey. The underside of willow leaves is silver white.*

[171] **crow-flowers**   *also called 'fair maid of France'. The symbolism here is thought to be 'crow-flowers' – a fair maid, 'nettles' – stung to the quick, 'daisies' – in her maiden bloom, 'long purples' – touched by the cold fingers of death.*

[172] **liberal**   *coarse obscene*
     grosser name   *more obscene name*

[174] **coronet weeds**   *crown of flowers*

[175] **envious**   *malicious*
     sliver   *small sprout, twig*

[179] **snatches**   *parts*
     old lauds   *old psalms, hymns*

[180] **incapable**   *ignorant, unaware*

[181] **native**   *belonging, born to*
     indued   *brought up in, educated to*

We'll make a solemn wager on your cunnings –
I ha't.
When in your motion you are hot and dry
(As make your bouts more violent to that end)   160
And that he calls for drink, I'll have
     preferred him
A chalice for the nonce, whereon but sipping,
If he by chance escape your venomed stuck,
Our purpose may hold there. But stay, what
     noise?

Enter QUEEN

QUEEN One woe doth tread upon another's heel
          So fast they follow. Your sister's drowned
               Laertes.
LAERTES Drowned! O, where?
QUEEN There is a willow grows aslant the brook
          That shows his hoar leaves in the glassy stream.
          Therewith fantastic garlands did she make   170
          Of crow-flowers, nettles, daisies, and long
               purples
          That liberal shepherds give a grosser name,
          But our cold maids do dead men's fingers
               call them.
          There, on the pendant boughs her coronet
               weeds
          Clamb'ring to hang, an envious sliver broke,
          When down her weedy trophies and herself
          Fell in the weeping brook. Her clothes spread
               wide
          And, mermaid-like, awhile they bore her up,
          Which time she chanted snatches of old lauds,
          As one incapable of her own distress,   180
          Or like a creature native and indued
          Unto that element. But long it could not be
          Till that her garments, heavy with their drink,

[189] trick   *habit, custom*

[190–1] When these...out   *When these tears are over this female passion will have left me*

[192] fain   *eagerly gladly*

[193] douts it   *extinguishes it, puts it out*

      Pulled the poor wretch from her melodious lay
      To muddy death.

LAERTES   Alas, then she is drowned?

QUEEN Drowned, drowned.

LAERTES Too much of water hast thou, poor Ophelia,
      And therefore I forbid my tears. But yet
      It is our trick. Nature her custom holds,
      Let shame say what it will. When these are
        gone   190
      The woman will be out. Adieu, my lord.
      I have a speech o'fire that fain would blaze
      But that this folly douts it.

                                      [*Exit*

KING   Let's follow, Gertrude.
      How much I had to do to calm his rage.
      Now fear I this will give it start again;
      Therefore let's follow.

                                    [*Exeunt*

ACT FIVE, scene 1

[1] buried in Christian burial *given a Christian burial in con-secrated ground*

[2] wilfully *in self-willed fashion, passionately, contrary to reason*

seeks her own salvation *seeks the saving of her soul in heaven by killing herself*

[4] straight *straight away, immediately*

crowner hath sat on her *the coroner's court has sat to consider her case and its verdict is . . . A coroner is a legal official who holds an inquiry on the bodies of those who die by violence or accident.*

[7–9] in her own defence . . . 'se offendendo' *The legal point involved has been best explained by W. L. Rushton: 'It seems that Shakespeare has made the first clown confound a "felo de se", or one who is guilty of self-murder, with a person who commits homicide "se defendendo", in his own defence, or, as he miscalls it "se offend-endo" . . . his reasoning, although it may appear absurd, is good law for he evidently means, that if the water comes to a man and drowns him, not wittingly, but against his inclination, he is as innocent of suicide as that man is innocent of murder who, "se defendendo", in his own defence, kills another who, "felleo animo" (with angry or evil intent), presses upon him'.*

[11] an act, and an act hath three branches *Shakespeare appears to be using the example of the case of Hales v. Petit (1561) where the verdict of suicide on Sir James Hales was contested by his widow since the estate of suicides was forfeit to the crown. In this suit Serjeant Walsh divided an act into three parts: the imagination, the resolution and the perfection or execution. The point is whether it was Ophelia's intention to kill herself or not. If it was her intention and she did not perform it she would be innocent. If she performed it but had no evil intention she would be equally innocent. Only if she performed it with the intention of suicide would she be guilty.*

[12] Argal *for Latin 'ergo', therefore*

[13] wittingly *knowingly, intentionally*

[14] Goodman Delver *good master digger*

[15] leave *leave to speak, let me continue*

[17] will he, nill he *willingly or unwillingly*

[23] quest *inquest*

[28] countenance *permission, approval*

[29–30] even Christen *equally Christian fellows*

[32] hold up *support, continue*

ACT FIVE

Scene 1. *Enter two* CLOWNS

CLOWN Is she to be buried in Christian burial when she wilfully seeks her own salvation?

OTHER I tell thee she is. Therefore make her grave straight. The crowner hath sat on her, and finds it Christian burial.

CLOWN How can that be, unless she drowned herself in her own defence?

OTHER Why, 'tis found so.

CLOWN It must be *se offendendo*, it cannot be else. For here lies the point: if I drown myself wittingly, it argues an act, and an act hath three branches – it is to act, to do, to perform. Argal, she drowned herself wittingly.

OTHER Nay, but hear you, Goodman Delver.

CLOWN Give me leave. Here lies the water; good. Here stands the man; good. If the man go to this water and drown himself, it is, will he, nill he, he goes – mark you that; but if the water come to him and drown him, he drowns not himself. Argal, he that is not guilty of his own death shortens not his own life.

OTHER But is this law?

CLOWN Ay, marry is't; crowner's quest law.

OTHER Will you ha the truth on't? If this had not been a gentlewoman, she should have been buried out of Christian burial.

CLOWN Why, there thou say'st. And the more pity that great folk should have countenance in this world to drown or hang themselves more than their even Christen. Come, my spade. There is no ancient gentlemen but gard'ners, ditchers, and gravemakers. They hold up Adam's profession.

OTHER Was he a gentleman?

[34] bore arms   *a) had a coat of arms, b) possessed the physical parts of the body*

[40] confess thyself   *make your confession of sins. The phrase normally continues ' and be hanged'.*

[41] Go to   *a shortened and therefore more polite form of 'go to the devil'*

[47] does well   *a) fits the riddle well, b) fits, is a suitable punishment for evil doers*

[50] To't   *Go to it, try, proceed*

[53] unyoke   *cease from labour (of thinking about it)*

[54] Marry   *To be sure, originally, 'By the Virgin Mary'*

[56] Mass   *By the mass*

[57] Cudgel   *Beat, drive your brains*

[58] mend his pace   *increase his pace, go faster*

[61] Yaughan   *presumably an innkeeper. If a joke or topical allusion was connected with the name, it has been lost.*

[63] In youth   *This song is an adaptation of a poem in Tottel's Miscellany (1557) now attributed to Thomas Lord Vaux which begins 'I loathe that I did love/In youth that I thought sweet'. The Clown transforms a song about death and the leaving of life into one that unites love and death in its imagery – like the graveyard scene itself.*

CLOWN He was the first that ever bore arms.

OTHER Why, he had none.

CLOWN What, art a heathen? How dost thou understand the Scripture? The Scripture says Adam
digged. Could he dig without arms? I'll put another
question to thee. If thou answerest me not to the
purpose confess thyself – 40

OTHER Go to.

CLOWN What is he that builds stronger than either
the mason, the shipwright, or the carpenter?

OTHER The gallows-maker – for that frame outlives a
thousand tenants.

CLOWN I like thy wit well. In good faith, the gallows
does well. But how does it well? It does well to
those that do ill. Now thou dost ill to say the gallows is built stronger than the church; argal, the
gallows may do well to thee. To't again, come. 50

OTHER Who builds stronger than a mason, a shipwright, or a carpenter?

CLOWN Ay, tell me that, and unyoke.

OTHER Marry, now I can tell.

CLOWN To't.

OTHER Mass, I cannot tell.

Enter HAMLET *and* HORATIO *afar off*

CLOWN Cudgel thy brains no more about it, for your
dull ass will not mend his pace with beating; and
when you are asked this question next, say 'a grave-
maker' – the houses he makes lasts till doomsday. 60
Go, get thee to Yaughan; fetch me a stoup of
liquor.

[*Exit* OTHER

Song

In youth when I did love, did love,
    Methought it was very sweet,
To contract o the time for a my behove,
    O methought there a was nothing a meet.

253

[69] a property of easiness   *something that belongs to carelessness or indifference, hence, a matter of indifference*

[71] daintier sense   *more delicate, fastidious, sense of touch*

[76-7] could sing once   *and by singing show that its owner was part of the harmony of nature—cf. Hamlet with the recorders*

[77] jowls   *strikes, knocks it to the ground (used especially of hitting the head against something)*

[78] Cain's jawbone   *Cain was traditionally supposed to have used an ass's jawbone (presumably transferred from the Samson story) to murder his brother Abel.*

[79] pate   *head, skull*
politician   *cunning schemer, intelligent manipulator*

[80] o'erreaches   *has the advantage over. Overreaching in the sense of outwit, get the better of, was the business of politicians.*
One   *A politician*
circumvent   *get round, cheat, deceive*

[89] chapless   *without the lower jaw*
mazzard   *head*

[90] revolution   *complete change of circumstance*

[91] trick   *art*

[90-1] cost no more the breeding   *cost no more time, trouble and expense to bring up*

[92] loggats   *a game on which money could be wagered played with pieces of wood thrown as close to a jack as possible*

HAMLET Has this fellow no feeling of his business,
that he sings at grave-making?

HORATIO Custom hath made it in him a property of
easiness.

HAMLET 'Tis e'en so. The hand of little employment   70
hath the daintier sense.

CLOWN

[*Sings*] But age, with his stealing steps,
      Hath clawed me in his clutch,
     And hath shipped me into the land,
      As if I had never been such.

Throws up a skull

HAMLET That skull had a tongue in it, and could sing
once. How the knave jowls it to the ground, as if it
were Cain's jawbone, that did the first murder. This
might be the pate of a politician, which this ass now
o'erreaches. One that would circumvent God, might   80
it not?

HORATIO It might, my lord.

HAMLET Or of a courtier: which could say, 'Good
morrow, sweet lord. How dost thou, sweet lord?'
This might be my Lord Such-a-one, that praised
my Lord Such-a-one's horse, when he meant to beg
it – might it not?

HORATIO Ay, my lord.

HAMLET Why, e'en so; and now my Lady Worm's –
chapless, and knocked about the mazzard with a
sexton's spade. Here's fine revolution, an we had   90
the trick to see't. Did these bones cost no more the
breeding but to play at loggats with them? Mine
ache to think on't.

CLOWN

[*Sings*] A pickaxe and a spade, a spade,
      For and a shrouding sheet,
    O a pit of clay for to be made,
      For such a guest is meet.

[99] quiddities *subtle distinctions*

[100] quillets *refined differentiations of meaning*

 cases *law cases*

 tenures *cases concerned with the occupation of property*

 tricks *legal skill – sometimes associated with sharp practice*

[102] sconce *head*

[103] action of battery *civil action for the use of unlawful violence*

[105] statutes *security for money affecting property, a bond by which the creditor could hold the debtor's land in case of default*

 recognizances *bond or legal obligation to observe certain conditions with a sum of money forfeited if they are not observed*

 fines *the compromise of a fictitious suit for the possession of land used as a means of transfering property which was in some way restricted, to descendants, for example*

[105–6] double vouchers *Two witnesses were required to vouch for or guarantee a transfer by a fine.*

[106] recoveries *the process by which a man buying an estate was protected from future actions for recovery by the descendants of the original owner*

[106–8] Is this the fine of his fines . . . dirt? *Is this the end of his fines and what he regains from his recoveries to have his handsome head filled with the last dirt that will ever occupy it? Implying, as W. L. Rushton points out, that his head has been filled with dirt for some time.*

[110] a pair of indentures *an agreement drawn up on a pair of identical documents so that each party can keep a copy. They were originally divided in such a way that only if they fitted exactly were they regarded as genuine. The indentures now purchased are the crooked or indented winding sheets.*

[111] conveyances *documents which show his title and purchase*

[117] assurance *a) legal evidence of the transfer of property, b) confidence, guarantee. There can be no guarantee of property or possessions since death removes the possessor. The activities of the politician, who gains property by stratagem, the courtier who obtains it by flattery, and the lawyer, who obtains it by legal manipulation, are all frustrated by death.*

[123] liest *tell lies, falsehoods*

[124] lie *a) remain inactive, idle, b) speak a lie*

[125] lie *a) lie like a dead body, b) speak a lie*

[127] quick *living*

[129] quick *rapid, acute, vigorous*

Throws up another skull

HAMLET There's another. Why may not that be the
skull of a lawyer. Where be his quiddities now, his
quillets, his cases, his tenures, and his tricks? Why 100
does he suffer this rude knave now to knock him
about the sconce with a dirty shovel, and will not
tell him of his action of battery? Hum, this fellow
might be in's time a great buyer of land, with his
statutes, his recognizances, his fines, his double
vouchers, his recoveries. Is this the fine of his fines,
and the recovery of his recoveries, to have his fine
pate full of fine dirt? Will his vouchers vouch him
no more of his purchases, and double ones too, than
the length and breadth of a pair of indentures? The 110
very conveyances of his lands will scarcely lie in this
box; and must th'inheritor himself have no more,
ha?

HORATIO Not a jot more, my lord.

HAMLET Is not parchment made of sheep-skins?

HORATIO Ay, my lord, and of calves' skins too.

HAMLET They are sheep and calves which seek out
assurance in that. I will speak to this fellow. Whose
grave's this, sirrah?

CLOWN Mine, sir. 120

[*Sings*] O, a pit of clay for to be made,
For such a guest is meet.

HAMLET I think it be thine indeed, for thou liest in't.

CLOWN You lie out on't, sir, and therefore 'tis not
yours. For my part, I do not lie in't, yet it is mine.

HAMLET Thou dost lie in't, to be in't and say it is
thine. 'Tis for the dead, not for the quick. Therefore thou liest.

CLOWN 'Tis a quick lie, sir; 'twill away again from me
to you. 130

HAMLET What man dost thou dig it for?

[138] absolute   *treats words in their absolute state – literally, without reference to the context*

[138–9] by the card   *according to the compass – be as accurate in our words as if we followed their meaning by a mariner's compass*

[139] equivocation   *the double meanings, ambiguity, of words will destroy us. Answering in a double sense was thought to be the particular practice of the Jesuit missionaries in England.*

[141] picked   *select, refined, fastidious*

[142–3] galls his kibe   *rubs, irritates the sore spot at the back of his heel. Peasants and courtiers are becoming indistinguishable in intellect and manners.*

[160] ground   *reason, occasion*

[162] thirty years   *so that Hamlet ought to be thirty years old*

[165] pocky   *infected with venereal disease – which had become more virulent and was on the increase throughout Europe*

[166] hold the laying in   *hold together without decaying during the period the body is kept before burial*

　　　　laying in   *storage*

[167] tanner   *treater of skins to convert them into leather*

CLOWN For no man, sir.

HAMLET What woman, then?

CLOWN For none neither.

HAMLET Who is to be buried in't?

CLOWN One that was a woman, sir; but, rest her soul, she's dead.

HAMLET How absolute the knave is. We must speak by the card or equivocation will undo us. By the Lord, Horatio, this three years I have took note of it: the age is grown so picked that the toe of the peasant comes so near the heel of the courtier, he galls his kibe. How long hast thou been a grave-maker? 140

CLOWN Of all the days i'th'year, I came to't that day that our last King Hamlet overcame Fortinbras.

HAMLET How long is that since?

CLOWN Cannot you tell that? Every fool can tell that. It was that very day that young Hamlet was born – he that is mad, and sent into England.

HAMLET Ay, marry, why was he sent into England? 150

CLOWN Why, because he was mad. He shall recover his wits there; or, if he do not, 'tis no great matter there.

HAMLET Why?

CLOWN 'Twill not be seen in him there. There the men are as mad as he.

HAMLET How came he mad?

CLOWN Very strangely, they say.

HAMLET How strangely?

CLOWN Faith, e'en with losing his wits.

HAMLET Upon what ground? 160

CLOWN Why, here in Denmark. I have been sexton here, man and boy, thirty years.

HAMLET How long will a man lie i'th'earth ere he rot?

CLOWN Faith, if he be not rotten before he die (as we have many pocky corses now-a-days that will scarce hold the laying in) he will last you some eight year or nine year. A tanner will last you nine year.

HAMLET Why he more than another.

[171] sore   *great, excessive*
   whoreson   *son of a whore – a mild swear word*

[179] Rhenish   *wine from the vineyards of the Rhine*

[187] gorge   *the contents of the stomach – I feel sick*

[189] gibes   *rough jokes, sarcasms*
   gambols   *antics*

[192] chap-fallen   *a) with the lower jaw hanging down, dejected, dispirited, out of countenance, b) with the lower jaw fallen off, dead*
[194] favour   *appearance, beauty*

[197] Alexander   *Alexander the Great, King of Macedon (356–323 B.C.) who conquered the then known world, was an image of imperial power for the Renaissance.*

[204] bung hole   *hole in the bulge of a barrel through which it is filled and usually stopped with a cork or clay*

CLOWN Why, sir, his hide is so tanned with his trade
that he will keep out water a great while – and your 170
water is a sore decayer of your whoreson dead body.
Here's a skull now. This skull has lien you i'th'earth
three and twenty years.

HAMLET Whose was it?

CLOWN A whoreson mad fellow's it was. Whose do
you think it was?

HAMLET Nay, I know not.

CLOWN A pestilence on him for a mad rogue! He
poured a flagon of Rhenish on my head once. This
same skull, sir, was, sir, Yorick's skull, the King's 180
jester.

HAMLET This?

CLOWN E'en that.

HAMLET Let me see. Alas, poor Yorick. I knew him,
Horatio: a fellow of infinite jest, of most excellent
fancy; he hath borne me on his back a thousand
times. And now how abhorred in my imagination it
is. My gorge rises at it. Here hung those lips that I
have kissed I know not how oft. Where be your
gibes now, your gambols, your songs, your flashes
of merriment that were wont to set the table on a 190
roar? Not one now to mock your own grinning –
quite chap-fallen? Now get you to my lady's chamber, and tell her, let her paint an inch thick, to this
favour she must come. Make her laugh at that.
Prithee, Horatio, tell me one thing.

HORATIO What's that, my lord?

HAMLET Dost thou think Alexander looked o'this
fashion i'th'earth?

HORATIO E'en so.

HAMLET And smelt so? Pah! 200

HORATIO E'en so, my lord.

HAMLET To what base uses we may return, Horatio.
Why may not imagination trace the noble dust of
Alexander till he find it stopping a bung hole?

261

[205] too curiously   *too minutely, strangely, inquisitively*

[208] modesty enough   *sufficient freedom from exaggeration, excess*

   likelihood   *probability*

[216] flaw   *squall, gust of wind*

[219] maimèd rites   *mutilated, incomplete ceremony*
[220] desperate   *a) despairing, b) violent*
[221] Fordo   *Destroy*
   estate   *rank, importance*
[226] obsequies   *funeral rites and ceremonies*
   enlarged   *extended*
[227] warranty   *justifying reason, grounds*
   doubtful   *involved in doubt and uncertainty, of a questionable nature. It was uncertain whether she killed herself or not.*
[228] great command   *powerful command – powerful because it comes from a great man, the King*
   o'ersways   *overcomes, changes by superior authority*
   the order   *order, form, of burial suitable to such a case*
[230] last trumpet   *In the Revelation of St John the day of judgement is preceded by seven angels blowing seven trumpets.*
[231] Shards   *Pieces of broken pottery*
[232] crants   *garlands, crowns – either on the coffin or hung in church as a sign that as a virgin she would be crowned in heaven*
[233] maiden strewments   *flowers symbolising virginity decorating the coffin*
   bringing home   *The tolling bell and the burial rites announce that she has arrived at her last home or long home, the grave.*

HORATIO 'Twere to consider too curiously to consider
so.

HAMLET No, faith, not a jot – but to follow him thither
with modesty enough, and likelihood to lead it, as
thus: Alexander died, Alexander was buried,
Alexander returneth to dust; the dust is earth, of 210
earth we make loam, and why of that loam whereto
he was converted might they not stop a beer-barrel?
Imperious Caesar, dead and turned to clay,
Might stop a hole to keep the wind away.
O that this earth which kept the world in awe
Should patch a wall t'expel the winter's flaw –
But soft, but soft awhile. Here comes the King,

Enter KING, QUEEN, LAERTES *and a coffin, with*
LORDS ATTENDANT

    The Queen, the courtiers. Who is this they
      follow,
    And with such maimèd rites? This doth
      betoken
    The corse they follow did with desperate hand 220
    Fordo it own life. 'Twas of some estate.
    Couch we awhile and mark.

LAERTES What ceremony else?

HAMLET That is Laertes, a very noble youth. Mark.

LAERTES What ceremony else?

PRIEST Her obsequies have been as far enlarged
    As we have warranty. Her death was doubtful,
    And, but that great command o'ersways the
      order,
    She should in ground unsanctified have lodged
    Till the last trumpet. For charitable prayers, 230
    Shards, flints, and pebbles, should be thrown
      on her
    Yet here she is allowed her virgin crants,
    Her maiden strewments, and the bringing
      home

[236] profane .desecrate, treat with unholy contempt

[237] sage requiem   a solemn requiem mass sung for the souls of the dead that they may rest in peace

[238] peace-parted souls   souls which leave their bodies having made their peace with God

[240] violets   the flowers of love, faithfulness and spring
          churlish   uncharitable

[241] minist'ring   giving aid, charitable

[242] howling   in the torments of hell

[243] Sweets to the sweet   The Queen clearly strews flowers in the grave.

[245] decked   adorned. The bridal bed was traditionally decorated for the first night of marriage.

[248] ingenious sense   noble and intelligent reason

[251] quick   living

[252] flat   flat area, plain

[253] Pelion   In Greek mythology the race of Giants piled the mountain Pelion upon Ossa in order to reach Olympus and cast Zeus from his throne.

[254] Olympus   in Greek mythology the home of the sky gods whose ruler was Zeus

[255] emphasis   intensity of force or feeling – a term of rhetoric meaning that more is implied by words than is actually said
          phrase of sorrow   particular way of speaking, uttering, his sorrow

[256] Conjures   Charm, bewitch by incantation. His language is so powerful that it causes the planets to stop and listen.
          wand'ring stars   the planets

[257] wonder-wounded   struck with wonder, astonishment

[258] Hamlet the Dane   Hamlet from Denmark. But this is also the royal title, Hamlet, King of Denmark

Of bell and burial.

LAERTES Must there no more be done?

PRIEST   No more be done.
We should profane the service of the dead
To sing sage requiem and such rest to her
As to peace-parted souls.

LAERTES   Lay her i'th'earth,
And from her fair and unpolluted flesh
May violets spring. I tell thee, churlish priest, 240
A minist'ring angel shall my sister be
When thou liest howling.

HAMLET   What – the fair Ophelia?

QUEEN Sweets to the sweet – farewell!
I hoped thou shouldst have been my Hamlet's
 wife.
I thought thy bride bed to have decked, sweet
 maid,
And not have strewed thy grave.

LAERTES   O, treble woe
Fall ten times treble on that cursed head
Whose wicked deed thy most ingenious sense
Deprived thee of! Hold off the earth awhile
Till I have caught her once more in my arms. 250

Leaps in the grave

Now pile your dust upon the quick and dead,
Till of this flat a mountain you have made
T'o'ertop old Pelion or the skyish head
Of blue Olympus.

HAMLET   What is he whose grief
Bears such an emphasis, whose phrase of
 sorrow
Conjures the wand'ring stars, and makes
 them stand
Like wonder-wounded hearers? This is I,
Hamlet the Dane.

LAERTES The devil take thy soul!

[261] splenative *given to fits of anger*
   rash *hasty*

[268] theme *subject – their love for Ophelia*
[269] wag *open and shut – until he is dead*

[275] forbear *have patience with him, show indulgence, refrain from injuring him*
[276] 'Swounds *By Christ's wounds!*
[278] eisel *vinegar. The drinking of vinegar was thought to induce melancholy.*

   eat a crocodile *The crocodile was thought to shed tears as it ate its victims. Crocodile tears are thus hypocritical and Laertes is accused of hypocrisy in this oblique fashion – Hamlet considers his grief a show that a man might play.*

[282] prate *talk idly*
[284] Singeing his pate . . . zone *Burns its head by reaching the burning sphere of the sun*
[285] Make Ossa . . . wart *Make Ossa, the mountain on which the giants piled Pelion, look like a human wart by comparison*

   mouth *open your mouth in an extravagant fashion of speech, act badly*
[286] rant *shout and storm in imitation passion, like a bad actor*
[288] female dove *the emblem of peace and tranquillity*
[289] golden couplets *couple, pair, of golden nestlings. The dove is said to lay and hatch only two eggs at one time and be a particularly careful mother.*

   disclosed *hatched (cf. III. 1. 169). The Queen attempts to protect Hamlet by continuing the fiction that he is mad, and her support at this moment is of considerable dramatic significance.*

266

HAMLET   Thou pray'st not well.
 I prithee take thy fingers from my throat; 260
 For, though I am not splenative and rash,
 Yet have I in me something dangerous,
 Which let thy wiseness fear. Hold off thy hand.

KING Pluck them asunder!

QUEEN Hamlet, Hamlet!

ALL Gentlemen!

HORATIO Good my lord, be quiet.

HAMLET Why, I will fight with him upon this theme
 Until my eyelids will no longer wag.

QUEEN O my son, what theme? 270

HAMLET I loved Ophelia. Forty thousand brothers
 Could not, with all their quantity of love,
 Make up my sum. What wilt thou do for her?

KING O, he is mad, Laertes.

QUEEN For love of God, forbear him.

HAMLET 'Swounds, show me what thou't do.
 Woo't weep, woo't fight, woo't fast, woo't
  tear thyself,
 Woo't drink up eisel, eat a crocodile?
 I'll do't. Dost come here to whine?
 To outface me with leaping in her grave? 280
 Be buried quick with her, and so will I;
 And, if thou prate of mountains, let them
  throw
 Millions of acres on us, till our ground,
 Singeing his pate against the burning zone,
 Make Ossa like a wart! Nay, an thou'lt mouth,
 I'll rant as well as thou.

QUEEN   This is mere madness,
 And thus awhile the fit will work on him;
 Anon, as patient as the female dove
 When that her golden couplets are disclosed,
 His silence will sit drooping.

HAMLET   Hear you, sir: 290
 What is the reason that you use me thus?

267

[293-4] Let Hercules . . . day *Even a hero like Hercules cannot prevent a cat from complaining or a dog from having his day of triumph – so how can I hope to stop you? Hamlet again compares himself unfavourably to Hercules at the very moment that he is about to cleanse the Augean stable of the court.*

[296] in our last night's speech *by, or with, what we said last night*

[297] present push *immediate trial or attempt*

[299] living *enduring. The King, and Shakespeare, are thinking of the famous line from Horace, 'exegi monumentum aere perennius' – I have completed a monument more enduring than bronze – the more enduring or living monument in their case is the act of poetic justice and revenge.*

ACT FIVE, scene 2

[6] mutines in the bilboes *mutineers held in their fetters*
    Rashly *Hastily, unadvisedly, without due consideration*
[7] let us know *let us acknowledge*
[8] indiscretion *lack of judgement, imprudence*
[9] deep plots *carefully laid and concealed plots*
    pall *become pale, fail*
    learn us *teach us*
[10] divinity *some divine power or providence*
    shapes *gives final form or act to our intentions*
[11] Rough-hew them how we will *whatever first rough attempt we make to plan or realise them*
    The words carry a more sinister meaning – there is a divine power which gives the exact form to our deaths although we can contribute the first hacking strokes. It can express a belief in providence or in a more primitive fate.
[13] scarfed *wrapped*
[15] Fingered *Stole*
    in fine *in conclusion*

I loved you ever. But it is no matter.
Let Hercules himself do what he may,
The cat will mew, and dog will have his day.

[*Exit*

KING I pray thee, good Horatio, wait upon him.

[*Exit* HORATIO

Strengthen your patience in our last night's
speech,
We'll put the matter to the present push.
Good Gertrude, set some watch over your son.
This grave shall have a living monument
An hour of quiet shortly shall we see,   300
Till then in patience our proceeding be.

[*Exeunt*

Scene 2. *Enter* HAMLET *and* HORATIO

HAMLET So much for this, sir; now shall you see the
other.
You do remember all the circumstance?

HORATIO Remember it, my lord!

HAMLET Sir, in my heart there was a kind of fighting
That would not let me sleep. Methought I lay
Worse than the mutines in the bilboes. Rashly,
And praised be rashness for it – let us know,
Our indiscretion sometime serves us well,
When our deep plots do pall; and that should
learn us
There's a divinity that shapes our ends,   10
Rough-hew them how we will.

HORATIO   That is most certain.

HAMLET Up from my cabin,
My sea-gown scarfed about me, in the dark
Groped I to find out them, had my desire,
Fingered their packet, and in fine withdrew
To mine own room again, making so bold
(My fears forgetting manners) to unseal

269

[20] Larded   *Made fat with superfluous phrases, padded*
     several   *different*
[21] Importing   *Signifying*
[22] bugs   *bugbear, hobgoblin, object of terror*
[23] on the supervise   *as soon as it had been looked over*
     no leisure bated   *no time for delay subtracted from the*
immediacy of the execution
[24] stay   *wait for*

[29] benetted round   *completely ensnared*
[30–1] Ere . . . play   *Before I could write a prologue to start my*
brains acting they had actually started on the performance of the play
itself

[33] statists   *politicians, statesmen, men of great estate or rank*
[34] baseness   *a sign of base breeding or low birth*

[36] yeoman's service   *good and faithful service. A yeoman was*
a) a royal servant, b) a man below the rank of gentleman who was yet
independant because he owned his own land.

[38] conjuration   *exhortation, solemn appeal, entreaty*
[39] faithful tributary   *one who paid tribute and owed obedience*

[40] palm   *the emblem of peace and love*

[42] a comma   *like a comma, as punctuation for their love joining*
it together
[43] charge   *weight, importance*

[47] shriving-time   *time to confess their sins and receive absolution*

270

Their grand commission; where I found,
  Horatio,
Ah, royal knavery! an exact command,
Larded with many several sorts of reasons,   20
Importing Denmark's health and England's
  too,
With ho! such bugs and goblins in my life,
That, on the supervise, no leisure bated,
No, not to stay the grinding of the axe,
My head should be struck off.

HORATIO   Is't possible?

HAMLET Here's the commission, read it at more
  leisure.
But wilt thou hear now how I did proceed?

HORATIO I beseech you.

HAMLET Being thus benetted round with villainies –
  Ere I could make a prologue to my brains,   30
They had begun the play – I sat me down;
Devised a new commission, wrote it fair,
I once did hold it, as our statists do,
A baseness to write fair, and laboured much
How to forget that learning; but, sir, now
It did me yeoman's service. Wilt thou know
Th'effect of what I wrote?

HORATIO   Ay, good my lord.

HAMLET An earnest conjuration from the King,
As England was his faithful tributary,
As love between them like the palm might
  flourish,   40
As peace should still her wheaten garland wear
And stand a comma 'tween their amitites,
And many suck like as-es of great charge,
That, on the view and knowing of these
  contents,
Without debatement further more or less,
He should those bearers put to sudden death,
Not shriving-time allowed.

[48] ordinant   *regulating, directing matters*

[52] Subscribed it   *Signed it*

gave 't th'impression   *impression of the seal, sealed it*

[53] changeling   *a child who has been changed by fairies, a fairy child left in place of a human – hence anything which has been changed beyond recognition while still appearing the same on the surface*

[54] sequent   *consequent, the following result*

[56] go to't   *go to their deaths*

[57] employment   *special errand or commission – but to 'employ' a woman is to make love to her, so they were as eager to act for the King as they are to enter a brothel.*

[58] near   *close to, touching, affecting*

[59] insinuation   *stealthy insertion of themselves into this business, attempt to creep into favour, winding in – often used, like 'defeat', in a sexual sense. Their ruin comes from making love and insinuation to this employment. Hence their 'baser nature'.*

[60] baser nature   *a) the inferior, more servile nature, b) the less legitimate, bastard*

[60–1] comes/Between   *interposes between the sword points*

[61] pass   *thrust*

fell incensed   *savagely angry, angry to the point of giving deadly or death-dealing strokes*

[62] mighty opposites   *great, powerful, high-born opponents*

[63] stand me now upon   *now concern me, be necessary, imperative for me. Hamlet is about to say that now it is essential and justified to kill the King, but breaks off the construction in considering again the character of Claudius.*

[65] Popped in   *Come suddenly or unexpectedly. Not only has he whored Gertrude but also Denmark since to 'pop in' also means to have sexual intercourse.*

[66] Thrown out his angle   *Cast his fishing line and hook to entrap*

proper   *own*

[67] coz'nage   *cheating, deception, fraud*

perfect conscience   *completely in accord with a good conscience*

[68] quit him   *acquit him of his debts, settle his debts, kill him*

[69] canker   *a spreading sore or ulcer, a grangrene, cancer*

[73] interim   *intervening time*

[74] one   *the first in a series of passes or strokes with the rapier*

HORATIO   How was this sealed?

HAMLET Why, even in that was heaven ordinant,
     I had my father's signet in my purse,
     Which was the model of that Danish seal;   50
     Folded the writ up in the form of th'other;
     Subscribed it, gave't th'impression, placed it
       safely,
     The changeling never known. Now, the next day
     Was our sea-fight – and what to this was
       sequent
     Thou knowest already.

HORATIO So Guildenstern and Rosencrantz go to't?

HAMLET Why, man, they did make love to this
       employment!
     They are not near by conscience. Their defeat
     Does by their own insinuation grow.
     'Tis dangerous when the baser nature comes   60
     Between the pass and fell incensed points
     Of mighty opposites.

HORATIO   Why, what a king is this!

HAMLET Does it not, think thee, stand me now upon –
     He that hath killed my king and whored my
       mother,
     Popped in between th'election and my hopes,
     Thrown out his angle for my proper life,
     And with such coz'nage – is't not perfect
       conscience
     To quit him with this arm? And is't not to be
       damned
     To let this canker of our nature come
     In further evil?   70

HORATIO It must be shortly known to him from
       England
     What is the issue of the business there.

HAMLET It will be short, the interim is mine.
     And a man's life no more than to say 'one'.
     But I am very sorry, good Horatio,

[77] image   *idea, conception, representation as in a picture*

[78] portraiture   *act of painting, making a likeness*

*Hamlet says that a) he understands the nature of Laertes'
cause from the idea or conception that he has of his own, b) beside the
picture which represents his own cause he can see a picture being
painted by Laertes which is very like it.*

[79] bravery   *display, show, ostentation*

[83] water fly   *fly skipping from place to place on water, idler,
trifler*

[87] crib   *barred trough for cattle fodder*

[88] mess   *at the King's table − a man who owns enough cattle
even if he is himself no better than a beast can be sure of eating with the
King*

   chough   *chattering jackdaw*

[89] spacious   *widely extensive*

[93] bonnet   *hat. Osric is evidently bowing with his hat off as if
Hamlet were the King.*

[98] complexion   *temperament, constitution*

[104] for my ease   *ease of mind and body − that he is behaving
with due respect*

[106] absolute   *perfect*

That to Laertes I forgot myself;
For by the image of my cause I see
The portraiture of his. I'll court his favours.
But sure the bravery of his grief did put me
Into a tow'ring passion.

HORATIO   Peace, who comes here?   80

Enter young OSRIC

OSRIC Your lordship is right welcome back to Denmark.

HAMLET I humbly thank you, sir.
    Dost know this water fly?

HORATIO No, my good lord.

HAMLET Thy state is the more gracious, for 'tis a vice to know him. He hath much land, and fertile. Let a beast be lord of beasts, and his crib shall stand at the King's mess. 'Tis a chough; but, as I say, spacious in the possession of dirt.

OSRIC Sweet lord, if your lordship were at leisure, I   90
should impart a thing to you from his Majesty.

HAMLET I will receive it, sir, with all diligence of spirit. Put your bonnet to his right use – 'tis for the head.

OSRIC I thank your lordship, it is very hot.

HAMLET No, believe me, 'tis very cold. The wind is northerly.

OSRIC It is indifferent cold, my lord, indeed.

HAMLET But yet methinks it is very sultry and hot for my complexion.

OSRIC Exceedingly, my lord; it is very sultry, as 'twere – I cannot tell how. But, my lord, his Majesty bade   100
me signify to you that he has laid a great wager on your head. Sir, this is the matter –

HAMLET I beseech you, remember.

OSRIC Nay, good my lord, for my ease, in good faith. Sir, here is newly come to court Laertes; believe me, an absolute gentleman, full of most excellent

[108] feelingly *a) appropriately, with just perception, b) from personal knowledge or experience*

card *compass card, someone who must be followed*

[109] calendar *guide, directory, example, model*

gentry *gentle behaviour, good manners*

[110] continent *that which comprises or sums up*

part *quality*

would see *would wish to see – as he is the compass or directory of good manners so you will find in him whatever country or area of manners you are looking for*

[111] definement *definition,*

[112] divide him inventorially *divide up and make an inventory or list of his good qualities*

[113] dozy *make dizzy*

th'arithmetic of memory *the computation, reckoning of memory*

[114] yaw *and still do nothing but steer from one side to the other compared to his quick sailing*

[115–16] of great article *of great importance*

[116] infusion *temperament given by nature*

dearth *glory, splendour, high price*

rareness *scarcity, uncommon excellence*

[117] to make true diction *give a true account of him*

[117–18] his semblable is his mirror *his likeness is his own faithful reflection – the only thing that is actually like him is his own reflection in a mirror. If he were a mirror for courtesy (i.e. a model, pattern) others might imitate him and become like him. Hamlet says he is so courteous that only his actual reflection resembles him.*

[118] trace *follow, copy*

[121] concernancy *the business concerning Laertes. What is the relevance of Laertes to your business?*

[123] Is't not possible . . . tongue? *Isn't it possible for Osric to understand his affected language when another person speaks it (as if it were a foreign language)?*

[124] do't *succeed in creating a language he cannot understand*

[125] What imports . . . gentleman? *What does the naming of this gentleman signify?*

[139] in his meed *in the praise which he rightly receives (as a reward for excellence) he is unmatched. It has been suggested that 'them in his meed' = those in his pay, his retinue.*

276

differences, of very soft society and great showing.
Indeed, to speak feelingly of him, he is the card or
calendar of gentry, for you shall find in him the
continent of what part a gentleman would see.   110

HAMLET Sir, his definement suffers no perdition in
you; though, I know, to divide him inventorially
would dozy th'arithmetic of memory, and yet but
yaw neither in respect of his quick sail. But, in the
verity of extolment, I take him to be a soul of great
article, and his infusion of such dearth and rareness,
as to make true diction of him, his semblable is his
mirror, and who else would trace him, his umbrage,
nothing more.

OSRIC Your lordship speaks most infallibly of him.   120

HAMLET The concernancy sir? Why do we wrap the
gentleman in our more rawer breath?

OSRIC Sir?

HORATIO Is't not possible to understand in another
tongue? You will do't, sir, really.

HAMLET What imports the nomination of this gentleman?

OSRIC Of Laertes?

HORATIO [*Aside to* HAMLET] His purse is empty already
– all's golden words are spent.

HAMLET Of him, sir.   130

OSRIC I know you are not ignorant –

HAMLET I would you did, sir. Yet, in faith, if you did,
it would not much approve me. Well, sir?

OSRIC You are not ignorant of what excellence
Laertes is –

HAMLET I dare not confess that, lest I should compare
with him in excellence; but to know a man well were
to know himself.

OSRIC I mean, sir, for his weapon; but in the impu-
tation laid on him by them, in his meed he's un-
fellowed.

HAMLET What's his weapon?   140

[142] two of his weapons   *The new style of fencing imported by the continental fencing masters used rapier and dagger. The old English style simply employed a rapier.*

[144] Barbary   *North African. Arab stallions were famous then as now.*

imponed   *staked, wagered*

[145] poniards   *daggers*

[146] assigns   *the equipment belonging to them*

girdle   *decorated sword belt*

hangers   *loops or straps on the belt from which the sword or sword scabbard was hung – often highly ornamented*

[147] carriages   *hangers*

dear to fancy   *pleasing to the imagination, very tasteful*

[148] responsive to the hilts   *a) respond to any movement of the hilt – they swing very fashionably when the sword is in them, or b) they correspond in design and ornament to the hilts*

delicate   *finely constructed*

[149] very liberal conceit   *very elegantly conceived, designed. It is significant that Osric judges the swords by their extraneous ornament; an Elizabethan swordsman would look at the temper and weighting of the blade.*

[151–2] edified by the margent   *improved or instructed by a note in the margin of a book, i.e. require a note*

[154] germane   *closely akin, relevant*

[155] cannon   *were mounted on carriages. Hamlet is again objecting to a new term affected by those who practised the foreign style of fencing.*

[162–3] exceed you three hits   *be more than three hits ahead of you*

[163] He hath laid on twelve for nine   *i.e. Laertes has wagered on nine hits out of twelve*

twelve for nine   *Odds at this time merely express an unequal bet without the modern mathematics of ratio and proportion. As J. A. Kilby explains, 'in order to win the stake impawned by the King, Laertes must score nine or more hits. In order to avoid losing what he himself has impawned, Laertes must score at least three more hits than Hamlet does.' A pass, of course, may end with no hit being scored.*

[164] trial   *determination – of the result*

[165] vouchsafe the answer   *grant the defence*

[170] breathing time   *time for exercise*

[175] redeliver   *report what you say*

OSRIC Rapier and dagger.

HAMLET That's two of his weapons – but well?

OSRIC The King, sir, hath wagered with him six
Barbary horses; against the which he has imponed,
as I take it, six French rapiers and poniards, with
their assigns, as girdle, hangers, and so – three of
the carriages, in faith, are very dear to fancy, very
responsive to the hilts, most delicate carriages, and
of very liberal conceit.

HAMLET What call you the carriages?   150

HORATIO [*Aside to* HAMLET] I knew you must be edified by the margent ere you had done.

OSRIC The carriages, sir, are the hangers.

HAMLET The phrase would be more germane to the
matter if we could carry a cannon by our sides. I
would it might be hangers till then. But on: six
Barbary horses against six French swords, their
assigns, and three liberal conceited carriages; that's
the French bet against the Danish. Why is this all
'imponed', as you call it?   160

OSRIC The King, sir, hath laid, sir, that in a dozen
passes between yourself and him he shall not exceed you three hits. He hath laid on twelve for nine,
and it would come to immediate trial if your lordship would vouchsafe the answer.

HAMLET How if I answer no?

OSRIC I mean, my lord, the opposition of your person
in trial.

HAMLET Sir, I will walk here in the hall. If it please
his Majesty, it is the breathing time of day with me. 170
Let the foils be brought, the gentleman willing, and
the King hold his purpose, I will win for him an I
can; if not, I will gain nothing but my shame and
the odd hits.

OSRIC Shall I redeliver you e'en so?

HAMLET To this effect, sir, after what flourish your
nature will.

[177] I commend my duty *I offer my duty*

[179] commend *praise*

[181] lapwing *A lapwing was regularly supposed to move as soon as it could, still carrying its shell. Horatio means that Osric is barely hatched in experience of the world.*

[182] comply *bow ceremoniously to*

    dug *nipple of the breast*

[184] bevy *a group of quails or other birds*

    drossy *mixed with waste and worthless matter – used especially of metals, particularly gold*

[185] tune of the time *is only in tune with this time, not in harmony with the universe*

[185–6] outward habit of encounter *exterior fashions of society*

[186] yesty collection *frothy mass of yeast. The image is from the brewing of beer. Osric and his companions are like the yeast who are carried through the clear and separated liquid and have to be blown off the top as the yeasty head (which emits great bubbles of gas with a hissing sound) before it is fit to drink.*

[187] fined *left to stand until it is bright and free from turbidity or impurity*

[188] winnowed *blown with a current of air until all impurities (in this case the yeast froth) have been separated out*

    do but blow them to their trial *when it comes to the testing moment of blowing air across the beer vat, their bubbles (of vain opinion) burst*

[190] commended *sent his greetings – and a request*

[194] constant to my purposes *a) unchanged in my intention (to fence), b) steadfast, faithful to my cause*

[194–5] follow the King's pleasure *a) they attend upon, wait for, serve the King's desire, b) they pursue, hunt, the King's lust*

[195] fitness speaks *a) if he says he is ready – for the fencing, b) if his mind and soul are prepared – for our last contest*

[196] able *fit, prepared*

[198] In happy time *At a fortunate, opportune moment*

[199–200] entertainment *give a courteous reception to*

    fall to play *begin to fence*

[204–5] win at the odds *win given the unequal nature of the fight Hamlet means that the odds are in his favour, the audience knows they are against him.*

[205] ill *ill at ease, foreboding, ominous*

OSRIC I commend my duty to your lordship.

HAMLET Yours, yours.

[*Exit* OSRIC

He does well to commend it himself, there are no
tongues else for's turn.   180

HORATIO This lapwing runs away with the shell on
his head.

HAMLET He did comply, sir, with his dug before he
sucked it. Thus has he, and many more of the same
bevy, that I know the drossy age dotes on, only
got the tune of the time and outward habit of encounter – a kind of yesty collection, which carries
them through and through the most fined and
winnowed opinions; and do but blow them to their
trial, the bubbles are out.

Enter a LORD

LORD My lord, his Majesty commended him to you 190
by young Osric, who brings back to him that you
attend him in the hall. He sends to know if your
pleasure hold to play with Laertes, or that you will
take longer time.

HAMLET I am constant to my purposes, they follow
the King's pleasure. If his fitness speaks, mine is
ready now – or whensoever – provided I be so able
as now.

LORD The King and Queen and all are coming down.

HAMLET In happy time.

LORD The Queen desires you to use some gentle entertainment to Laertes before you fall to play.   200

HAMLET She well instructs me.

[*Exit* LORD

HORATIO You will lose this wager, my lord.

HAMLET I do not think so; since he went into France
I have been in continual practice. I shall win at the
odds. But thou wouldst not think how ill all's here
about my heart; but it is no matter.

[208-9] gain giving   *misgiving, warning, premonition*

[211] forestall   *prevent*
      repair   *coming*

[212] augury   *divination, the art of reading signs and omens to ortell the future*

[212-13] special providence . . . sparrow   *God's providence is concerned even with the death of a sparrow: 'Are not two sparrows sold for a farthing? and one of them shall not fall on the ground without your Father . . .' (Matthew 10.29)*

[214] it   *death and the day of judgement*

[215] readiness   *preparedness, fitness for death or judgement and redemption (Matthew 24. 44) 'Therefore be ye also ready: for in such an hour as ye think not, the Son of Man cometh.'*

[216] no man owes of what he leaves   *death pays all debts*

[217] betimes   *early in life*

foils and gauntlets *Evidently the English method of fencing with single rapier parried by using a glove or gauntlet and catching or fending off the opponent's blade was to be used, rather than a rapier and dagger.*

[221] This presence   *Those in the presence of the King, the court*

[222] punished   *afflicted*

[223] sore distraction   *severe disturbance, cause of confusion*

[224] exception   *objection, dislike, dissatisfaction*

[226] Was't Hamlet . . .   *Hamlet pleads madness but he uses madness not as a corrupt way of avoiding his responsibility but as a term which covers the mad and murderous world of the court. As in the case of Ophelia, what matters is the intention as well as the act. It was never Hamlet's intention to kill Polonius. He imagined he was acting against a trap set by the King.*

[231] faction   *party (to a lawsuit), one of the people wronged*

HORATIO Nay, good my lord –

HAMLET It is but foolery; but it is such a kind of gain-
giving as would perhaps trouble a woman.

HORATIO If your mind dislike anything, obey it. I will 210
forestall their repair hither, and say you are not fit.

HAMLET Not a whit, we defy augury. There is a special
providence in the fall of a sparrow. If it be now, 'tis
not to come; if it be not to come, it will be now; if it
be not now, yet it will come – the readiness is all.
Since no man owes of aught he leaves, what is't to
leave betimes? Let be.

Enter KING, QUEEN, LAERTES *and* LORDS *with
other* ATTENDANTS *with foils and gauntlets,
a table and flagons of wine on it*

KING Come, Hamlet, come, and take this hand from
me.

HAMLET Give me your pardon, sir. I have done you
wrong;
But pardon 't, as you are a gentleman.   220
This presence knows,
And you must needs have heard how I am
punished
With a sore distraction. What I have done
That might your nature, honour and
exception
Roughly awake, I here proclaim was madness.
Was't Hamlet wronged Laertes? Never
Hamlet.
If Hamlet from himself be ta'en away,
And when he's not himself does wrong
Laertes,
Then Hamlet does it not, Hamlet denies it.
Who does it, then? His madness. If't be so, 230
Hamlet is of the faction that is wronged;
His madness is poor Hamlet's enemy.
Sir, in this audience,

[234] my disclaiming from a purposed evil   *my claim that I had no evil purpose or intention*

[235] Free me so far   *Acquit, excuse me to this extent*

[236] arrow   *another symbol of the distance between an intention and its result in action. Cf. III. 2. 214-16.*

[237] in nature   *my natural feelings (of love for my father and desire to revenge his death)*

[238] motive   *cause, reason for action*
          stir   *move, excite, provoke*

[239] terms of honour   *conditions of honour. Laertes does not know whether it is honourable for a gentleman to accept such an apology without some satisfaction – such as a duel.*

[242] voice   *approval, supporting advice*

[243] ungored   *undamaged, unstained*

[248] your foil   *a sheet of metal placed behind glass to make a mirror, hence anything which shows off, reflects, something else*

[249] star i'th' darkest night   *As a star appears brighter in a dark night so Laertes will seem more skilful in comparison with Hamlet's poor performance.*

[256] bettered   *improved, made more excellent*

[258] These foils . . . all a length?   *Are these foils all the same length?*

[260] stoups   *cups, flagons – also a vessel containing holy water*

Let my disclaiming from a purposed evil
Free me so far in your most generous thoughts
That I have shot my arrow o'er the house
And hurt my brother.

LAERTES   I am satisfied in nature,
Whose motive in this case should stir me most
To my revenge; but in my terms of honour
I stand aloof, and will no reconcilement   240
Till by some elder masters of known honour
I have a voice and precedent of peace
To keep my name ungored – but till that time
I do receive your offered love like love,
And will not wrong it.

HAMLET   I embrace it freely;
And will this brother's wager frankly play.
Give us the foils. Come on.

LAERTES   Come, one for me.

HAMLET I'll be your foil, Laertes; in mine ignorance
Your skill shall, like a star i'th' darkest night,
Stick fiery off indeed.

LAERTES   You mock me, sir.   250

HAMLET No, by this hand.

KING Give them the foils, young Osric. Cousin
     Hamlet,
You know the wager?

HAMLET   Very well, my lord.
Your Grace has laid the odds a'th' weaker side.

KING I do not fear it: I have seen you both.
But since he's bettered, we have therefore
     odds.

LAERTES This is too heavy; let me see another.

HAMLET This likes me well. These foils have all a
     length?

                     [*They prepare to play*

OSRIC Ay, my good lord.

KING Set me the stoups of wine upon that table.   260
If Hamlet give the first or second hit,

[262] quit in answer   *returns an answering hit in repayment on the third bout*

[264] better breath   *a) better breathing to allow him to sustain his exertions, b) better life – which, for the King, means his death*

[265] union   *a pearl which is the only one found in a particular oyster and is thus of exceptional size and quality*

[268] kettle   *kettle drum*

[269] cannoneer   *artillery officer in charge of a battery of guns*

[278] palpable   *easily perceived, plain, evident. Since it also means to feel by touch it implies that Laertes must have felt it.*

Or quit in answer of the third exchange,
Let all the battlements their ordnance fire;
The King shall drink to Hamlet's better
   breath,
And in the cup an union shall he throw,
Richer than that which four successive kings
In Denmark's crown have worn. Give me the
   cups,
And let the kettle to the trumpet speak,
The trumpet to the cannoneer without,
The cannons to the heavens, the heaven to
   earth,   270
'Now the King drinks to Hamlet'. Come,
   begin –
And you, the judges, bear a wary eye.

Trumpets the while

HAMLET Come on sir.
LAERTES Come, my lord.

                            [They play

HAMLET One.
LAERTES No.
HAMLET Judgement?
OSRIC A hit, a very palpable hit.
LAERTES Well, again.
KING Stay, give me drink. Hamlet, this pearl is thine. 280

       Drum, trumpets and shot.
       Flourish, a piece goes off

Here's to thy health. Give him the cup.
HAMLET I'll play this bout first, set it by awhile.
   Come.

                            [They play

   Another hit, what say you?
LAERTES A touch, a touch, I do confess't.
KING Our son shall win.

[287] fat   *out of condition, sweaty – which is why she offers her handkerchief*

[288] napkin   *handkerchief*

[289] carouses   *drinks a health – one of the most vital theatrical moments in the play when Claudius could save her life but does not do so. See Introduction p. 26.*

[297] against my conscience   *Most editors assume that this is an aside. Said to the King it indicates that his control over his most vital instrument is slipping.*

[298] dally   *trifle, play with me*

[299] violence   *forceful skill*

[300] make a wanton   *make a child – treat me as if I were a child by not fencing as well as you are able*

[303] Have at you now!   *The bout is over and Hamlet has certainly dropped his guard and should probably have turned his back when Laertes strikes with the same sort of exclamation as Hamlet's 'rat', uttered when he killed Polonius.*

scuffling   *The change of rapiers is easily managed if each is using his gloved hand to catch and hold the other's weapon. Such exchanges were common and recognized in fencing manuals.*

[304] incensed   *enraged, have lost their tempers. The King reacts quickly to Hamlet's possession of the poisoned sword.*

[309] springe   *trap, snare. Woodcocks were used to decoy birds to a trap, but coming too near were sometimes snared themselves.*

QUEEN He's fat, and scant of breath.
Here Hamlet, take my napkin, rub thy brows.
The Queen carouses to thy fortune, Hamlet.
HAMLET Good madam.   290
KING Gertrude! Do not drink.
QUEEN I will, my lord. I pray you pardon me.
KING [*Aside*] It is the poisoned cup. It is too late.
HAMLET I dare not drink yet, madam; by and by.
QUEEN Come, let me wipe thy face.
LAERTES My lord, I'll hit him now.
KING   I do not think't.
LAERTES And yet it is almost against my conscience.
HAMLET Come, for the third. Laertes, you do but
dally.
I pray you pass with your best violence.
I am afeard you make a wanton of me.   300
LAERTES Say you so? Come on.

[*They play*

OSRIC Nothing, neither way.
LAERTES Have at you now!

In scuffling they change rapiers

KING Part them! They are incensed!
HAMLET Nay, come again.
OSRIC Look to the Queen there, ho!
HORATIO They bleed on both sides. How is it, my
lord?
OSRIC How is't, Laertes?
LAERTES Why, as a woodcock to mine own springe,
Osric.
I am justly killed with mine own treachery.   310
HAMLET How does the Queen?
KING She swoons to see them bleed.
QUEEN No, no, the drink, the drink! O my dear
Hamlet!
The drink, the drink. I am poisoned!

[QUEEN *dies*

[320] in thy hand   *the sword, which he holds in his hand*
[321] Unbated   *Not blunted*
envenomed   *poisoned*
practice   *a) exercise, b) plot, stratagem*

[330] union   *a) pearl, b) marriage. Hamlet forces him to drink the poisoned cup.*
[331] served   *a) served with the drink, b) punished as he deserved*
[332] tempered   *mixed, prepared*
[334] come not upon thee   *let them not be a weight or sin on your soul to damn you*
Laertes dies first because he has been killed by a sword thrust rather than merely scratched by the poisoned point.

[339] mutes   *actors who say nothing*
audience   *are like spectators or a theatre audience*
[340] fell sergeant Death   *deadly officer death. 'Sergeant' is either a) an officer of a court who summons or arrests those who have to appear before it or have been sentenced by it, or b) the sergeant-at-arms, an officer of the crown who arrested on charges of treason.*
[344] unsatisfied   *not satisfied in knowledge or understanding*
[345] antique Roman   *an ancient Roman with the stoic philosophy which holds that a man may end his misery by suicide*

HAMLET O villainy. Ho, let the door be locked!
    Treachery, seek it out.

LAERTES It is here Hamlet. Hamlet, thou art slain.
    No med'cine in the world can do thee good.
    In thee there is not half an hour's life.
    The treacherous instrument is in thy hand,   320
    Unbated and envenomed. The foul practice
    Hath turned itself on me. Lo, here I lie,
    Never to rise again. Thy mother's poisoned.
    I can no more. The King, the King's to blame.

HAMLET The point envenomed too?
    Then, venom, to thy work.

                                [Hurts the KING

ALL Treason, treason!

KING O, yet defend me, friends; I am but hurt.

HAMLET Here, thou incestuous, murd'rous, damnèd
        Dane,
    Drink off this potion. Is thy union here?   330
    Follow my mother.

                                      *[*KING *dies*

LAERTES   He is justly served.
    It is a poison tempered by himself.
    Exchange forgiveness with me, noble Hamlet.
    Mine and my father's death come not upon
        thee,
    Nor thine on me.   *[Dies*

HAMLET Heaven make thee free of it. I follow thee.
    I am dead, Horatio. Wretched Queen, adieu.
    You that look pale and tremble at this chance,
    That are but mutes or audience to this act,
    Had I but time, as this fell sergeant Death   340
    Is strict in his arrest, O, I could tell you –
    But let it be. Horatio, I am dead:
    Thou livest; report me and my cause aright
    To the unsatisfied.

HORATIO   Never believe it.
    I am more an antique Roman than a Dane.

[348] wounded name   *damaged reputation*

[351] felicity   *the happiness of death*

[357] o'er-crows   *triumphs over, overcomes*

[359] election lights   *the choice alights on, selects*
[360] voice   *vote*

[362] solicited   *a) disturbed, b) urged. The sentence is unfinished.*

[367] woe and wonder   *grief and destruction*
[368] quarry   *dead bodies of animals displayed at the end of a hunt*
    cries on   *painfully announces*
    havoc   *no quarter or mercy having been given*

Here's yet some liquor left.

HAMLET   As th'art a man
Give me the cup. Let go. By heaven, I'll ha't.
O God. Horatio, what a wounded name,
Things standing thus unknown, shall live
    behind me.
If thou did'st ever hold me in thy heart,   350
Absent thee from felicity awhile,
And in this harsh world draw thy breath in
    pain,
To tell my story.

    March far off, and shot within

        What warlike noise is this?
OSRIC Young Fortinbras, with conquest come from
    Poland,
To th'ambassadors of England gives
This warlike volley.
HAMLET   O, I die, Horatio!
The potent poison quite o'er-crows my spirit.
I cannot live to hear the news from England,
But I do prophesy th'election lights
On Fortinbras. He has my dying voice.   360
So tell him, with th'occurrents, more and less,
Which have solicited – the rest is silence. [*Dies*
HORATIO Now cracks a noble heart. Good night,
    sweet prince,
And flights of angels sing thee to thy rest.
Why does the drum come hither?

Enter FORTINBRAS *and* ENGLISH AMBASSADORS
   with drum, colours, and ATTENDANTS

FORTINBRAS Where is this sight?
HORATIO   What is it you would see?
If aught of woe or wonder, cease your search.
FORTINBRAS This quarry cries on havoc. O proud
    death,

[379] jump *immediately, just at this point*

[382] stage *platform*

[385] carnal *lustful, bodily, fleshly*
[386] accidental judgements *mistaken or chance decisions*
 casual slaughters *random, accidental murders*
[387] put on *inflicted*
 forced cause *imperative, compelling reason, necessary reason*
[388] upshot *result, conclusion*
 purposes mistook *intentions taken the wrong path*
[389] inventors' *devisers'*

[393] rights of memory *unforgotten rights, rights justified by memory*
[394] vantage *opportunity, chance, position of superiority*

[396] from his mouth *Hamlet's vote for Fortinbras will persuade others to vote for him.*

[397] presently *immediately*

What feast is toward in thine eternal cell
That thou so many princes at a shot   370
So bloodily hast struck?

AMBASSADOR   The sight is dismal,
And our affairs from England come too late:
The ears are senseless that should give us
    hearing
To tell him his commandment is fulfilled,
That Rosencrantz and Guildenstern are dead.
Where should we have our thanks?

HORATIO   Not from his mouth,
Had it th'ability of life to thank you.
He never gave commandment for their death.
But since, so jump upon this bloody question,
You from the Polack wars, and you from
    England,   380
Are here arrived, give order that these bodies
High on a stage be placed to the view;
And let me speak to th'yet unknowing world
How these things came about. So shall you
    hear
Of carnal, bloody, and unnatural acts;
Of accidental judgements, casual slaughters,
Of deaths put on by cunning and forced cause;
And, in this upshot, purposes mistook
Fall'n on th'inventors' heads – all this can I
Truly deliver.

FORTINBRAS   Let us haste to hear it,   390
And call the noblest to the audience.
For me, with sorrow I embrace my fortune;
I have some rights of memory in this kingdom,
Which now to claim my vantage doth invite
    me.

HORATIO   Of that I shall have also cause to speak,
And from his mouth whose voice will draw on
    more.
But let this same be presently performed,

[398] wild   *restive, unsteady, unrestrained*

[401] put on   *put to the test of kingship*
[402] passage   *rite of passage, funeral rites, burial service*

[404] Speak loudly   a) *Be played loudly for him, b) sound his praise loudly*
[406] Becomes the field   *Is a suitable sight for a battlefield*
[407] shoot   *fire a volley from cannon in salute*

    Even while men's minds are wild, lest more
      mischance
    On plots and errors happen.

FORTINBRAS   Let four captains
    Bear Hamlet like a soldier to the stage;   400
    For he was likely, had he been put on,
    To have proved most royal; and for his passage
    The soldier's music and the rite of war
    Speak loudly for him.
    Take up the bodies. Such a sight as this
    Becomes the field, but here shows much amiss.
    Go, bid the soldiers shoot.

*   Exeunt marching, after the which a peal of
           ordinance are shot off*